Praise for *Teachers Without Borders?*

"Shining a light into a little known and largely unexamined corner of the contemporary maze of policy proposals and practices known as 'school reform,' Alyssa Hadley Dunn illuminates the wreckage and the rubble that characterizes ideologically-driven school change. In this brilliantly rendered case, we see the human consequences—up-close and personal—when advocates adopt profit-driven strategies, assume quick-fix solutions to profound challenges, and embrace an arid view of teaching and learning and the toxic logic of student and community deficit. We can also glimpse beneath the devastation and the damage, the confusion and the chaos, pathways toward creating a system capable of educating all children in our wildly diverse democracy."

—**William Ayers**, educator and bestselling author of *To Teach, Third Edition,* and co-author of *Teaching the Taboo*

"Masterfully sorting fact from fiction, Dunn's study is timely, compelling, and downright fascinating—a flip side reality check, in many respects, to the fulsome mythology of Thomas Friedman's *The World Is Flat*. Written in an engaging, informative, and moving narrative, *Teachers Without Borders?* opens a new window on the complex realities of cultural literacy in our schools, the challenges of culturally responsive pedagogy in our classrooms, and the still promising opportunities for reform today."

—**Jeff Biggers**, author of *State Out of the Union: Arizona and the Final Showdown Over the American Dream*

"This highly-readable and moving book couples compelling case studies with hard-hitting social and political critique. In a sensitive yet unflinching analysis, Alyssa Hadley Dunn exposes the complex economic, professional, and humanitarian issues involved in international teacher recruitment. Although many readers will not be aware of this problem before reading the book, they will never be able to forget it once they do."

—**Marilyn Cochran-Smith**, Cawthorne Professor of Teacher Education, Lynch School of Education, Boston College

"I really like this book! *Teachers Without Borders?* informs u education hidden behind the neoliberal argument that, witl international teachers, students in urban schools will have i aware and have pedagogical content knowledge appropriate Dunn reveals this is not so. She argues that both students ar misled. This is an excellent and important study."

—**Carl A. Grant**, Hoefs-Bascom Professor, University Wisconsin–Madison

"*Teachers Without Borders?* will transport you through the local and the global, interweaving nuanced portraits of teachers from abroad with troubling unveilings of the bigger picture behind teacher recruitment and school reform. Alyssa Hadley Dunn compels us to address an insidious system that exploits teachers and harms children, even while those very teachers strive to enact liberatory pedagogies in urban communities. Insightful, passionate, and expansive, this book is a must-read."

—**Kevin Kumashiro**, University of Illinois at Chicago, and author of *Bad Teacher! How Blaming Teachers Distorts the Bigger Picture*

"*Teachers Without Borders?* documents the advent of hiring international teachers to fill shortages in urban schools, primarily serving African American students in a low income area. Dunn's extraordinary analysis shows the lack of preparation of the teachers in understanding the cultural, social, political, and pedagogical context in which they find themselves. And, as important, she teaches us how to build the kind of support that will transform this kind of teacher recruitment into a system that matters for students, their schools, and their communities."

—**Ann Lieberman**, Senior Scholar, Stanford University, and co-editor of
Teachers in Professional Communities and co-author of *How Teachers Become Leaders*

"*Teachers Without Borders?* makes a valuable contribution to understanding one of the lesser-studied dimensions of neoliberal privatization and deregulation that is infecting every last part of public education today—foreign and domestic teacher labor exploitation masquerading as feel-good cultural exchange and cosmopolitanism. Dunn highlights the ways that the international teaching rackets contribute to a broad-based symbolic assault on teachers' work and students' cultures, undermine a professional and unionized teacher labor force, and participate in the current craze for selling off and selling out public schools, teachers, and students."

—**Kenneth J. Saltman**, DePaul University, Chicago,
and author of *The Failure of Corporate School Reform*

"In this highly readable case study, Dunn exposes how the rhetoric of 'cultural awareness' used to justify hiring temporary international teachers masks a deeper devaluation of teachers, students of color, and pedagogical knowledge. Dunn skillfully portrays teaching as a cultural activity, showing how superficial understandings of culture support practices that jeopardize the education of urban youth while simultaneously exploiting international teachers."

—**Christine Sleeter**, professor emerita, California State University, Monterey Bay,
and co-editor of *Teaching with Vision:
Culturally Responsive Teaching in Standards-Based Classrooms*

MULTICULTURAL EDUCATION SERIES

James A. Banks, *Series Editor*

(continued)

Teachers Without Borders?

*The Hidden Consequences of
International Teachers in U.S. Schools*

ALYSSA HADLEY DUNN

FOREWORD BY
JACQUELINE JORDAN IRVINE

Teachers College
Columbia University
New York and London

Published by Teachers College Press, 1234 Amsterdam Avenue, New York, NY 10027

Library of Congress Cataloging-in-Publication Data

Dunn, Alyssa Hadley.
    Teachers without borders? : the hidden consequences of international teachers in U.S. schools / Alyssa Hadley Dunn ; foreword by Jacqueline Jordan Irvine.
        p. cm. — (Multicultural education series)
    Includes bibliographical references and index.
    ISBN 978-0-8077-5411-5 (pbk. : alk. paper)
    ISBN 978-0-8077-5433-7 (hardcover : alk. paper)
    1. Education, Urban—United States. 2. Teachers, Foreign—United States.
    3. Teaching—Social aspects—United States. I. Title.
    LC5115.D86 2013
    370.9173'2—dc23   2012045368

ISBN 978-0-8077-5411-5 (paperback)
ISBN 978-0-8077-5433-7 (hardcover)

Printed on acid-free paper

Manufactured in the United States of America

20 19 18 17 16 15 14 13   8 7 6 5 4 3 2 1

To my parents, David and Helen Hadley,
for giving me an incomparable education in and out of school

Financial responses alone won't ultimately safeguard our economic and social well-being.... Substantial, strategic investments in education are essential.... We cannot just bail ourselves out of this crisis. We must teach our way out.

—Linda Darling-Hammond, 2010

It is not enough to say that education is a political act just as it is not enough to say that political acts are also educative. It is necessary to truly assume the political nature of education.... I cannot recognize the limits of the political-educative practice in which I am involved ... if I am not clear about in whose favor I work. Clarifying the question of in whose favor I practice puts me in a certain position ... in which I devise against whom I practice and, necessarily, for what reasons I practice—that is, the dream, the type of society on whose behalf I would like to intervene, act, and participate.

—Paulo Freire, 1998

Contents

    Gandhi, MLK, and Culturally Relevant Pedagogy   **65**

    Multiculturalism in India   66

    Culturally Relevant Pedagogy   74

    Translatable Skills: Common CRP of International Teachers   77

    "Trying to Speak the Same Language":
        Occasional CRP of International Teachers   82

    "Lost in Translation":
        Stated But Not Evident CRP of International Teachers   86

    "It's All Greek to Me":
        Missing CRP in International Teachers' Classrooms   90

    Building Foundation-Less Bridges   96

4. **Barriers to Success: Stymied Goals for**
    International Teacher Recruitment   **97**

    Meeting Teachers' Goals   98

    Meetings Goals for Students   104

    Meeting Schools' Goals   109

    Meeting District Goals   112

    Short-Term Goals Versus Long-Term Problems   116

5. **Pushing the Boundary and Crossing the Line:**
    Hidden Purposes and Consequences of Recruitment   **117**

    Political Spectacle   118

    Hidden Purposes   119

    Hidden Consequences   125

    Challenging the Spectacle   141

6. **Charting a Course:**
    The Future of International Teacher Recruitment   **142**

    Implications for Practice: Why Schools and Districts
        Should Support International Teachers   149

    Implications for Future Research:
        Why Researchers Should Investigate International Teachers   157

    Implications for Teacher Preparation: Why Teacher Educators
        Should Care About International Teachers   159

Series Foreword

This informative, timely, and engaging book describes the experiences of four international teachers from India who are recruited to teach in one of the nation's largest and most challenged urban school districts. Dunn uses the experiences of these teachers as a vehicle to describe the problems, opportunities, and complexities that occur when urban inner-city school districts try to solve their teacher shortage by recruiting teachers from distant lands. A significant lesson that readers will take from this sympathetic, cogent, and critical depiction of international teachers in inner-city schools is that although this strategy for resolving the problem of teacher flight from inner-city schools is promising, its positive outcomes are largely unrealized for many intractable reasons.

Dunn skillfully and compellingly challenges some of the major assumptions made by the agencies that recruit teachers from other lands to teach in U.S. schools. These recruiters contend that international teachers will serve as effective cultural ambassadors who will enrich the cultural literacy of U.S. students by helping them to learn about the cultures in their nations. They also assert that international teachers will be able to understand the cultures of ethnic minority youths in the United States and to implement culturally responsive pedagogy because they come from different nations and cultures and therefore have unique cultural eyes and dispositions. Dunn deconstructs each of these claims and adduces logical and empirical evidence that indicates how they are inaccurate, misleading, and educationally unsound.

Despite her penetrating and insightful critique of the ways in which international teachers are recruited and the difficult experiences they have in the school district that she studied, Dunn is optimistic about the feasibility of implementing reforms that will enable international teachers to enrich their experiences in U.S. schools, as well as the experiences of their American students. In the concluding chapter, Dunn recommends a number of promising strategies for reforming the ways in which international teachers are recruited, in-serviced, and supported.

This revealing and practical book can help researchers, policymakers, and practicing educators to respond thoughtfully and creatively to the challenges and possibilities of recruiting international educators to teach in U.S. schools and to enrich the experiences of students from diverse groups, including immigrant students.

American classrooms are experiencing the largest influx of immigrant students since the beginning of the 20th century. Almost 14 million new immigrants—documented and undocumented—settled in the United States in the years from 2000 to 2010. Less than 10% came from nations in Europe. Most came from Mexico, nations in Asia, and nations in Latin America, the Caribbean, and Central America (Comarota, 2011). A large but undetermined number of undocumented immigrants enter the United States each year. The U.S. Department of Homeland Security (2010) estimated that in January 2010 10.8 million undocumented immigrants were living in the United States, which was a decrease from the estimated 11.8 million that resided in the United States in January 2007. In 2007, approximately 3.2 million children and young adults were among the 11.8 million undocumented immigrants in the United States, most of whom grew up in this country (Perez, 2011). The influence of an increasingly ethnically diverse population on U.S. schools, colleges, and universities is and will continue to be enormous.

Schools in the United States are more diverse today than they have been since the early 1900s when a multitude of immigrants entered the United States from Southern, Central, and Eastern Europe. In the 20-year period between 1989 and 2009, the percentage of students of color in U.S. public schools increased from 32% to 45% (Aud, Hussar, Kena, Blanco, Frohlich, Kemp, & Tahan, 2011). If current trends continue, students of color will equal or exceed the percentage of White students in U.S. public schools within one or two decades. In 2010–2011, students of color exceeded the number of Whites students in the District of Columbia and in 13 states (listed in descending order of the percentage of ethnic minority students therein): Hawaii, California, New Mexico, Texas, Nevada, Arizona, Florida, Maryland, Mississippi, Georgia, Louisiana, Delaware, and New York. (Aud, Hussar, Johnson, Kena, Roth, Manning, Wang, & Zhang, 2012). In 2009, children of undocumented immigrants made up 6.8% of students in grades kindergarten through 12 (Perez, 2011).

Language and religious diversity is also increasing in the U.S. student population. The 2010 American Community Survey indicates that approximately 19.8% of the school-age population spoke a language at home other than English (U.S. Census Bureau, 2010). The Progressive Policy Institute (2008) estimated that 50 million Americans (out of 300 million) spoke a language at home other than English in 2008. Harvard professor Diana L. Eck (2001) calls the United States the "most religiously diverse nation on earth" (p. 4). Islam is now the fastest-growing religion in the United States, as well as in several European nations such as France, the United Kingdom, and The Netherlands (Banks, 2009; Cesari, 2004). Most teachers now in the classroom and in teacher education programs are likely to have students from diverse ethnic, racial, linguistic, and religious groups in their classrooms during their careers. This is true for both inner-city and suburban teachers in the United States, as well as in many other

Western nations such as Canada, Australia, and the United Kingdom (Banks, 2009).

The major purpose of the Multicultural Education Series is to provide preservice educators, practicing educators, graduate students, scholars, and policymakers with an interrelated and comprehensive set of books that summarizes and analyzes important research, theory, and practice related to the education of ethnic, racial, cultural, and linguistic groups in the United States and the education of mainstream students about diversity. The dimensions of multicultural education, developed by Banks (2004) and described in the *Handbook of Research on Multicultural Education* and in the *Encyclopedia of Diversity in Education* (Banks, 2012), provide the conceptual framework for the development of the publications in the Series. They are content integration, the knowledge construction process, prejudice reduction, an equity pedagogy, and an empowering institutional culture and social structure.

The books in the Series provide research, theoretical, and practical knowledge about the behaviors and learning characteristics of students of color, language minority students, and low-income students. They also provide knowledge about ways to improve academic achievement and race relations in educational settings. Multicultural education is consequently as important for middle-class White suburban students as it is for students of color who live in the inner city. Multicultural education fosters the public good and the overarching goals of the commonwealth.

In her careful and astute observations of Aleeza, Shrusty, Faria, and Samia in their classrooms and in her discussions with students and principals, Dunn concludes that these teachers wanted to do their best, were concerned about their students, but lacked the sociological and cultural knowledge about the complexity and nuances of African American youth culture that is required to effectively implement culturally responsive pedagogy. When they tried to actualize their ideas about culturally responsive pedagogy in the classroom, it often "faltered or crumbled."

Dunn's smart analyses and vivid descriptions of classroom interactions indicate why subject matter knowledge is necessary but not sufficient for effective teaching, why treating all students from different ethnic, cultural, and linguistic groups the same usually results in educational inequality, and why the "colorblind approach" to dealing with differences in the racialized context of the United States perpetuates racial and ethnic stratification (Pollock, 2004; Schofield, 2007). Dunn identifies the serious problems wrought by placing international teachers in U.S. schools without essential support and in-service education and describes promising and practical ways to deal with these problems. Dunn's innovative and realistic ideas for change and reform merit serious consideration by policymakers, school administrators, and classroom teachers.

James A. Banks

REFERENCES

Aud, S., Hussar, W., Johnson, F., Kena, G., Roth, E., Manning, E., Wang, X., & Zhang, J. (2012). *The condition of education 2012* (NCES 2012-045). Washington, DC: U.S. Department of Education, National Center for Education Statistics. Retrieved from http://nces.ed.gov/pubsearch

Aud, S., Hussar, W., Kena, G., Bianco, K., Frohlich, L., Kemp, J., & Tahan, K. (2011). *The condition of education 2011* (NCES 2011-033). U.S. Department of Education, National Center for Education Statistics. Washington, DC: U.S. Department of Education, National Center for Education Statistics Retrieved from http://nces.ed.gov/programs/coe/pdf/coe_1er.pdf

Banks, J. A. (2004). Multicultural education: Historical development, dimensions, and practice. In J. A. Banks & C. A. M. Banks (Eds.). *Handbook of research on multicultural education* (2nd ed., pp. 3–29). San Francisco: Jossey-Bass.

Banks, J. A. (Ed.). (2009). *The Routledge international companion to multicultural education.* New York and London: Routledge.

Banks, J. A. (2012). Multicultural education: Dimensions of. In J. A. Banks (Ed). *Encyclopedia of diversity in education* (vol. 3, pp. 1538–1547). Thousand Oaks, CA: Sage Publications.

Camarota, S. A. (2011, October). A *record-setting decade of immigration: 2000 to 2010.* Washintgton, DC: Center for Immigration Studies. Retrieved from http://cis.org/2000-2010-record-setting-decade-of-immigration

Cesari, J. (2004). *When Islam and democracy meet: Muslims in Europe and the United States.* New York: Pelgrave Macmillan.

Eck, D. L. (2001). *A new religious America: How a "Christian country" has become the world's most religiously diverse nation.* New York: HarperSanFrancisco.

Perez, W. (2011). *Americans by heart: Undocumented Latino students and the promise of higher education.* New York: Teachers College Press.

Pollock, M. (2004). *Colormute: Race talk dilemmas in an American classroom.* Princeton, NJ: Princeton University Press.

Progressive Policy Institute. (2008). *50 million Americans speak languages other than English at home.* Retrieved from http://www.ppionline.org/ppi_ci.cfm?knlgAreaID=108&subsecID=900003&contentID=254619

Schofield, J. W. (2007). The colorblind perspective in school: Causes and consequences. In J. A. Banks & C. A. M. Banks (Eds.), *Multicultural education: Issues and perspectives* (6th ed., pp. 271–295). Hoboken, NJ: Wiley.

U.S. Census Bureau. (2010). *2010 American community survey.* Retrieved from http://factfinder2.census.gov/faces/tableservices/jsf/pages/productview.xhtml?pid=ACS_10_1YR_S1603&prodType=table

U.S. Department of Homeland Security. (2010, February). *Estimates of the unauthorized immigrant population residing in the United States: January 2010.* Retrieved from http://www.dhs.gov/files/statistics/immigration.shtm

Foreword

One of the most recognized yet intractable problems in education is recruiting, training, and retaining quality teachers, particularly in low-performing schools that enroll low-income students. The reality is that most urban schools have difficulty with all aspects of hiring, supporting, and keeping teachers. Thirty-three percent of new teachers leave teaching within their first 3 years, and within 5 years, nearly half of all new teachers have left the profession (Ingersoll, 2003). National data show that annual turnover rates in urban high-poverty schools are nearly 70% higher than are the turnover rates in low-poverty schools (Ingersoll, 2004). In predominantly Black, Hispanic, high-poverty, urban schools, students are twice as likely as students in other schools to be taught by the most inexperienced teachers (Haycock, Jerald, & Huang, 2001). Additionally, teachers of students of color in high-poverty schools are more likely to be uncertified and teach subjects in which they do not even have a college minor (Haycock, 2002).

These issues are critically analyzed in Alyssa Hadley Dunn's *Teachers Without Borders?* She tackles conventional wisdom that urban education, international education, and culturally relevant teaching unquestionably share common beliefs and a common agenda. Dunn carefully unpacks this myth by thoroughly analyzing the complex and nuanced contextual issues related to the recruitment and retention of urban teachers—like culture, race, and nationality.

Dunn makes her points clear that the recruitment of international teachers for urban schools that serve African American students is based on a set of faulty assumptions. First, school administrators and international recruiters assume that mastery of content knowledge is the most important variable needed to teach diverse students. Second, there is the perception that international teachers understand the cultural and social context of teaching and learning in the urban schools where they are frequently placed. Dunn argues that the international teachers in her study were competent, often exemplary, in their knowledge of the content. However, this strength was not enough to make them effective with their students, because their knowledge of African American culture was practically nonexistent.

The social and cultural context of teaching and learning are important matters to address in classroom practice. Students are not passive recipients of teaching or blank cultural slates. They have preferences for the subject matter they are taught, how it is taught, and the people who teach them. Teachers are also not cultural blank slates. They bring their values, opinions, and beliefs, prior socialization, present experiences, their race, gender, ethnicity, and social class into their classrooms. The educators in Dunn's text demonstrate the degree to which teachers' beliefs are embedded in their practice, even in a new cultural context. Although it would be unfair to imply that teachers and students are solely a product of these traits and prior experiences, it would be equally naive to assume that teaching and learning are unaffected by the influences of culture and ethnicity.

Teachers Without Borders? underscores the need for teacher educators and district personnel to incorporate culturally relevant pedagogy into their programs and professional support. Culturally relevant pedagogy builds on the premise that learning may differ across cultures, and teachers can enhance students' success by acquiring knowledge of their cultural backgrounds and translating this knowledge into instruction. Culturally relevant teaching allows teachers to employ multiple representations of their content knowledge by using students' everyday lived experiences to motivate and assist them in connecting new knowledge to home, community, and global settings.

Finally, Dunn emphasizes that the problems of recruiting and retaining international teachers for challenging urban schools is not simply a pedagogical issue solved by more professional development and better recruitment strategies. The problems are more complex. In an era of neoliberal agendas and attacks on the teaching profession, teachers from the United States or abroad are more likely to be affected by policies that undermine progressive visions of education. These problems signal weak commitment and leadership by local, state, and national policymakers who appear oblivious to issues of social justice and equality that Dunn illustrates are vital for all teachers and students.

Jacqueline Jordan Irvine

REFERENCES

Haycock, K. (2002). Toward a fair distribution of teacher talent. *Educational Leadership, 60*(4), 11–15.

Haycock, K., Jerald, C., & Huang, S. (2001). Closing the gap: Done in a decade. *Thinking K–16, 5*(2), 3–21, Retrieved from http://64.224.125.0/main/documents/_k16_ spring01.pdf

Ingersoll, R. M. (2003). *Is there really a teacher shortage?* Seattle, WA: Center for the Study of Teaching and Policy.

Ingersoll, R. M. (2004). *Why do high-poverty schools have difficulty staffing their classrooms with qualified teachers?* Washington, DC: Center for American Progress and the Institute for America's Future.

Acknowledgments

The easiest part of writing this book was crafting the acknowledgments because I have an abundance of wonderful supporters who made this work—and all of my work—possible. Because of their love and encouragement, I am able to share this book with you.

I owe tremendous thanks to the talented group at Teachers College Press, especially editor Brian Ellerbeck. The dedicated team of Meg Hartmann, Beverly Rivero, Aureliano Vazquez, Michael McGann, and the copy editor of the manuscript made this publication process incredibly smooth. It is always a delight to work with Kendra Millis of Millis Indexing. For giving me such an outstanding opportunity so early in my career, I am indebted to Jim Banks. To be included in the James Banks's Multicultural Education Series, a series that has featured the work of scholars who inspire me daily, is gratifying and humbling. Additional thanks are extended to Marilyn Cochran-Smith, Kevin Kumashiro, and Christine Sleeter for the time and care they spent reviewing this text.

For writing the foreword to this text, I am grateful to Jacqueline Jordan Irvine. Her profound guidance through the years has informed the way I research and teach for social justice. Carole Hahn continues to be a powerful example of what an advisor can be. The support of these two amazing mentors is something I can only hope to pass on to my own students. I would also like to thank Bob Jensen, Joseph Cadray, and Aiden Downey of Emory University for their early reading of this work and their support through my doctoral program.

I owe a debt of gratitude to all of my participants, including the teachers, principals, and district officials of "Glendale" and the representatives from the American Federation of Teachers. Most importantly, my teachers welcomed me into their classrooms and shared their stories with honesty and courage. Their hard work and resilience is a continuous inspiration.

I am blessed to be part of a community of educators whose careers and lives center on the fight for educational equity and justice. They have made be a better person and a better scholar. I am lucky to call these colleagues from Emory University and Georgia State University my dear friends. Thank you to my Emory family, now dispersed throughout the country, especially Nadia Behizadeh, Saundra Deltac, Jillian Ford, Keisha Green, David Morris, Michelle Purdy, Laura Quaynor,

Mari Ann Roberts, Ana Solano-Campos, and Vera Stenhouse. Erica Dotson, who has helped to fill the past 8 years with laughter and friendship, treated this project as if it was her own and I am eternally thankful.

Thank you also to my fellow Panthers who have read portions of this work, offered important suggestions, and welcomed me into the community, especially Stephanie Behm Cross, Kara Kavanagh, and DaShaunda Patterson. Dana Fox, the chair of the Department of Middle-Secondary Education and Instructional Technology, ensured that I had the time and support to complete this project. My graduate research assistants, Morgin Jones Williams and Natasha Thornton, were instrumental in the development of this book. I look forward to seeing the gifted scholars they become. Though this work has been read and critiqued by many colleagues and reviewers, I take responsibility for any errors or gaps contained within.

Finally, I am immeasurably grateful for the support and love of my friends and family, whom I do not see nearly as much as I would like but who are always close to my heart, including my grandparents; aunts, uncles, and cousins; brother Brian; and my in-laws. Most especially, I thank my parents, David and Helen Hadley. My parents were my first and best teachers, and they instilled in me a passion for education and justice. My mother's tremendous ability to balance work and family is a skill I seek to emulate every day. Coming from a long line of strong, successful women, she is my hero. My father instilled in me a love of reading and writing and, as a child, I would sometimes read a book a day. Each time I finished, I would seek him out and proudly tell him that I finished another book. I am very happy to say again: Daddy, I finished my book! I dedicate this book to them.

My closest ally in writing and in life is my best friend and husband, John Dunn. My voice is stronger because John helped me find and nurture it. For his diligent editing skills, thoughtful critique, and never-ending devotion to my work, he is a perfect research partner. For his loyalty, laughter, and love, he is my perfect life partner. To me, he is all-powerful.

Teachers Without Borders?

Introduction

Crossing Oceans

Teaching is a tough job in America, don't you think so?
—Samina, English teacher from India

So many international teachers like us come to America, the land of opportunity, with these big American dreams, and then our dreams are shattered by reality.
—Shrusty, special education teacher from India

When I first met Padma, she looked as terrified as I felt. It was late August 2007, the first day back for teachers, who straggled intermittently into the stuffy school library that had been closed up all summer. Sitting at a table waiting for the meeting to begin, I listened to a veteran teacher talk about how much she missed summer already, even though she had only been back to work for half an hour. It was my first day teaching at this school and, like any new teacher, I was battling a complex mix of terror, hope, excitement, and post-summer exhaustion—and the students had not even returned yet! Padma came in shortly thereafter, stepping through the door and blinking as she adjusted to the flicker of fluorescent lights and the smell of aged books. She stood in place for several minutes, unsure of where to go or what to do. By this time, there were perhaps 20 other teachers in the room, and no one said anything to her. Guessing she was as nervous as I, I smiled and waved her over to our table. She hurried over and sank into a chair in a way that made me think she had not sat down all morning. And, sure enough, she had not. She had already walked 3 miles to school that morning because she knew no other way to get there.

Padma was an international teacher who had arrived from India several days before the start of the school year. In a heavy Indian accent, she told us that she had been hired by an agency to work in our district. She went on to tell us that the agency had placed her and three other Indian teachers in an apartment but had not provided them with any means to get to school. No one had told her about the public buses, so she walked that morning, rising at 5:00 a.m. to ensure she arrived on time.

After that day, I rarely saw Padma around the school, but I certainly heard about her. Many of my 11th-grade American literature students were also in her science class, which, unfortunately for everyone, met in the tiniest room of the school, in the basement, with windows that had to be propped open with old textbooks. There was little air-conditioning in the summer or heat in the winter. Unless students were absent, there were not enough desks or books to go around. I heard students discussing how Padma had "no control" over the students and how they "gave her hell" because she was an easy target. About 2 months into the year, I went to visit Padma in her classroom after school to see how she was doing. I found her trying to clean permanent marker from the desks, where students had written names, initials, curses, and gang signs. During our conversation, we realized that we lived close to each other, and Padma asked if I would be willing to drive her to and from school each day if she paid me. Since her first day of walking, she had either been taking the bus, a cab, or riding home with other science teachers if they had time. I was happy to do it without reimbursement, and I am fortunate that I did.

On our rides to and from school each day, I learned about Padma's life in India and how she had come to the United States. Although Padma is not a participant in the research presented here, she *is* part of the story.

PADMA'S STORY

This is Padma's story, but it also is not, because Padma's story, I would later discover, would be told by others. In India, a teacher begins thinking about the world outside her crowded village, about an opportunity to explore new horizons and, if possible, provide for her family in the process. Across the globe, a city administrator in the United States sifts through paperwork and tries to determine how he is going to fill next year's vacant positions, the result of high teacher turnover and a stretched budget. They both access the Internet and, within moments, appear to have found a solution: a company promising to be, at once, both an employment agency and an educational service that will bring the Indian teacher to the American school. Though this company will charge both the teacher and the administrator thousands of dollars each, the cost seems worth it. Several months later, the teacher has secured a visa, proven her English skills and teaching experience to a panel of U.S. recruiters, and been placed in a city school the following autumn. Although they do not meet before her first day, the school's principal is assured of the teacher's competence by the administrator and the recruitment agency, who both promise that not only will she fill the much-needed role of a science teacher, but she will also serve as a "cultural ambassador" to his African American student population.

The new teacher is given a teacher's edition of the state-mandated textbook and expected to plan her curriculum in the 3 "pre-planning" days before the students arrive. She attempts to do this in all her "free time" between finding an apartment, learning the public transportation system because she does not have a U.S. driver's license, orienting herself to a new city far away from her family, and receiving a "crash course" in U.S. school policies. In the latter, in a single afternoon, she learns about topics like high-stakes testing, classroom management, zero tolerance policies, and special education guidelines. She feels overwhelmed by the amount of information she is expected to internalize in such a short time, but thinks positively; it will get better when the students arrive and she is "in her element." She was, after all, recognized as an outstanding educator in India, and her students there cried when she told them she was leaving.

But when the students arrive, spilling into the classroom in a commotion of bodies and laughter, it does not get better. Instead, the teacher feels more overwhelmed. The school is overcrowded; the classroom is stuffed with 35 desks, even though it was built for 22. The students say they do not understand the teacher's accent, and they do not seem to want to sit still and raise their hands like her Indian students. She is in charge of preparing them for high-stakes exams; if they do not pass, not only will they not graduate, but it will reflect poorly on her teaching performance. Is this really the "American experience" that she constantly heard she would encounter? On the contrary, it is as if everything she read about culture shock is coming true. No one understands her but the other international teachers; she lives in a small apartment with three other Indian teachers, but they are all placed at different schools, so there is no one to help her during the day.

Her difficulties do not subside after a few months as her agency promised, and she is worried about approaching the principal. What if he thinks she is incompetent? She is already here on a temporary visa and does not want to give anyone a reason to send her home early, as she signed a year-long contract. It is especially difficult when she calls her family in India, as her 6-year-old son does not understand why his mother is not home, with him. The agency said it would help her bring her husband and son next year, if she could just make it through the first one alone. One day, she hopes, her son will understand that she did it for him. The salary here is five times what she made in India. The only problem is that she gets paid 2 weeks later than everyone else, because the agency receives her paycheck first and deducts all the requisite fees, which can sometimes amount to hundreds of dollars, and then sends what is left to her.

In February, as her fellow teachers receive their contracts for the following year, the principal tells Padma that she has to wait because he does not make the ultimate decision; the agency does. It is not until 1 week before school is finished that she is told she will not be rehired at her original school. She is given the option to move to another school in the same district, but she is too emotionally and physically overwhelmed to consider starting over again in a new place. On her last day, she thinks again about her Indian students and how they cried when she left. Here, she thinks everyone will throw a party, and she does not know why. She used to be a good teacher.

Though this is one teacher's story, Padma is far from alone. The themes that emerge—a desire for an "American experience," lack of support, culture shock, classroom management challenges, and more—speak to the broader trends in the personal and professional experiences of foreign teachers[1] who are recruited for and placed in U.S. urban schools. These teachers are promoted as "cultural ambassadors" who can better prepare American students for an increasingly globalized world. But does being from another country automatically qualify someone to teach students from diverse groups? Many administrators in urban districts have assumed that it does, as they face a supposed teacher shortage that may require nearly 4 million teachers by the year 2020, with the largest growth in student population occurring in public schools (National Center for Education Statistics, 2011). As a result, corporate agencies that recruit teachers for critically understaffed urban schools have proliferated, placing almost 20,000 foreign-trained educators per year in U.S. schools (American Federation of Teachers, 2009).

The majority of new teachers will be needed in urban areas that are traditionally hard to staff with quality educators. This perennial "teacher shortage" is better defined as a problem of teacher misdistribution, because the most highly qualified and the greatest number of teachers are hired in suburban, well-paying districts, while many urban centers are left behind (Ingersoll, 2002; Ingersoll & Smith, 2003). Federal, state, and local governments have developed various initiatives to address teacher shortages, including easing teacher certification requirements, supporting alternative certification and financial incentive initiatives, and championing recruitment programs that strive to bring mid-career professionals, military veterans, and minorities into the classroom. The most recent strategy to alleviate the teacher shortage is the recruitment of teachers from other nations.

International teacher recruitment is literally being "sold" as both a solution to the shortage and as a way to provide students of color with more world exposure. Usually when we talk about minority students, we talk about Black students as having culture and White students not, but in this case for some reason, we presume that Black students need more cultural exposure. The irony of such rhetoric is that students of color are understood as having a cultural deficit, while White students, who themselves often believe they are "culture free," are not thought to need the "cultural assistance" of international educators. Two discourses, the need to fill open spots and the need for "cultured" students of color, are dovetailing into one strategy.

Although in a much different form from today, international teachers have been a part of U.S. classrooms for decades, as part of university faculty or teacher exchange programs like the Fulbright Teacher Exchange Program. Although some empirical research has been conducted on teacher exchange programs, this is not the case for international teacher recruitment. From national statements, we have some statistics on the number of teachers who are recruited, but we do not often know where or for how long they stay or what motivates them to stay or go. We know very little about what happens during their recruitment, transition, and orientation process, and even less about what happens in their classrooms as they work to engage urban students. We do not know what brings them joy, what challenges them, or what makes them wish they were home again. We do not know how their students feel about having an international teacher or how this influences instruction or the classroom environment. Nor do we know what their American colleagues and principals think about the recruitment and instructional practices of teachers from abroad. Thus, we do not know if and how international teacher recruitment fulfills any of the goals of agencies, districts, or teachers themselves. These lacunae about very critical components of the teachers' experiences are only slightly filled by personal stories and reflections in newspaper and magazine periodicals (e.g., Coates, 2005; Neufeld, 2005; Peterson, 2005). *Teachers Without Borders?* fills this void in the literature by examining international teachers' recruitment, experiences, and pedagogy; in particular, this book uncovers what happens, culturally, in their urban classrooms. It also determines why, among the myriad possibilities that exist to solve the supposed teacher shortage, this type of teacher recruitment has become one of the favored policy solutions.

WHY INTERNATIONAL TEACHERS? WHY NOW?

Each year, millions of teachers are needed to staff public schools around the country. Researchers have shown that, contrary to popular opinion, enough teachers *are* being prepared; rather, the shortage is a problem of teacher turnover and teacher distribution (Hansen, 2001; Ingersoll, 2002; National Education Association, 2003). This perceived lack of teachers is exacerbated by the fact that the biggest shortages are where highly qualified teachers are needed most: in underfunded and under-resourced urban schools. In fact, in these urban public schools, the student population was expected to grow to almost 50 million by 2014, an increase of more than 20% since 1989 (Council for the Great City Schools, 2012; National Center for Education Statistics, 2012). Inevitably, many more teachers are needed to deal with this influx of new students, many of whom are immigrants and refugees. One can imagine many solutions to an increasing student population and perceived teacher shortage; and indeed many solutions were tried and tested (and mostly failed) for the past several decades. Therefore, why were international teachers being proffered as a resolution in the 2000s and 2010s? One reason is the preponderance of post-*x* ideologies. In an era of post-sexist, post-racial/racist, post-injustice rhetoric (e.g., Bonilla-Silva, 2006; Wise, 2010), it is easy to see how international teachers fit into this picture. Recruitment agencies capitalize on neoliberal beliefs about the importance of transcending borders and offer cheap, movable labor. Popular opinion dictates that it does not matter where this labor comes from because, thanks to globalization, we are moving even beyond post-race and into post-nation. But what else about the political, educational, and global climates made this "solution" to the shortage and this acceptance of post-nation ideology seem feasible and popular, yet allowed it to remain remarkably under-researched? It is my hope that *Teachers Without Borders?* answers those questions and challenges the feasibility of creating and building a post-culture, post-border world.

FROM THE GLOBAL TO THE LOCAL: SETTING AND PARTICIPANTS

Though this book offers descriptions of international teachers around the country, the primary sources of information and those teachers whose voices you will hear will be from a major metropolitan school district in the southeastern United States. In 2010, I conducted a qualitative case study, using interviews and classroom observations with teachers in a school district I will call Glendale. (See Appendix for more details on the methodology.) In order for you to fully understand the context in which these participants were placed, I will briefly outline the setting before describing the participants themselves.

Glendale School District

Glendale is massive in size, one of the largest systems in the southeastern United States. At the time of this writing, Glendale has approximately 140 schools and 13,000 employees, serving more than 102,000 students. The district spends approximately $8,000 per student per year, slightly less than the average spending in surrounding districts and states. In addition to traditional elementary, middle, and high schools, the district is also home to magnet, charter, theme, special education, Montessori, alternative, vocational, and international schools. Spread over approximately 260 square miles, these schools serve a variety of student populations. Yet socially, historically, and politically, Glendale is a district divided.

The student population of Glendale is over 70% Black and largely low-income; over 60% of students are on free or reduced-price lunch. Like many urban districts, Glendale is highly segregated, a vestige of decades-long segregation and more recent gentrification (Purdy, 2011). Though White students make up 10% of the population, they are clustered at only several schools in the north of the district. Many of the schools in south Glendale are severely segregated, or what Kozol (2005) calls apartheid schools, serving more than 98% students of color.

Glendale schools exhibit the "typical" problems of schools in urban environments, including lack of resources; bureaucratic hurdles; strict disciplinary plans and policing; high dropout, remediation, and school failure rates; student poverty; and teacher attrition (Kopetz, Lease, & Warren-King, 2005; Stairs, Donnell, & Dunn, 2011). Unique local problems also contribute to the difficulties faced by

Glendale teachers and students. At the time of this writing, several school-level administrators were indicted for cheating on the state examinations and district officials were in the midst of multiple lawsuits. A previous superintendent was embroiled in a criminal investigation, and redistricting plans pitted parents from the north against parents from the south as the nine-member Board of Education executed plans to close schools around the district. Though Glendale's website listed "a balanced budget" as one of their strengths, they were, in fact, in a deficit of more than $110 million, faced with closing schools (primarily in the southern part of the district), firing central office staff and other employees, and furloughing teachers. Teachers were increasingly concerned that new teacher effectiveness measures would endanger their jobs, as the state sought to tie student test scores to teacher evaluations. It is into this turbulent context—fraught with past and present cultural debates—that international teachers were placed.

The district employed between 60 and 100 foreign teachers each year; in 2009–2010, there were 74 foreign teachers. Forty-nine of the teachers were recruited by the agency discussed in this book, referred to as International Recruitment, Incorporated (IRI). The remaining 25 teachers were from another regional agency. The majority of teachers were recruited for secondary math, special education, and science positions.

Forty-six schools employed at least one international teacher, and many employed two or three teachers. Unsurprisingly, 97.3% of international educators working in Glendale in the 2009–2010 school year were placed in schools categorized as urban in the south side of the district, which served primarily poor, African American students and traditionally had more difficulty hiring and retaining teachers. The district's four top high schools and two top middle schools, all of which serve a majority of White students from the northern part of the district, did not employ any international teachers. The four teachers whose stories are shared here reflected the trend of international teachers being placed on Glendale's south side, as each of their south side schools served 99% students of color, and the average percentage of students on free or reduced-price lunch was 65%.

The Teachers

Glendale School District used two regional agencies to recruit international teachers, both of which recruited primarily from India. The four teachers in this study were employed by IRI and all were from India's Hyderabad area. As is typical of international teachers, all possessed a J-1 International Exchange visa, renewable for up to 3 years. All of the participants lived in the same apartment complex where they were originally placed by IRI, or the neighboring complex. The complexes were located in the north of the district, approximately 30 minutes from each of their schools, and were primarily home to other Indian and East Asian immigrants.

Aleeza. If you walked into Aleeza's classroom, you would not immediately have known that she was an international teacher. The room, like others at Tubman High School, was crowded with 35 desks, an overhead projector, a teacher's lab table and computer desk, cabinets, and a whiteboard. The leaning tower of paperwork was piled on the teacher's desk, cascading into skyscrapers of notebooks, binders, and folders. Small piles of crumpled paper decorated student desks, room corners, and even the top of cabinets far out of human reach, as if, as a colleague once noted, the paper fairy had come overnight and left trails of paper balls in her wake. On a bulletin board in the back of the classroom, there were sections for state standards, assignment rubrics, and examples of student work from her 10th- and 11th-grade chemistry and physical science classes. Colorful posters with hand-drawn electrons and atoms adorned the wall. On blinds (which were shuttered), big student-crafted posters said "elements and compounds," "changes in matter," and "properties of matter." On the front board, there were sections labeled for Agenda, Opening (divided into standard, essential question, and bell ringer), Work Period, and Closing. As students strolled in before the bell rang for their first-period class to begin, they picked up a textbook from the tilting pile and a notebook from underneath the lab table. Students did not have assigned seats, and when I asked one if I was in his seat, he said, "No, I am just thinking of where I want to sit." When the bell rang at 8:10 a.m., the teacher, Aleeza, entered from the hallway and shut the door.

In her third year in the United States, Aleeza was in her first year at Tubman, having been transferred from Douglass, a nearby school where she worked with another international teacher. At Tubman High School, Aleeza worked under Mr. Clark, an African American male, who was in his first year at the school, but had previously been her principal at Douglass. Tubman, a Title I school, had a graduation rate of approximately 70% and had difficulty making adequate yearly progress (AYP) on state assessments. Mr. Clark said that Tubman's biggest strength was its students, who may not realize all they can accomplish, but whom he saw as having "unlimited potential." Though others in the district may have "underestimated" Tubman, he claimed it was an "untapped gold mine." He identified the school's challenges as needing to raise test scores, improve the level of instruction for all students, and deal with discipline issues "common to all urban schools."

Before coming to the United States, Aleeza had 2 years of experience teaching middle school in India, where she received two bachelor's degrees in science and education of science, plus a master's degree in English. She decided to switch to teaching high school in the United States because she wanted to provide more in-depth science instruction. Unique to the teachers discussed here, Aleeza had traveled and lived outside India, in the Middle East and Europe, before coming to the United States. This particular morning, she looked at her 17 students, though by the end of the period there would be 28. If everyone attended, she told me later, there would not be enough desks for each student. With the exception of two students who appeared to be multiracial, all the others appeared to be Black. She said quietly, as Mr. Clark came over the loud speaker to read the morning announcements, "Okay, you need to start on your bell ringer." The students talked to each other and did not heed her request. She repeated herself with a bit more force, and then there appeared the only indication that something was different from any other urban classroom: A student called out, "Miss, I don't understand you and your accent sometimes. What did you say?"

Faria. During second period, 5 miles away at Woodson High School, Faria's high school math classroom looked remarkably similar. Here, too, there were clearly demarcated sections on the board, demonstrating her compliance with the district's mandates for organizing instructional time. This revealed the three different subjects she taught: Geometry, Algebra I, and Algebra II. All 30 students in this algebra class appeared to be Black and, just as the bell rang, they moved hurriedly into her classroom from the noisy hallway, which was littered with piles of trash because it was one of the school's "locker cleanout" days. Students had either "missed" the trash bins, or the bins had overflowed onto the floor, and one had to wade through piles of discarded paper to enter the room.

Woodson High School was a Title I school in the south of the district. Led by Mr. Norman, an African American male in his fourth year as principal, Woodson graduated 85% of its seniors. The school frequently made AYP. Mr. Norman attributed this to teachers' high level of retention, commitment to the school, and devotion to the community. Challenges identified by Mr. Norman included the transitory nature of the community, which did not allow for a consistent student body; the need for students to contribute to their household income, which meant students were often tired or unprepared for each school day; and discipline problems common in other public schools. Woodson High School attempted to control for these challenges by offering extra tutorials and Saturday school.

Students in Faria's classroom shifted around the large boxes at the back of the room, which had been packed for her move to a new space in the newly constructed wing. As a result of the move, which she told me was already delayed 1 month, there was nothing on the stark white walls except for chipping paint. Faria readjusted her head scarf and rapped on the board with a marker. "Look here," she called to her students over the din, "get started on your Do Now." Most students continued talking to each other and sharing photographs on their cell phones.

Faria was in her third year at Woodson High School. In India, she received her bachelor of education in mathematics and physical science. She had seven years of experience teaching similar subjects, plus physical science, at an Indian private school. She had never traveled outside her state or country before, but she was given the chance to teach in either the United States or Oman. She chose the United States because it was "the land of opportunity."

Samina. Seven miles from Faria's classroom, Samina opened the classroom door and escorted in her third-period, 6th-grade language arts students from the cafeteria at Chisholm Middle School. Every day, she had to pick them up from lunch and walk them in a straight line back to her classroom. This was the school policy implemented by Mr. Sutherland, the principal of the Title I school and the feeder school for Douglass High. Mr. Sutherland, an African American male, was in his third year at Chisholm. He explained that the school's strengths were dedicated teachers and students who "come to school every day and they come prepared to learn, the majority of them." The challenge, however, according to Mr. Sutherland, was that, because many parents worked several jobs, it was difficult to get parents involved in school decisions and classroom life. Other students had abusive or unsupportive home situations that had "a profound impact on their lives at school because they come to school sometimes very angry. They act out because of what has happened the night before or a week before." One way the school accommodated students and families with these challenges was to make full use of the Title I community liaison position, filled by a school counselor, to reach out to parents and find ways to get them involved in their child's education.

In Samina's classroom, boys sat on one side of the room, girls on the other, all in rows, according to her policy for classroom organization. Here, too, the floor was littered with tissues, pen caps, notebooks, and stray paper. In India, Samina had received two bachelor's degrees, one in science and one in education, and a master's degree in English. She taught for 7 years, including 6th through 9th grades and an adult spoken English class. Though she had more experience teaching science, she was hired to teach English at Chisholm; she was one of the only foreign teachers ever hired to teach English in the district.

While she hurriedly took attendance on the computer at the front of the room, one student passed out composition books to her classmates, all 28 of whom appeared to be Black. Samina moved to the front of the room near the whiteboard, which, like Faria and Aleeza's, was marked with standards and instructions for each section of the class period. The first one that Samina pointed to was silent reading. She tried to get students' attention by clapping her hands and walking to a milk crate filled with paperback books. "It is time for reading now," she yelled. "No talking! This is a classroom, not a zoo. Now is reading time! You know this!" Three of the 28 students reached into their backpacks and pulled out a book; two walked over to the milk crate and selected a book. The rest continued talking to each other.

Shrusty. Just 3 miles up the street at Douglass High School, Shrusty escorted her students back into their classroom from Adaptive Physical Education. She was accompanied by two male paraprofessionals and seven students, all appearing to be Black. Three students were in wheelchairs. The four students who could do so sat in desks labeled with their names in large block letters. Her space here reminded Shrusty of home. In India, she had been trained in special education and, with her family, operated a special education "center" for disabled students for 2 years before her departure. She also taught computer programming to adults in India and had previously worked as a call center manager for a major U.S. online company. When I met her, she had been in the United States for 3 years and was the "mother" of a group of international teachers. She "knew the ropes" and had learned enough about her school and local community that she drove other teachers to and from schools nearby.

Shrusty's principal at Douglass High School was Mr. Scott, an African American male. Though he had been a principal for 4 years, it was his first year at Douglass, where the district had transferred him to "improve" the school. Douglass was one of the largest high schools in the district, qualified for Title I status, and had not made AYP for 7 years. When asked about the school's strengths, Mr. Scott answered, "Athletics . . . I do not know of any others." When asked about challenges, however, he provided an extensive list of difficulties, including academic performance, student apathy and teacher apathy stemming from a dysfunctional school culture, student misbehavior stemming from lack of parental involvement, and high teacher and administrative turnover.

On this afternoon, Shrusty rolled one student's wheelchair into place, and then all students faced the television on the wall. It was mounted above the teacher's desk, near the entrance to the private bathroom. The students were silent as Shrusty turned on *The Lion King*, which they had presumably begun watching earlier, as it picked up in the middle of the movie. One student squealed out loud as the characters began singing on screen. Shrusty moved around the classroom, tending to various tasks: putting formula into one student's feeding tube; taking one student to be changed in the bathroom; entering attendance records on the computer in the back of the classroom; adjusting one student's headphones so that he was better able to hear Britney Spears. Their classroom was at the end of a long hallway, a considerable distance from the center of the school; they had to be near a side entrance, Shrusty explained later, so the adapted school buses could pick students up at the door. It was a world that felt far removed from the bustle of school dismissal for the other 1,000 students.

The Decision Makers

A large part of the story of international recruitment in Glendale depends on the decision makers. To include this portion of the story, I also interviewed the principals mentioned in the teacher profiles above, district officials, and recruiters. Ms. Muller and Ms. Jefferson were district-level personnel who served in the human resources department. They were involved in the international teacher recruitment process at varying points throughout the year. They were able to speak to the district's reasons for recruitment, overall hiring processes, and orientation and professional development programs for foreign teachers. Each had been in her current position for several years.

The founder and owner of IRI, Ms. Jain, agreed to be interviewed for this project. IRI places approximately 60 teachers per year in one state in the Southeast, and Ms. Jain was the sole person responsible for interviewing and hiring teachers in India; coordinating their departure, arrival, and orientation in the United States; and maintaining communication throughout their tenure in the country. Throughout the book, her statements about her agency and teachers are compared to the comments of teachers, principals, and district officials, and to my observations.

The Allies

International teachers around the country are not alone in their fight for better treatment. Indeed, two of the only groups to write about international teachers have become their staunch advocates. In addition to the National Education Association's 2003 report on foreign teachers, the American Federation of Teachers (AFT) wrote a more recent report. These two unions are currently representing international teachers in several labor dispute cases, but they are not representing the teachers in Glendale.

To contextualize the policy framework in which teacher recruitment exists, I interviewed three AFT representatives. Ms. Dougherty and Mr. Adams (pseudonyms) were specifically selected because of their work on a 2009 report about foreign teachers. Mr. McNeil (real name) served as legal counsel for a lawsuit against a recruitment agency in Louisiana. They provided important facts and opinions about equitable hiring processes, fair treatment in the workplace, and the future of recruitment.

I see myself as an ally for international teachers and their students. While I went into this research open to promising results and successful possibilities and hoping that that Padma's experience was an exception to the rule, I did not find either of those things. Instead, I found a group of teachers who were not trained or supported for U.S. urban schools and whom I believe to be representative of a larger group around the country. I found teachers who wanted to do their best, but did not know how. I found principals who yearned for a way to connect their students to the world outside Glendale, but had been misled into thinking that international teachers were that solution and whose problematic deficit perspectives and quest for "control" of urban students exacerbated the problems. I found some students who connected with their international teachers, but more who did not. I found district officials who created convenient ways to deny the problems that were happening in their schools and a recruiter who lied to her teachers and to me. What I did not find, disappointingly, were very many activists fighting to help the teachers find their voice and their rights.

In many cases, the lack of concerned advocates may be merely because people do not know what is happening. When I tell people this story, they commonly ask, "Why didn't I know this was going on?" or "Why is no one talking about this?" There are nearly twice as many international teachers as there are Teach for America (TFA) corps members (approximately 5,000 new corps members per year, for 10,000 corps members at one time if all are retained into their second year in the program, as compared to 19,000 international teachers in any given year), but it is rare these days to meet a teacher or scholar who does not know about and have strong opinions on TFA (American Federation of Teachers, 2009; Teach for America, 2012). It cannot be just about numbers. Perhaps it is because, unlike TFA, which has been championed by policymakers, international teacher recruitment remains under the radar of those policymakers who create the master narrative of urban school reform.

In the process of working with these teachers, I frequently fought the "scholar" versus "activist" debate with others and myself. Could I fight for their rights and remain "objective" in my research? In the end, I decided that my scholarship can be objective even if it leads me to a position that is not. I can be impassioned by my research without being biased during the research. Thus, though I make a research-based and data-driven argument, my goals are not neutral. I want others to be shocked and outraged with what they read, and I hope this outrage incites both personal indignation and a professional refusal to stand idly by while yet another group of teachers and students is left behind in urban schools. Thus, I write this text with the hope that, in a future edition perhaps, the section on allies and scholar-activists will be longer.

HOW THIS BOOK IS ORGANIZED

This text is organized around the theme of borders, barriers, and boundaries and, as suggested by the question mark in the title, explores whether or not international teachers actually *are* without borders. This is not to suggest that the borders are merely or literally geographic—rather, the metaphorical borders that international teachers face are also cultural and social. The barriers they face are also political and historical, which are much harder to see than physical boundaries. Chapter 1, *Climbing Mountains,* examines the trends, benefits, and challenges of teacher recruitment, paying close attention to current educational policies that push globalization and neoliberal reforms. I argue that the mountains of challenges inhibit teachers' ability to achieve the "American Dream" through temporary recruitment. Chapter 2, *The Continental Divide,* explains the similarities and differences between teachers' U.S. and Indian classroom contexts. Further, I explore the effect these similarities and differences have on teachers' practice and interpersonal relationships. Here, I assert that teachers' lack of understanding about U.S. school culture leads to deficit views of urban students and that an instrumental factor in their ability to remain in the United States is the support of American allies and international colleagues.

Chapter 3, *Trying to Build Cultural Bridges,* provides a window into the teachers' classrooms, gleaned from observations and interviews, and illustrates their challenges working with African American students in urban environments. I present their culturally relevant pedagogical practices as a continuum, arguing that while international teachers exhibit some characteristics of effective teaching, their lack of historic background knowledge and competence makes true cultural relevance nearly impossible. As their ability to work with diverse students is touted as one of the goals of recruitment, Chapter 4, *Barriers to Success,* discusses how, if at all, recruitment achieves stated goals—ranging from making more money to preparing students for a global marketplace to solving the teacher shortage—for teachers, students, schools, and districts. I argue that, by ignoring the unique needs of international teachers and buying into neoliberal ideology, various stakeholders systematically undercut teachers' goals and destroy the possibility of a successful outcome for teachers and their students.

Chapter 5, *Pushing the Boundary and Crossing the Line,* analyzes the obstacles that teachers and schools have in achieving their goals, including the perilous consequences of recruitment. Using related stories from high-profile cases of migrant teacher exploitation, including Filipino and Caribbean teachers around the United States, I uncover the tendency for districts to overlook exploitation and the troubling, illegal practices of some recruitment agencies. Finally, a concluding chapter, *Charting a Course,* presents an extended set of recommendations for research, policy, teacher education, and classroom practice that will allow for the promise and possibility of international recruitment to be fulfilled while ensuring that teachers are treated equitably and students are provided with the best educators possible. Overall, I argue that international teacher recruitment, as it currently exists, is unjust for teachers and students. The challenges faced by foreign educators are exacerbated by neoliberal policies and practices that ignore the importance of cultural context and instead perpetuate a hegemonic discourse about a border-free world.

ONE

Climbing Mountains

Trends, Benefits, and Challenges of Recruitment

We import just about everything else—why not teaching talent as well?
—Wolff and Glaser, 1986

After climbing a great hill, one only finds there are many more hills to climb.
—Nelson Mandela, 1995

Living as an international teacher requires a delicate balance of strength, determination, grit, and finesse. As they cross borders, teachers may encounter mountains that require them to face their climbs with no rope, climbing partners, or map. In the tricky and treacherous terrain of border-crossing education, they often climb one mountain and, relieved to reach the peak and joyful at their ascent, only find a sprawling landscape of other peaks in the distance. Teachers experience this metaphorical climb as they negotiate the benefits and challenges of working as an international educator in U.S. urban schools.

This chapter describes the national trends, benefits, and challenges of international teacher recruitment, drawing primarily upon union reports and mass media sources, as there is little empirical research on the topic. The experiences of my four participants will ground the discussion by highlighting their reasons for coming to the United States, what they saw as benefits of recruitment, and what challenges they expected and experienced. Overall, I argue that the overwhelming challenges outweigh the benefits of recruitment and that the current neoliberal policy context creates even more mountains in the teachers' paths.

As with all educational policy decisions, the movement toward hiring more teachers from abroad does not occur in a vacuum. The climate of neoliberalism that allows charter and voucher programs to flourish—and to be seen as the only alternative to "failing" public schools—is the same climate that makes it possible for districts to outsource their hiring procedures (e.g., Apple, 2006). The same climate, ironically, nurtures arguments for anti-immigration policies, "secured borders," and a unifying national identity or assimilation. As policymakers and urban administrators are decrying a teacher "shortage," they are taking steps to import teachers from abroad. According to the American Federation of Teachers

(2009), "while the hiring of overseas-trained teachers may be a Band-aid treating the symptom of the teacher shortage, it is in no way a cure for the conditions that caused the shortage in the first place" (p. 25). Those conditions—difficult working environments and overwhelming bureaucracy, for example—are fed by two contextual factors: (1) definitions and revisions of teacher education and recruitment and (2) neoliberal education policies and reforms.

DEFINITIONS AND REVISIONS OF
TEACHER EDUCATION AND RECRUITMENT

As a result of the No Child Left Behind Act (NCLB) and its supplement, Race to the Top (RTTT), urban districts are in even greater need of high-quality teachers to prepare students for high-stakes testing than in the past. In recent decades, there has been, in fact, no shortage of programs designed to remedy the problem of recruiting and preparing more teachers for U.S. classrooms. The reigning discourse is that urban schools simply need more teachers and that if the government removes the barriers standing in the teachers' way (primarily finances and certification requirements), the problem will be solved. Strategies center around three areas, all of which attempt to bring greater numbers of teachers into the education profession: financial incentives; reduced certification requirements; and recruitment of nontraditional teaching populations. International teacher recruitment aligns with the ideology of all three of these tactics.

First, states and districts utilize financial incentives, especially in the recruitment of teachers to high-need locales and subjects. Despite research that has shown that teachers would prefer better working conditions over higher pay (Public Agenda, 2000), states have not ceased attempts to attract more teachers by offering financial rewards, though the rewards do not actually increase teachers' salaries. Incentives include student loan deferment or cancellation for teaching in "critical needs" areas; mortgage and housing down payment assistance; and "combat pay" or "hazard pay" for teachers willing to work and remain in urban districts. International teachers are also offered financial incentives for working in U.S. schools—mainly higher salaries than they made in their home countries. Though states continue to develop financial incentives to recruit more teachers, they are doing so without any research base. The Education Commission of the States recognized as early as 2000 that in all instances of loan-forgiveness programs, signing bonuses, housing allowances, and salary increases, "no data [were] available on whether . . . recipients remain[ed] in these high-need assignments or in the teaching profession longer than average" (n.p.).

A second revision to teacher recruitment and preparation is that teacher licensure requirements have been altered and reduced. The U.S. government has long been a proponent of easing what it calls "barriers" to certification (Paige, 2002), and as a result, states and universities have created alternative preparation programs designed to expedite the certification process. Instead of training through a traditional 4-year undergraduate teacher preparation program or a graduate teacher certification program, many teachers have been able to enter the classroom after enrolling in an alternative program. Alternative certification requirements vary by state and program, but the majority of them compress the amount of time pre-service teachers (who have bachelor's degrees in subjects other than education) must spend in coursework and student teaching before entering their own classrooms. Some "fast-track" programs allow teachers to enter the classroom *before* they receive state certification. From the outset, the federal government has supported alternative preparation of teachers in many states. During his tenure as Secretary of Education under President George W. Bush, Rod Paige (2002) championed the development of alternative certification routes, which would alleviate "burdensome requirements" of teacher education and bring "thousands of talented soldiers of democracy into our schools" (p. vi). Paige's successors Margaret Spellings and Arne Duncan have followed his lead and championed alternative routes. Most notably, Duncan, speaking to a group of teacher educators and future students, claimed that traditional teacher education was doing a "mediocre job" and needed "revolutionary change" to meet the needs of today's schools. Similarly to alternatively certified U.S.-born teachers, when international teachers arrive in U.S. schools, most have already taken a certification exam that proves that they meet the minimum requirements for teacher licensure. However, most have not been educated about U.S. school history, culture, or curriculum.

Despite the federal and state push for alternative programs, research continues to show that alternative certification is not as rigorous or effective as traditional teacher preparation programs (e.g., Darling-Hammond, Holtzman, Gatlin, & Heilig, 2003; Feistritzer, 2007; Hansen, 2001; Johnson, Birkeland, & Peske, 2003). Advocates of alternative certification, as Zeichner (2003) notes, argue that "teachers' subject matter knowledge and verbal ability are the main determinants of teaching success" and that many teacher training classes' themes and methods could be better learned through on-the-job training (p. 503). Yet, Zeichner claims that alternative certification is really part of a "deregulation agenda" by school reform advocates hoping to break the "monopoly" of teacher education colleges. However, "majoring in a subject or passing a subject matter test," as Zeichner demonstrates, "even if the bar is set high, is no guarantee that teachers understand the central concepts in their discipline and have the pedagogical content knowledge needed to transform content to promote understanding by diverse learners" (pp. 505–6).

Using a combination of alternative certification and financial incentives, other recruitment programs bring nontraditional populations into teaching. These programs, the most famous of which is Teach for America (TFA), are designed to attract recent college graduates and mid-career switchers into the education profession. TFA's approaches resemble international teacher recruitment in that the current rhetoric of finding "the best and the brightest" (domestically and abroad) ignores the need for teachers to have a more contextualized understanding of schools and students (Dunn & Kavanagh, 2012). In all of these revisions of teacher recruitment and education, policymakers fail to recognize that the most effective teachers are the ones who have an understanding of subject matter, pedagogy, and students' cultures, especially if they are entering a school where the students' cultures are dramatically different from their own (Ladson-Billings, 1997). Understanding students' funds of knowledge and their engagement in out-of-school contexts is also important for understanding the whole child (Behizadeh, 2012; Ford, 2011; K. Green, 2011). None of these recruitment methods addresses the more fundamental problem of teacher retention. Rather, they are primarily concerned with drawing teachers to urban schools, not with keeping them there and preparing them for success with urban students.

NEOLIBERAL EDUCATION POLICIES AND REFORMS

Neoliberal ideology, or a set of economic beliefs in favor of market-based competition, privatization, and globalization, has developed a stronghold in political and educational discourse. Though neoliberalism is not the only dogma that influences schools, its proponents exercise a major force in shaping current policy by arguing that their strategies are the best solutions to problems that plague urban schools. The crux of neoliberal beliefs lies in capitalism and centers goals for society and the economy around market forces. Policies are then legitimized and prioritized based on their relationship to these market forces.

The language of the "market" comes from economics and business, and it typically refers to the volume of buyers for a particular product or service. When neoliberal market principles are applied to education, parents and students become the buyers or consumers, and instruction (and thus instructors) become the products and services rendered. According to Fitzsimons (2002), "for neoliberals, it is not sufficient that there is a market; there must be nothing which is not the market" (p. 2). McCarthy, Pitton, Kim, and Monje (2009) call neoliberalism "the universalization of the enterprise ethic" (p. 39). Schools will improve, too, according to this philosophy, if they are in competition with one another and we allow market forces to commodify education, thus, as Chomsky says, valuing profit over people (Apple, 2001; Chomsky, 1999; Giroux, 2004; Saltman, 2007).

The pervasiveness of market discourse is evident in the new language of education, through what Saltman (2007) calls omnipresent and nebulous market terms. For example, in the Glendale district, teachers attend workshops on "customer service" and "efficiency" to better "serve their clients." Chief executive officers, chief operating officers, and executive directors staff the district and school offices and are in charge of maintaining "transparency" within the district's "culture of accountability." They complete tasks such as "employee verification audits" and "strategic plans." In one strategic plan for how to improve the district, the Glendale School Board claimed it was

> fully committed to a process of managed instruction and performance/
> empowerment for the operation of schools as determined by appropriate
> criteria. Complementary to this commitment is the implementation of an
> aligned management system for continuous improvement and differentiated
> compensation and recognition based on demonstrated effectiveness for
> student growth and achievement.

Such a strategic plan hides behind business lingo of operational efficiency and management and obscures a very controversial reform: pay-for-performance. Glendale had aligned with state legislation to pay teachers based on "student growth and achievement" (which they measure as scores on state-mandated standardized tests) under the guise of improving the efficiency of a school system. Further, the imprecise and jargon-laden statement makes it difficult for the most important people in a school system—students, parents, and teachers—to understand the reality of such a plan. What is even more troubling than the language itself is the fact that the school board unquestionably adopted such business models without considering why schools are ill-fitted to be run as businesses. This opened the door for public resources to be allocated to private entities, among them for-profit recruiters of international teachers. A display of neoliberalism at the highest levels of education occurred when I called the U.S. Department of Education and was greeted with the automated message, "Thank you for calling the U.S. Department of Education, where we aim to serve our customers well" (March 29, 2010). This increasing and unexamined commodification means that "under neoliberalism, everything either is for sale or plundered for profit" (Giroux, 2004, p. xiii), even people, like international teachers.

Neoliberals also believe in privatization of schools because of their ongoing suspicion of public services and, as a result, have influenced policy in such a way that investments in public education have decreased or shifted to the private sphere (Giroux, 2004; Saltman, 2007). Neoliberals argue that the state should not be involved in economic or social life. For them, public resources are at risk because the state is too large and bureaucratic, whereas the private sector has the freedom to be more efficient and responsive to individual needs (Saltman, 2007). Privatizing public spheres seems a sensible solution if one accepts the "central neoliberal tenet that all problems are private rather than social in nature" (Giroux, 2004, p. 9), ignoring issues of systemic discrimination. If problems are private, then solutions can be private, too. Saltman (2007) offers an extensive list of the forms that neoliberal privatization takes in education, including:

for-profit management of schools, performance contracting, for-profit charter schools, school vouchers, school commercialism, for-profit online education, online home-schooling, test publishing and textbook industries, electronic and computer-based software curriculum, for-profit remediation, educational contracting for food, transportation, and financial services. (p. 53)

We can add international teacher recruitment to his list, in which districts "hire out" their employment functions and outsource their human resources role to for-profit recruitment agencies. The role of finding highly qualified teachers moves from the public sphere to the private.

One of the reasons that neoliberalism is so expansive and resilient is because it grounds itself in conceptions of freedom and liberty, and broad ranges of individuals find that liberty appealing (Robertson, 2008). Though progressive reformers argue that neoliberalism is inherently undemocratic, advocates of neoliberalism often closely link market rhetoric with democratic language—in this case, democracy is seen as the "freedom to consume and own within a capitalist society (Wells, Slayton, & Scott, 2002, p. 338). For example, Wells et al. studied a charter school's board that made decisions based on the understanding that their students and parents were "consumers with the economic, political, and social efficacy to make demands" (p. 338). Neoliberalism flourishes because many groups that would have otherwise remained disparate hear the language of democratic choice and see it as sensible (Apple, 2001; Giroux, 2004). For example, elite White Republicans and working-class Black parents do not typically agree on social policy, yet neoliberal rhetoric about "choice" for charter schools and vouchers appeals to both groups. Though many scholars and educationalists recognize that neoliberal doctrine is "crafted and employed for reasons of power and profit" (Chomsky, 1999, p. 39) as opposed to the welfare of the country's neediest citizens, the general public—and indeed many politicians, administrators, and others with control over education—remain under the illusion that neoliberal doctrines are designed as the great equalizer in a broken educational system. Yet, as Bowles and Gintis (1976) argued decades ago, it is still true that "the major characteristics of the educational system in the United States today flow directly from its role in producing a workforce able and willing to staff occupational positions in the capitalist system" (p. 265).

The inevitable question, then, becomes, so what *is* wrong with a system that wants to give parents, students, and schools the choice between private and public providers? If parents are not happy with their children's school options, or if administrators are not happy with their hiring options, is it not their right to look for other alternatives? I would argue that, while alternative paradigms and solutions may sometimes be necessary, the danger is that neoliberalism is often framed as the *only* alternative to urban school "failure." And it is one alternative whose ends do not justify the means. The ends of neoliberal policies in education are the dismantling of public schools, the commodification of teachers, and the blaming of children for "the global economic race to the bottom" (Saltman, 2007, p. 12). One of the dangers of neoliberal education policy, as well as neoconservative policies that stress a return to "the basics" and a general disregard for issues of privilege and oppression, is that "civic engagement now appears impotent as corporations privatize public space and disconnect power from issues of equity, social justice, and civic responsibility" (Giroux, 2004 pp. 5–6). Privatizing public schools and the teaching forces within them threatens the very nature of a democracy—chiefly the families' and teachers' ability to participate in organizing, governing, and unionizing efforts to make their voices be heard. For this democratic education to be realized through "the creation of an equal and liberating school system," there must be "a revolutionary transformation of economic life" (Bowles & Gintis, 1976, p. 265). Urban students and teachers are being further marginalized by policies that claim to give them power; instead, these key stakeholders and their values are being co-opted for private interests and slogans while their decision-making power is becoming more and more negligible. In the words of a former Idaho teacher union president, Sherri Wood, and the buttons and bumper stickers that have captured the feelings of millions of teachers around the country: "You can't put students first if you put teachers last."

GLOBALIZATION AND 21ST-CENTURY SKILLS

Neoliberal reforms—and thus the recruitment of international educators— are supported by the rhetoric of globalization and the purported need for the United States to achieve a competitive advantage in the world marketplace. What Friedman (2005) views as the "flattening" of the marketplace, neoliberals see as an opportunity to restore the United States to its "rightful place" as an international leader. For neoliberals, globalization's "rapid intensification of migration, the amplification of electronic mediation, the movement of economic and cultural capital across borders, and the deepening and stretching of interconnectivity around the world," is a political landscape ripe for the picking (McCarthy et al., 2009, p. 39). This is not to say that all aspects of globalization are bad or dangerous, but that when neoliberals use globalization to argue for the commodification of people, globalization's possibilities run the risk of disenfranchising the very individuals for whom globalization holds the most promise.

Globalization often leads to "glocalization" (Bauman, 1998; Weber, 2007), where the global becomes local, and the local, global, because of rapid consumerism across borders. For Bauman (1998), glocalization is a "process of world-wide re-stratification, in the course of which a new world-wide socio-cultural hierarchy is put together" (p. 43). Such a tension between global-local relationships is reflected in the recruitment of international teachers. Unsurprisingly, this "world as a supermarket ripe for consumer (and producer) competition" is appealing to parents and educators concerned for their students' success (Apple, Au, & Gandin,

2009, p. 10) because they see no alternative to this hegemonic discourse that has become enormously engrained in our cultural milieu (Giroux, 2004). What parents and educators need to realize, however, is that students are being increasingly viewed as human capital (Apple et al., 2009). Schools are forced to respond to neoliberal reforms in a way that allows their students to be successful, but the impact of vouchers, charters, and other reforms is that student identities are "constructed in and by the market" (McCarthy et al., 2009, p. 40). Instead of developing children as thoughtful citizens or giving them access to multicultural practices that researchers have shown can make a difference (Banks, 1994, 2004; Ladson-Billings, 1997), schooling is reduced merely to economic ends and, like in Glendale, teachers are reduced to human capital transmitters and "investments."

In the face of this pressure, when states are stepping back from their investment in public education, what is a school district to do except look for a solution, for a way to legitimize itself? They seek any reform to solve the problem. International teacher recruitment, which promises to prepare students for a new, globalized world with invisible borders, while filling empty positions, is one such reform.

INTERNATIONAL TEACHERS BY THE NUMBERS

As far back as the 1980s, some school district policymakers were asking how they might harness international teaching talent for U.S. students: "we import just about everything else—why not teaching talent as well" (Wolff & Glaser, 1986, p. 27). Yet despite the length of time for which recruitment has been considered and used, there are few national data on recruitment trends. Two national reports shed light onto the preponderance of such recruitment.

First is Barber's (2003) report for the National Education Association, in which he uses data from Immigration and Naturalization Services (now the U.S. Citizenship and Immigration Services), the U.S. Labor Department, the State Department, and various teacher placement agencies to estimate that around 15,000 international teachers were employed in U.S. schools in the 2002–2003 school year. Of these, around 10,000 were employed in public school settings. Most of the teachers were placed in states with large urban districts that were members of the Council of the Great City Schools, such as California, Florida, Georgia, Illinois, Maryland, New Jersey, Ohio, and Texas (Council of the Great City Schools, 2012).

Next, Barber's report describes third-party recruitment, placement, and employment agencies for international teachers.[1] Most school districts pay agencies between $11,000 and $14,000 per year. Barber notes that the districts, many of which are already stretched monetarily, find ways to include this expense in their budgets because foreign teachers do not require retirement, health care, or Social Security benefits (because the teachers pay their own costs through fees charged by recruitment agencies).

The American Federation of Teachers (AFT), expanding Barber's report, updated the number of international teachers in the United States to almost 20,000, and synthesized the process, perils, and international impact of recruitment (American Federation of Teachers, 2009). Aptly titled *Importing Educators*, the report highlights recruitment dangers such as visa fraud, indentured servitude, unequal benefits, culture shock, and communication barriers, which will be discussed in future chapters. It also identifies one of the major challenges of tracking international teachers: the lack of systematized reporting and record-keeping for educators' visas.

International teachers have to possess either an H-1B visa or a J-1 visa to enter the United States. Both visas, by definition, are temporary and are not intended to lead to permanent residency or citizenship. Data from the Department of State, the Department of Labor, and the U.S. Citizenship and Immigration Services are difficult to access and are not published as frequently as mandated by law, but the most recent statistics available illustrate that there was an increase in international teacher visas in the last 10 years (American Federation of Teachers, 2009).

H-1B visas, designed as Specialty Occupation Work visas, are valid for 3 years and can be renewed once, allowing the holder to remain in the United States for up to 6 years. Teachers have to then return to their home countries for at least 1 year before getting another H-1B. Several recruitment agencies supply their teachers with H-1B visas, as the only requirement is that the holder possesses a bachelor's degree and expertise in a "highly specialized body of knowledge" (U.S. Department of Labor, 2012). In 2007, the last year for which data are available, there were 6,085 new H-1B teacher visas issued; data were not available, however, on how many total H-1B visas were used for teachers each year.

Another type, the J-1 Exchange Visitor visa, is valid for 1 year and can be renewed twice, allowing the holder to remain in the United States for up to 3 years. Teachers have to then return to their home countries for at least 2 years before getting another J-1. Holders of J-1 visas have to "be a primary or secondary teacher in their last legal residence; satisfy the standards of the state in which they will be working; be of good reputation and character; want to teach primary or secondary school in the United States full-time; and have a minimum of 3 years teaching experience" (National Archives and Record Administration, 2012). Approved sponsors provide information and orientations for each teacher; in 2008, there were 64 sponsors, including IRI, other recruitment agencies, state and local Departments of Education, intercultural nonprofits, and other groups.

For school districts to sponsor an international teacher under the J-1 Exchange visa program, the districts have to ensure teacher proficiency in English, a provision of medical insurance, and program orientation, both pre- and post-arrival in the United States. In addition, the districts are required to monitor teachers' welfare and progress, file an annual report with the U.S. State Department, and confirm that the teaching position is, in fact, temporary (Barber, 2003). Specific orientation information is required, including information about life and customs in the United States; community resources, including public transportation, schools, and banks; health care and insurance; outlines of program rules, structure, and representatives; and official materials from the State Department (Barber, 2003). It is unclear whether the "required" information is actually ever distributed to international teachers or if and how other requirements are monitored.

The problem with both H-1B and J-1 visa data is that significant amounts of necessary information are not collected, and thus, it is difficult to track the increase in foreign teacher recruitment over time. Based on the number of new visas issued each year, the AFT (2009) estimated that in 5 years, between 2003 and 2008, the number of international teachers working in the United States increased by at least 30%. They were unable, however, to track how long each of the teachers stayed. Did they renew their visas the maximum number of times and stay 3 or 6 years? Further, how many teachers applied for visa extensions or waivers? How many later returned on a second visa or became permanent residents? Unless more complete and timely data are compiled by relevant governmental departments and made more accessible to the public, it will remain difficult to gauge the true impact of international teachers on U.S. retention problems.

WHERE IN THE WORLD?
INTERNATIONAL TEACHER MIGRATION PATTERNS

The migration of teachers across borders is not solely a U.S. or an Indian phenomenon. In fact, the United States and India are but two pieces of a much larger puzzle of worker migration. Teacher migration around the world, similar to other highly skilled labor movements like nursing, information technology, and customer service, has increased with globalization. There are an estimated 200 million migrant workers around the world today. These workers come disproportionately from developing nations that need to retain their highly educated citizenry. For example, 50% to 80% of all highly educated citizens from several developing countries in African and the Caribbean live and work abroad, and one in seven Filipinos works abroad (American Federation of Teachers, 2009; Manik, Maharaj, & Sookrajh, 2006; Commonwealth Secretariat, 2004). The monetary impact of their migration is undeniable: Migrant workers send home an estimated $300 billion a year (DeParle, 2007). This amount is nearly three times the world's combined foreign-aid budgets. In the Philippines alone, overseas workers account for more than $1 billion a month in remittances back to the Philippines (American Federation of Teachers, 2009). Gutierrez (2012) argues that "the Philippines' institutionalized export-labor program, commodification of women's labor, and the historical colonial relationship to the U.S. have created the pathway for this recent large-scale migration" (n.p).

In addition to the monetary benefits, researchers have found other reasons that impel workers to leave their homes for work abroad. These "push" and "pull" factors are outlined in the AFT's 2009 report. "Push" factors, or the negative environmental factors in one's home country that make it desirable to leave, include low compensation and benefits, family obligations, political instability, poor working and living conditions, and the lack of jobs and job security. Conversely, "pull" factors are positive environmental factors abroad that tempt workers to migrate. These reasons could be higher compensation and benefits; more job opportunities; more political, economic, and social stability; better living and working conditions; professional development interests; and a desire to see the world. Recruiters often inflate the significance of both push and pull factors in trying to attract potential clients (American Federation of Teachers, 2009).

It is easier, of course, to recruit from developing nations with economic and social instability and fewer opportunities for career advancement, but it is not solely about workers from developing nations moving to "First World" countries. For example, Appleton, Morgan, and Sives (2006) studied the migration of teachers in four countries—Botswana, England, Jamaica, and South Africa—and found significant international teacher mobility in each nation. Jamaica and South Africa were identified as "sending countries," and Botswana and England as "receiving countries." They also found that roughly half of all teachers in each country were interested in migrating to other countries to teach. The United Kingdom receives many teachers from within and outside the Commonwealth, including those from Australia, Canada, New Zealand, South Africa, Commonwealth Africa, South Asia, and the Pacific islands. In 2003, the United Kingdom sent 26,000 new teachers into the workforce—and roughly 10,000 of them, or 38%, were international teachers (Ratterree, 2006). Though demand for international teachers is decreasing in the United Kingdom, in 2003, roughly 1–2% of the entire teaching force was foreign-born.

In some situations, countries can serve as both sending and receiving countries. For example, as South Africa is sending teachers to the United Kingdom, they are also receiving teachers from East and West Africa. And as Indian teachers are crossing oceans to teach in the United States, teachers from the Seychelles are headed to India to fill their open positions (Ratterree, 2006).

LIVING THE AMERICAN DREAM: BENEFITS OF RECRUITMENT

In 2007, the same year I met Padma, the teacher mentioned in the introduction, I was teaching American literature to 11th-graders at an urban high school. One of the state-mandated standards that I was supposed to teach dealt with American literature related to the "American Dream." I wondered how my students—over 95% of whom were students of color and over 50% of whom were immigrants or refugees—would feel about the topic. They saw evidence of the American Dream on television, in sitcoms with two-(always heterosexual)-parent households, picket fences, and abundant opportunities for leisure and education. They heard it in songs with lyrics that glorified wealth, beauty, and opportunity. And now they had to read about it in literature class, when everything else in their lives was pointing to the commonsense conclusion that the American Dream was a myth. Unsurprisingly, when I presented the group with a variety of quotations about the American Dream, from writers, politicians, celebrities, philosophers, and teachers, they agreed that it is only available to a select few who, through no hard work of their own, have been granted privileges and access to society's largely upper-middle-class "dreams." In the words of one student: "How can anyone believe the American Dream is real for everyone? Just turn on the news or read the paper!" Though they wanted to believe in Martin Luther King, Jr.'s dream, their lived experiences offered a stark contrast to his dream of the equal opportunity red hills of Georgia.

Yet, at the very same time that I was teaching this unit, Padma was in a classroom one floor below, working diligently to achieve her own version of the American Dream. She believed that coming to the United States would offer her and her family a chance at the illustrious vision of success that the United States had worked so hard to convince the rest of the world was accessible and available. Like other international teachers, Padma's desire for the American Dream was intricately linked to money and access to a global network of possibilities.

Benefits for Teachers

Articles about international teachers mention monetary incentives most often because "teaching in the United States means a lot more than just a job" (Graham, 2001, p. 2). As with most immigrant workers, the pay is much higher in the United States than in their home countries. In the Philippines, for example, teachers made between $9,000 and $12,000 per year, whereas if they were hired in Baltimore, they made $45,000 (Coates, 2005, p. 65). According to Vaishnav (2001), "a big motivation for some of the teachers [was that] they planned to send money back home" (p. 3). However, the teachers in Glendale only found monetary benefit if they were able to save enough to repay their debt in India, accrued to pay IRI's finders' fees. Aleeza pointed out, "being from a good family, I do not have [a] lot of problem to pay her [IRI] the money that I paid to come here. But some of the teachers, they have debts there. And they have borrowed money from people to come here so that they can at least work for 3 years, then save some money for their family." (See Chapter 5 for more discussion on monetary incentives.)

The teachers also came because they wanted to experience American life and culture or face a new challenge or get out of their comfort zone (Coates, 2005; Henry, 2001; Neufield, 2005; Sack, 2001; Shapira, 2005; Vaishnav, 2001). Speaking wistfully and looking off into the distance, as if hoping for a window instead of four cinderblock walls, Faria recounted that she had the option of teaching in the United States or Oman, but chose this country because "[the] United States is the land of opportunity." Samina said she was "really interested in working [in] different areas, like working with different people, different cultures, that excites me. . . . I would love to work with different people and gain as much experiences and knowledge because, you know, learning never stops."

Benefits for Schools and Students

"Where it was once uncommon to cross state lines in pursuit of new teachers," Sack (2001) writes, "recruiters now do not blink at crossing oceans" (p. 8). While many journalists writing about international recruitment frame the issue as a last-resort strategy that districts turn to only after they could not find qualified local candidates, others cite clear and distinct benefits of hiring international teachers. Some districts find the teachers highly qualified and representative of the diversity of student populations. For administrators in urban schools in Baltimore, for example, Filipino teachers are "attractive candidates: they're highly educated—many have advanced degrees—they have tons of classroom experience and most are fluent in English" (Coates, 2005, p. 65). To test their English proficiency, administrators in some districts ask international teachers about their favorite movie or actor and give them unexpected questions to test how intelligible their language would be to K–12 American students.

Very few recruitment agencies publish detailed descriptions of how, specifically, their employees would benefit U.S. schools and students. One program that does is Visiting International Faculty (VIF), based in Chapel Hill, North Carolina, the largest and most-reviewed international teacher recruitment program. Founded by brothers David and Alan Young in 1987, VIF was initially intended as a cultural exchange program for college faculty, but by 2005, the program had grown into the largest K–12 international teacher placement organization in the country (Keller, 2005). VIF claims that, since its founding, "8,500 educators from more than 70 nations[2] . . . have worked in more than 1,500 U.S. schools in North Carolina, South Carolina, Georgia, Virginia, Florida, Colorado, Maryland and California" (Visiting International Faculty Program, 2012). According to Keller (2005), one-fourth of all North Carolina public schools host a VIF international teacher. VIF recruits teachers of all subjects and grade levels, though they specialize in mathematics, science, foreign language, special education, and bilingual education.

VIF imagines themselves as a different kind of recruitment program than other for-profit recruiters. Though VIF recruits for hard-to-staff schools, its predominant mission espoused in program materials is for teachers to "share the heritage of your home nation with U.S. students, educators and members of host communities, opening their eyes to the world beyond their borders. Upon returning home, you'll contribute fresh perspectives in education and act as goodwill ambassadors on behalf of the United States" (Visiting International Faculty Program, 2012). Keller (2005) reports that "company leaders insist . . . VIF is a cultural exchange program first and a recruiting business second" (p. 8). The experience is sold as one of cultural immersion and broadened horizons:

> Imagine your students listening attentively as their South African-born teacher shares his experiences during the last days of apartheid; a German teacher discusses the fall of the Berlin Wall; or a Spanish teacher demonstrates Flamenco . . . to an after-school club. Extraordinary teachers sharing the world with your students—that's the essence of . . . VIF. (Visiting International Faculty Program, 2012)

The Young brothers, in a letter to the editor of *Education Week* (2001), state that, "instead of merely filling vacant teaching positions, properly selected teachers from other countries expose our students to the world beyond our borders, thus preparing them to thrive both professionally and personally in our increasingly diverse and interconnected society" (Young & Young, 2001, p. 1). VIF's basic application requirements include English language proficiency; the equivalent of a U.S. bachelor's degree; teacher training and experience in K–12 classrooms; and a valid driver's license. Program materials do not specify how much training and teaching experience are actually necessary to be selected by VIF. VIF's selection procedures increased in intensity over time. For example, in 2005, Keller reported that one in ten teachers was selected "after a winnowing process that include[d] essays, interviews, recommendations, and criminal background checks" (p. 8). By 2012, however, according to the VIF website, the program had developed "valid assessment tools using behaviorally-benchmarked scoring to predict a candidate's potential for success in the classroom" (Visiting International Faculty, 2012). They argue that six competencies were necessary for success as an international teacher (cultural adjustment and fit, professionalism, contributions to school and community, instruction planning and implementation, classroom management and organization, and assessing and monitoring performance), and that they test these competencies through "a series of selection hurdles," like an application screening, a structured phone interview, and an in-person interview with "a lesson plan presentation, a writing sample submission, an in-basket exercise, and a structured personal interview" (Visiting International Faculty, 2012). It is unclear whether VIF believes these requirements are the only ones that make a teacher "highly qualified" and why local candidates fall short of these minimal prerequisites.

VIF makes accommodations for foreign teachers' travel arrangements, visas, certifications, and health insurance. Other program components include predeparture preparation and guidance, travel stipends, arrival pickup in host country, housing location assistance, professional orientation sessions, interest-free relocation loans, and automobile leasing and insurance. These components are identified in list form and thus the pre-departure training and professional orientation sessions are not explained in detail, though Keller (2005) reports that one VIF teacher had only a 3-day orientation session. Throughout the international teachers' tenure, VIF also provides health, disability, and life insurance; professional development; cultural-education guides and training; 24-hour emergency support; travel opportunities; support from a local advisor; and an alumni email network. Again, no specifications are given for any continued support activities, and when I attempted to obtain materials from VIF for this research, I was told "all materials are proprietary" and would not be released.

VIF teachers' success is unclear and debated. Charney (2009) asserts that VIF teachers bring added value to schools in North Carolina. VIF claims that it has a "high rate of success," including a "95 percent success rate of VIF participants. And schools rate more than 80 percent of VIF participants as 'outstanding' or 'above average'" (Visiting International Faculty, 2006). There is no systemically collected evidence to support this assertion (or, if there was, it was not released through VIF), and most of the proof given was anecdotal. Keller (2005) interviewed two principals in North Carolina public schools, one of whom said VIF teachers "filled a big void, came with experience, . . . are very flexible, . . . and are so eager to participate in the program" (p. 8). Another principal said "the diversity of backgrounds makes her school stronger" because the student population was increasingly foreign-born (p. 8). In the article, neither principal explained how she knew VIF teachers were successful with students. In a VIF press release, the company reports that an analysis by the SAS Institute, a for-profit business software developer in North Carolina, showed that "VIF teachers match U.S. teachers on student test scores" and are "equally successful . . . in promoting student achievement on standardized tests" (Visiting International Faculty, 2006). The only details provided about the SAS study are that the institute analyzed test scores on final tests for each grade and course in the Guilford County Schools in North Carolina. The results of VIF teachers' students are compared "anonymously by grade level and course" with the scores of U.S. teachers' students. The press release does not note if researchers controlled for prior achievement or out-of-classroom effects like gender and socioeconomic status. Principals also argue, however, that "test scores have gone up," and foreign teachers had "dramatic positive results on student learning" (Visiting International Faculty, 2006).

CHALLENGING THE AMERICAN DREAM: STRUGGLES OF RECRUITMENT

The challenges of international teacher recruitment are also noted in popular press articles, though most of the challenges are carefully balanced with positive, personal anecdotes. First, many critics of hiring international teachers argue that it is a short-term solution that does not address the real problems behind the teacher shortage (Henry, 2001). Mildred Hudson, of Recruiting New Teachers, Inc., states that the trend is a "reactive and emergency measure to rectify the problem" of a teacher shortage that the government knew was coming for over 10 years but they "didn't do enough to stop it" ("School districts import teachers," 2001, p. 1). In media articles, the most frequently identified challenges of recruitment include culture shock, communication difficulties, and family issues. The teachers in Glendale shared similar sentiments.

Culture Shock

Anyone who has traveled abroad knows the feelings associated with culture shock: confusion, anxiety, disorientation, and frustration. It may happen when you are trying to board a train and find you do not know the language or customs necessary to buy a ticket, let alone board the train and find your seat. It may happen when trying to purchase food from an outdoor market or a grocery store, when you do not recognize any of the goods around you. It may happen walking down the street, eating in a restaurant, touring a museum or landmark, or, more likely, all of the above. Culture shock is well defined for travelers who experience new cultures and customs for short periods, as well as for migrants and immigrants who experience cultural shifts over long periods of time.

In the case of international teachers, culture shock happens in their personal and professional lives. Coates (2005) discusses the culture shock for people who have worked in countries where "educators are accorded great respect" (p. 65). One teacher, according to Coates, only survived because of her prayers and support from the principal. Cook (2000) summarizes the story of Mexican and Filipino teachers in Dallas, who are not comfortable in the classroom with "disrespectful" American students: "They were well-qualified . . . but many were used to managing classrooms differently. They also had trouble passing a mandatory state test. The district would now rather spend its money to retain teachers and recruit locally" (p. 18).

VIF acknowledges that "culture shock is an almost unavoidable consequence . . . and a challenge every VIF teacher will experience" (Visiting International Faculty, 2006). The company outlines four stages of cultural adaptation as described by Oberg (1954), including euphoria, irritability, gradual adjustment, and adaptation. VIF also provides a list of cultural contrasts that may pose difficulties for international teachers. The dichotomies between the U.S. culture and many other cultures include: the child as an individual versus the child as part of a group, independence versus affiliation and helpfulness, fostering and self-esteem versus criticism to enable positive behavior, challenging versus listening to authority, personal choice versus group consensus, and flexibility in social roles versus stability in social roles (Visiting International Faculty, 2006). There is no discussion of how to help international teachers overcome culture shock or the difficult balance of these seeming dichotomies.

For Indian teachers in Glendale, culture shock began immediately upon entering the United States. Much of what they learned, teachers said, was absorbed "on the spot" during their first few days in the United States. In fact, when asked if they remembered their first days in the country, all four participants responded by saying, "Of course!" or "I could never forget it!" Aleeza lost her suitcase and had to learn where to buy new clothing. A quick trip to Macy's, her first visit to a department store, solved this dilemma. Faria arrived after many flight delays and was greeted by another foreign teacher at 6:30 p.m. on her first day and told that she would be picked up a mere 12 hours later for her first day at her new school. The abrupt introduction into this new culture was a demanding shock. Shrusty recalled her initial exposure:

> The [district] orientation started the day after we got here, and the thing was we had jet lag and we were trying to concentrate on what they were saying because of the accent. . . . Then the last day [of orientation] we were told to meet the principals [at our individual schools] and the problem was we didn't have a ride; we didn't know any places. We didn't know anything and our employer just left saying to search [for] somebody who can help you go there. . . . We had our new cell phones at least [to call someone to come pick us up], but we looked around, it was all a jungle. He came after 2 hours, so we were waiting outside for 2 hours.

Shrusty's sentiments concretely illustrate that recruitment agencies and often districts themselves do not offer enough preliminary support and preparation for teachers entering their schools. For teachers to be left without transportation in a new place is not only insensitive but dangerous. Compounding the problem is that the orientation itself was not enough to make teachers feel comfortable in their new places and roles. Shrusty still saw her new environment as a "jungle," both literally, because the area surrounding the school was forested, and figuratively because the environment itself seemed menacing. Finney, Torres, and Jurs (2002) explain related struggles for Spanish teachers who traveled on a teacher exchange to South Carolina. The researchers argue that foreign teachers were concerned about too little orientation time; difficulties in classroom management and discipline; lack of awareness about school procedures and policies; lack of standards for Spanish classes; improper placement of teachers in schools with "instructional philosophies different from their own"; difficulties understanding the grading system; and not enough networking and support (p. 96).

Samina's first day was also a shock for her. She arrived 2 weeks into the school year, when a substitute was running her classroom. She asked the substitute to stay throughout the first week, during which she observed the class and "did not say a word." Because she missed both the agency and the district orientations, she had to learn on her own through observation. As a result, "my first impression on them [the students] was not good because I did not know the rules. I was not aware of the rules and the consequences, of how to deal with them, how to talk with them."

In addition to challenging starts to their school years, the teachers experienced culture shock in their worlds outside the classroom. Aleeza, one of a few teachers allowed to bring her family to the United States after her first year, described the culture shock of her 9-year-old son, who was not used to seeing public displays of affection. She tried to explain to him that one culture was not better than the other, but even she was surprised by the "indecent exposure and girls and boys mixing it up [making out]" in the hallways of her school and in other public spaces like shopping malls. Other teachers agreed that they were surprised by the "amount of smooching in front of adults" and a general "lack of decency." Samina was surprised that American students "get pregnant at the age of 12, that babies were having babies" and did not know that "America is composed of so many Black people; especially in the South, we have so many Blacks." Shrusty noted that some culture shock was because the apartment complex where they were all placed was mostly inhabited by Indians and other Asians, so they "did not get to have a real American picture" immediately upon arrival.

Faria described seeing a young man with sagging pants on her first day in the United States:

> We could see what he was wearing inside; I was shocked! But I could not even ask anyone because I was just thinking it might be a problem with that person and he is just not caring about his dress. But to my shock, when I came to [my new school] the next morning, I saw the same thing in the cafeteria. . . . All I saw were saggy pants and huge personalities.

Much of what teachers noticed, such as teenage pregnancy, a large Black population, and sagging pants, they found to be in conflict with the picture of America they had seen in movies and in the news. The "urbanness" of their teaching contexts made their working situations unexpected and stressful. Though these issues were not directly related to classroom instruction, culture shock still contributed heavily to the teachers' overall adjustment and feelings of belonging.

Communication Difficulties

Communication difficulties were also challenging for teachers. Though Ms. Muller, a district official, claimed that, when interviewing potential candidates, "we listen a lot for fluency, if our children are going to be able to understand them," another representative, Ms. Jefferson, admitted that communication was frequently an issue with international educators. Concurring with anecdotal literature that teachers had difficulty with language and terminology (e.g., Basu, 2002), Principal Scott stated he had not had success with international teachers in the past "because of their language, just not being able to communicate to the kids, kids not being able to understand them, and written communication to the parents has been poor." Principal Sutherland said he sympathized with students who did not understand the teachers: "I had to call a help center [in India] for my McAfee [computer virus software] the other day. And I couldn't understand a word! I was frustrated after those 3 minutes, so imagine 55 minutes if you don't understand." These two principals said they frequently received calls from parents complaining that students did not understand what the teachers were saying.

Teachers themselves indicated that communication was sometimes an issue. According to Aleeza, language was "the main, topmost, important thing" and that "you basically have to learn their lingo and then you are good." For instance, Shrusty explained, "in our language we do not tend to say please every time . . . so we learned you have to add *please* because we really mean it but we do not say it." In addition to learning new slang and communicative strategies, the teachers' accent also proved to be a challenge. Faria said,

> The language was totally different from what I used to speak, so I had problems with that. . . . In math, we usually deal with terminology, which is the same thing [in India], so it was not that bad. But still, while you are speaking, sometimes you feel embarrassed when people ask you to repeat.

Samina also revealed that her accent contributed to her students' lack of respect for her: "They think I don't know anything because of my accent. I say, how do you tell me how to speak when you can't speak well? I tell them, do you know you are speaking to someone with a master's in English?" This comment, which shows teachers' frustration with students' lack of global awareness, seems to imply that the teachers have internalized the assumption that content knowledge and advanced degrees should make them effective educators, regardless of their pedagogy. This could have contributed to students' frustration and lack of respect if they did not agree with her assessment.

Family Issues

When I discuss this research with colleagues or at conferences, this is the part of the story where, inevitably, someone raises a hand in sheer confusion. How does it make sense, people wonder, to bring teachers into an entirely new context and expect them to succeed without any family present? Wouldn't having family nearby increase their likelihood of success? Common sense and research indicate that, yes, a ready-made, familial support system would undoubtedly help ease transitions. Some fear that hiring international teachers "could harm learning and result in wasted effort [because] educators unaccustomed to inner-city challenges . . . [may] get homesick and leave" (Cook, 2000, p. 18). However, recruiters and district officials in Glendale believed that having family would be "distracting" and inhibit the teachers' ability to adjust to a new culture if they were "more worried about family than about their students." When I pushed a bit, asking if, in fact, they would not be more worried about their family if they were a world apart and were trying to find convenient times to talk by phone or Internet, even if it meant waking in the middle of the night, I was quickly and summarily dismissed as "not understanding."

As with my friend Padma, Glendale teachers had to leave their families behind for at least their first year of teaching in the United States. Samina had a difficult time talking about her family; professionally, she was having a tough time adjusting to U.S. school culture and the absence of her family made the pain more acute. She explained, "I miss my family very much. When you have something like this, bad days, you feel it more. . . . It is stressful. I have lost so much weight. On the weekends, we go online. I see my son playing in the house. I talk to my husband and son every day. My son will be 6 in June." Sighing, she showed me a small picture of her son in her purse and said that she would be seeing him in a few months. "I just have to be patient," she concluded and, straightening her shoulders and attempting a small smile, stood up to prepare for her next class as the bell rang. In my researcher's journal that evening, I wrote:

> What must it take to make that decision? To leave your family, especially a small child, and go to another country in the hopes of making a better life for your child? You are leaving him to be raised by someone else while you go take care of other people's children. And then to have to pretend it's not MORE of a "distraction" that he's all the way across the world? Of course, the irony of it all is that the "better life" that she was promised—that they were ALL promised— doesn't appear to be a better life at all. She is stressed, exhausted, overworked, underpaid, and confused. I can't imagine making that choice to come here and then constantly wondering every day if you made the right one.

CONCLUSION

This chapter has covered a lot of ground—teacher education, neoliberal reform and globalization, migration trends, and the teachers themselves. I hope that this contextual information that situates international teachers within a sociopolitical narrative will inform your reading of future chapters in which teachers' stories are more centered. International teachers are essentially caught in a web of circumstances, the threads of which were spun long before they even arrived in the United States and that are profoundly affecting their lives and the lives of their students.

The Continental Divide

Similarities and Differences Between Indian and U.S. Education

Beloved community is formed not by the eradication of difference but by its affirmation, by each of us claiming the identities and cultural legacies that shape who we are and how we live in the world.

—bell hooks, 1995

On the first day, I had three gifts for my kids. . . . I brought something for them like a candy . . . to introduce [myself] to [the] class and then we played a game. I gave them a word on the board, and I asked them to make ten words out of the word, and I told them that whoever is going to make it first, the first three are going to get a gift. And there was a girl who made it, and I gave her a gift. She threw that candy right into the trashcan right in front of me! I never expected that! But then I was quiet and the whole class was quiet when she did that. . . . I was like okay, maybe that is the way they behave here. So that was my first experience on my first day.

—Aleeza, science teacher

From her first day onward, Aleeza's experience in U.S. urban schools was drastically different from her experience in Indian schools. Her first day, described above, provides a small glimpse into the different cultural expectations for students and teachers, but the disparities extended beyond cultural misunderstandings. Like Aleeza, the other international teachers were intensely aware of how students, teachers, administrators, and schools operated differently in the United States than in their home country. Yet, as illustrated in the classroom portraits in the previous chapter, in many ways, the classrooms in which international teachers work on a daily basis are not drastically different from the classrooms of American-born teachers. The students are similar, and the state standards require similar instructional strategies and structure. However, the most common theme that arose in teacher interviews was the radical difference between U.S. and Indian schools. Teachers described how every part of their lives in the United States, including living situations, attire, cultural habits, students' knowledge and behavior, school procedures, and even food, contributed to a feeling of "foreignness."

35

One participant, when asked about the similarities, responded, "What is that saying you people have? Apples or oranges? That is what it is like to compare [the] USA and India . . . like apples to oranges."

Here I present evidence from teacher interviews and observations on the similarities and differences between U.S. and Indian classrooms in order to illustrate the erroneous assumption made by recruiters, some policymakers, and administrators that there are no or few differences between teaching abroad and teaching in U.S. urban schools. Or, if there are differences, the assumption is made that they are not enough to merit specialized discussion and preparation for working in a new environment. I begin with a brief explanation of the prior knowledge and beliefs that participants held about "American" schools and culture, in order to demonstrate the ways in which they were or were not prepared. Then, I discuss reported similarities and differences between Indian and U.S. classrooms. Differences, which are more substantial than similarities, are categorized into seven themes: student behavior, resources, pedagogical strategies, curriculum, lack of cultural awareness, policies of school and state, and relations with parents and families. I argue that these numerous differences compelled teachers to change their practice and relationships with each other, other teachers, and their students. Many of the differences related to what teachers viewed as their students' "lack" of something—knowledge, focus, achievement—and this perspective served to reinforce the difficulty of working in U.S. urban schools.

PRIOR KNOWLEDGE OF AMERICAN SCHOOLS

There is no guidebook for international teachers, no Rick Steves or Lonely Planet manual to help teachers navigate the rugged terrain of a new culture and context. While in France in 2012, I realized firsthand how many aspects of American school culture can be lost, literally and figuratively, in translation. My colleague and I were in Montpellier, France, with a professor of teacher education and the director of the immigrant orientation program for Montpellier schools. As one of the women explained how the immigration programs received money from the government, I asked how they "proved" their success with the program in order to receive government funds. Did they conduct their own research? If so, did they collect test scores? Interview participants? Around and around we went (and not just because of my linguistic faltering), trying to explain why I would even have *thought* they needed proof and what types of "proof" are necessary in the United States. The ideas of accountability had become so engrained in the way I discuss education in the United States that I did not even realize my question was making a culturally relative assumption. A similar communication gap arose when we tried to explain high-stakes testing and annual yearly progress. Jaws open wide, confusion spread across their faces, they continued to question what we said: "Every year? Tests every year?" and "Failing means less money? Less money?" Though the French system is no stranger to major examinations, as they have the baccalaureate exam for admission to college, the notion of using test scores to determine K–12 school funding and teacher pay was completely foreign.

There are some practices, educational or otherwise, that require background knowledge from our French colleagues and for the Indian teachers with whom I work. But with little to no information provided by the recruiters and receiving districts—and certainly no back-and-forth conversations like those I engaged in with my French colleagues—international teachers have to rely on their own prior knowledge to make sense of novel environments and experiences. For example, Vaishnav (2001) describes one teacher who arrived in Boston 3 days before he was to begin teaching and all he knew about the United States was based on the Boston Celtics and the movie *Stand and Deliver*. Similarly, the teachers sent to Glendale used knowledge from media, personal research, friends' accounts, and the brief orientations provided by the district and their recruitment agency. Despite all of these sources, their prior knowledge of the United States was still too limited to make up for the cultural gaps between Indian and U.S. schools.

Media Portrayals

During another recent trip abroad, I was teaching about U.S. school culture in Malmö, Sweden. At the beginning of the first lecture in the series, I asked the students to tell me what they already knew and believed about education in the United States. From the audience came a variety of responses: "Schools care more about sports than academics. Poor schools are very different from rich schools. American schools are ethnocentric and students don't learn about much outside the United States. Urban schools are dangerous. Not a lot of students in the United States go to college." I wrote all of their ideas on the board and then asked how they had "learned" these things. At once, they responded: "Movies. Television shows. Newspapers. CNN."

The international teachers were no different, though one would hope their knowledge would have been supplemented by more academic sources before and after their arrival. They learned what little they knew about American culture and students from movies and the media. For example, Shrusty listed American movies, such as *Speed*, *Anaconda*, and *101 Dalmatians*, that helped her learn American English. Faria concurred, based on her viewing of American films about education:

> I did not know much about American schools, but I just had an impression that it is going to be a great experience when I go there and teach, and I could get an opportunity to use technology in the classrooms and to not have to use those conventional methods of teaching like I used back home.

Samina, too, anticipated that American students would be "more technically advanced" and "very logical, wanting me to give reasons behind everything" because of the media to which she had been exposed. I struggled for a while trying to figure out how the media had made U.S. students seem logical (because this is not what we in the United States see in the news, is it?) and then remembered the preponderance of teen movies and television shows in which adolescents act, speak, and think like adults. Some television shows, having ended in the United States years before, that were rising in popularity in India as the teachers were applying to travel abroad were *Beverly Hills 90210*, *Party of Five*, *Dawson's Creek*, and *Buffy the Vampire Slayer*. These shows portray teens in adult situations, carefully and sometimes painfully analyzing their every decision, action, and feeling. They also portray upper-middle-class schools with abundant resources. It is no wonder that some teachers from other countries came to the United States believing that their young students would be functioning at adult levels.

However, contrasting this optimistic vision of the great "American experience" was a media-generated image of school violence. Shrusty postulated that "it was not a safe place for a woman to stay alone. . . . It was a very wild culture . . . and you should not be talking to any males because they may take advantage." Faria, too, "had a kind of fear in my heart. . . . I mean like, I have heard about two or three stories about a student shooting a teacher because she did not give a good grade. I have heard about those stories." Both were relieved to learn that these rumors were false. It is interesting to note that the "violent" schools in the news media are drastically different from the abundantly resourced schools featured in films, yet the teachers somehow imagined that their schools would be both at once.

Personal Research

Aleeza conducted her own Internet research to learn more about American schools and students: "I YouTubed a lot of things . . . like classrooms in [the] USA and especially [the state] where I was coming." She said she learned interesting facts about what American students were like and what American chemistry labs looked like. Her research, she presumed, showed "the way I have to teach over there." The contrast between her expectations and reality is revealed in the opening quotation to this chapter.

Shrusty learned about American schools through her education coursework. Because special education "originated" in the United States, she had read "all American books, but we could not get a clear picture of what exactly was going on, but everything was like, okay this is how it works in America." All teachers indicated that no amount of personal research, even when combined with media and friends' accounts and orientations, fully prepared them for the new contexts into which they were placed.

Peers' Testimonies

Some of what the teachers learned came from other Indian teachers who had previously taught or worked in the United States. That was how many of the teachers who came to Glendale learned about international teaching in the first place, from friends or acquaintances who had taught in the United States and had since returned to India. Not all of this information was reliable, however. Shrusty told the story of a male Indian colleague who was in her "batch" of teachers. Before he left India, he was told that if he was alone in a room with a high school girl and did not do what she told him to do, "like put [her] grades up or something like that, then she may just say he raped her." Imagine not only the fear that this particular male teacher must have faced, but also what his other perceptions of the United States must have been for him to believe that such a sensational story could have been true.

Stories of international teachers who returned to India were included on many websites and blogs devoted to Indian culture and education. These personal anecdotes combined stories of success with gross exaggerations about urban students and schools. For example, Thomas (2003) wrote:

> Public schools in the U.S. and Britain are notorious turfs of over-aged children with serious psychological and motivation problems. Most inner-city school children are from broken homes and prone to chronic indiscipline and violence. Chronic indiscipline, racial abuse and aggressive behaviour . . . is the rule rather than exception in inner-city. . . . Whereas in India teachers usually have to cope with two or three students per class who pose behaviour problems, in most inner-city schools abroad only a handful are likely to observe the norms of propriety and good behaviour. Metal detectors are not uncommon and students are often not allowed to take even compass boxes into their classrooms. Some Indian teachers find the experience so stressful that they quit their jobs and return home. (p. 3)

These images connoted extreme violence, but what is even more dangerous is the stereotypes that are perpetuated through flagrant employment of deficit language about urban students' culture. With such accusations that they had serious psychological problems that contradicted "norms of propriety," it is unsurprising that some international teachers truly believed it was possible for female students to accuse male teachers of rape or students to shoot their teachers simply because of grade disputes. Though it was important to present future migrant teachers with the truth about American schools, including how the environment differed from the one they were accustomed to India, the generalizations and scare tactics used in such blogs could have prejudiced teachers before they even arrived in the United States.

Orientations

In the Glendale School District, there were two orientations that teachers should have attended. First was the recruitment agency orientation, conducted by IRI. Shrusty and Faria argued that this orientation, in which they were taught about American schools from their Indian employer, was slightly effective, but it was too brief and should have been conducted before their departure from India. Teachers also stressed the need for "real" stories about American classrooms, in the form of teacher testimonies or videoed lessons. Two of my four participants did not even attend orientation. As Samina arrived 2 weeks into the school year, she was unable to attend either orientation from the agency or the district. IRI provided "personal guidance" in the form of a brief conversation over the phone. This supposed "orientation" included a description of "the classroom setup . . . the three-stage lesson plan, like the opening period and closing, the grading system, the word wall, the rules and regulations and bulletin boards." From observations of their classrooms, it was quite clear that the teachers understood and implemented the required lesson plan format and setup of word walls and bulletin boards. According to the district's teacher evaluation instrument, the presence of a word wall and standards on the board counted as much as a lesson plan that engaged students or a clear understanding of one's content. For any teacher, international or American-born, this minimal, checklist-style feedback is not enough to help them become better educators. Yes, the international teachers' classrooms would have received a "satisfactory" evaluation, but what small victories amid a landscape of difficulties. In long run, these brief and logistical orientation sessions do little to ease the culture shock and difficulties of international teachers.

SIMILARITIES BETWEEN HOME AND ABROAD

In order to better understand international teachers' practice in the United States, we must first understand the way they conceptualized their home contexts. Thus, my interviews with the teachers in Glendale began with discussions of how the students and situations at Douglass, Chisholm, Woodson, and Tubman were similar to and different from their classrooms abroad. I discuss some of the history and policies of Indian education in the next chapter, specifically those that relate to working with students of diverse backgrounds, but I also believe that equally as important as the programmatic features are the ways the teachers themselves *think* about these features.

They were able to list only two similarities: that they were teaching students of the same age or with the same disabilities, and that schools in the United States, like in India, were economically disparate.

Similar Student Age and Disabilities

Though Samina, Shrusty, and Aleeza all had experience teaching adults, they also had practice working with younger students. The grades they taught in India were not always equivalent to the grades in U.S. schools, but the general age ranges were similar. For example, Samina taught 6th through 9th grades in India, and in the United States, she was working with 6th-graders. Though Faria noted that her American students did not always "use" their academic skills as much as their Indian counterparts, "they are the same age and just as smart."

Shrusty found the most similarities between her Indian and U.S. contexts because she worked with special education students in both countries. Though there were more severe cases of disability in U.S. schools, possibly because of the available resources and legislation, most of her students possessed similar disabilities and exhibited similar behaviors as she was accustomed to in India. "Autism is autism," she noted, "in India or [the] USA."

Economic Disparities

Growing up in India, Shrusty recalled that she was very aware of "those who had" and "those who did not have anything." She attended a school far away from her home, where she had to walk a distance to the bus stop, take a long bus ride, and then walk farther along to her school building. If she forgot her lunch, as she said she did many days, there was no way of getting one, and many of her classmates had nothing to share with her. However, in the same city, other students attended tuition-charging private schools. Thus, from a young age, she was aware of the economic disparities among Indian students and schools.

Aleeza found a similar situation in her Glendale classroom as she found in India. There were students who could afford to buy their own supplies, and those who could not. There were students who had to work long hours after school to contribute to their families' incomes, and those who did not. Similarly, in the public school where she taught in India, there were students of different castes. (The caste system will be discussed in more depth in Chapter 3.) What was surprising for her was not the difference among U.S. students' economic conditions, but the differences in conditions among U.S. schools.

According to the teachers, in India, the disparity in school funding existed between public and private schools. In the United States, the teachers discovered, the disparity also existed *among* public schools. For example, the schools in which the teachers taught were all located in the south side of the Glendale district, an area known to be underfunded and under-resourced. However, their apartments lay in the north side of the district, and thus, those teachers with elementary-age children sent their children each day to schools with significantly more resources than were available in the schools where they were teaching. "We are lucky we can send the kids there [to the north side schools]," Shrusty commented. "I think it would be different if they came here [to the south side schools]."

DIFFERENCES BETWEEN HOME AND ABROAD

Though they could list only two similarities, when I asked the teachers to discuss differences, they often laughed and spoke for over an hour. Teachers openly revealed the many struggles they faced as newcomers and how they quickly learned to "expect the unexpected." These challenges stemmed from the intensity and variety of experiences they faced, Samina said:

> There are a lot of hard parts because of a whole new culture with different people, a different way of teaching, different situations. Most importantly, there are different kids. You cannot even compare time; it is day here and night there. Dressing style is different; the way you speak and live is different. The way you express yourself is different. Nothing is similar.

Differences for these teachers can be grouped into seven categories shown in Table 2.1.

Student Behavior

Students' actions inside and outside of class were, by far, the most frequently cited difference between U.S. and Indian schools. Concurring with the anecdotal literature that international teachers have difficulty adjusting to "U.S. students [who] are not as motivated and tend to be discipline problems" (Henry, 2001, p. 2), all four teachers stated that their biggest challenge involved a complex interaction of student behavior, classroom management, and what they viewed as academic apathy. Though they had been "warned" in brief discussions with district or agency officials that American students behaved differently from the students they were used to, they were not fully prepared for the drastic difficulties that came as a result of these different cultural expectations for student behavior. For example, Faria said,

> I did not know much about American schools. I did not know none [sic] of the problems, and I just had an impression I would just have to go there and teach and it is going to be the same math. But then I came and saw this . . . [pauses] . . . I saw the same problems like I used to have back home, but the discipline issues are just a little bit more.

Table 2.1. Differences Between International Teachers' Home Classrooms and U.S. Classrooms

Category	Definition	Subcategories
Student behavior	The way students act in and outside the classroom in relationship to the teacher, peers, and academic content	• Lack of focus • Academic apathy • Lack of respect for school/ property/self/ others • Necessary management/ control techniques
Resources	Classroom materials and objects (either literally or theoretical) for educative purposes	• More materials • More money • More technology
Pedagogical strategies	Teaching techniques perceived as more appropriate for American students	• No lecture • More hands-on • Group work/discussion

Curriculum	Textbooks, lesson planning, standards, and the way standards are measured	• Scripted curriculum
		• Assessment
		  » Standardized tests
		  » Multiple choice

Lack of cultural awareness	Students' lack of or misinformation about non-U.S. people and cultures	• Knowledge of world outside the United States • Knowledge of Indian culture
Policies of school and state	Policies that are formed outside the classroom but which influence classroom dynamics	• Multiple chances and no consequences • School reform
Relations with parents and families	Dynamics between parents and students, parents and teachers, and parents and school officials that influence classroom dynamics	• Supporting versus challenging teachers' authority • Communication issues • Parents as part of the "problem"

Teachers attributed these difficulties to four key components of student behavior: students' lack of focus; academic apathy; a lack of respect for school, property, self, or others; and a lack of necessary management and self-control techniques. All participants, like those interviewed for news articles (Coates, 2005; Cook, 2000; Henry, 2001), discussed U.S. student behavior in contrast to the students' attitudes and academic focus in their home country. You will notice repetition of missing components of what the Indian teachers believed was important for school success; that is, the differences were not in things the American students *had*, but in things they *lacked*.

Lack of focus. Participants suggested that American students were not used to focusing for long periods of time and were too distracted by outside influences, thus inhibiting their academic achievement. For example, Faria said her students "have a lot of potential, a lot of abilities, but they do not utilize it. . . . [There are] a lot of distractions, like cell phones, iPods, and everything, so they are distracted a lot. . . . They do not care." Faria exhibited an interesting shift from discussing "distractions" to a lack of "care." During one classroom observation, her students' lack of focus was evident; within one class period, at least ten students, or one-third of the class, were using their cell phones for music or text messaging at any given time, a direct violation of district and school policy. Students in India, on the other hand, were more focused because of fewer distractions at home and school, she said. Faria said that it was never an issue for teachers to tell students to turn off their iPods in India, because the cultural expectation was that if students had personal technology devices at all, the devices were kept at home for afterschool amusement.

Another teacher, Samina, lamented that her American students' lack of focus was due to a school culture that did not enforce consequences for misbehavior: "Teaching is a tough job in America, don't you think so? They cannot sit still for 10 minutes. But nothing is done about it. No one cares." Whereas in India, "their future is in darkness" if they do not succeed and behave in school, the teachers saw American schools as offering too many second chances for students who misbehave or fail. I see this idea as connected to school and state policies and will discuss it further in a future section.

Academic apathy. Several teachers, when asked if they believed all students wanted to learn, replied with an emphatic "no." The reasons they cited were not much different from the reasons I hear from some U.S. teachers or the pre-service teachers with whom I work. As with many White or upper-middle-class teachers whose own educational experiences differ from their urban students' experiences, international teachers found it difficult to reconcile their previous experiences with what they were seeing every day in their schools (e.g., Dunn, 2010; Howard, 1999; Stairs, Donnell, & Dunn, 2011). Citing students who did not come to school, slept through class, talked during lessons, or did not turn in homework, teachers claimed that students did not care about their education as much as their students in India. One teacher said this was due to cultural expectations. In India, there was more competition among students that encouraged them to perform academically and made them more "keen learners," according to Aleeza. Faria held that this benefited the students because "they know if they do not work hard, they cannot be in the competition. They cannot get good jobs." She elaborated,

> [Students in India] work hard because they know if they do not, they cannot get good jobs. . . . You do not graduate to a higher class unless you pass all the subjects, but here, even if they fail, they can take some makeup classes and still catch up. Maybe that is a reason why they are so careless. I do not see but 40% of them trying to master the subject.

This sentiment shows Faria's belief that students' attitudes—in this case, their apathy—were intimately related to school policies. She hypothesized that students were apathetic because the school's policy of makeup classes was enabling them to eventually succeed even if they failed the first time. This idea is elaborated in the future section in this chapter on policies of school and state.

Despite the teachers' interactions with some successful students, they held lingering beliefs that American students were apathetic and did not care enough about their studies. Even toward the end of her third year of teaching, Aleeza commented,

> They are not interested to learn. . . . Maybe there are personal problems. There are a bunch of them in my third period who are not interested, whatever you do. They are *not* interested. I do not know the reason yet, but they are not interested.

Samina, who also felt strongly that her students did not care about education, developed what she called a solution for academic apathy, but it only worked some of the time. In accordance with what she had learned from other teachers, she saw for herself that "here, you have to keep reminding them that you are something." She explained that this reminder took the form of repeating "I am your teacher, I know better than you. . . . I am not going to play with you, this is not going to work with me, I am like this, I am a strict person." Even though Samina adamantly believed that she did not want to be strict, she claimed that the students' careless attitude was best countered with strictness.

Lack of respect. Participants argued that respect for teachers and administrators was neglected or missing from their schools. "It was not easy the first time I came into [an American] classroom," Aleeza remembered, "because I was used to the classroom in India. Everybody was talking to each other and I was like, I am the teacher, I am standing right here and they do not even care. . . . I did not feel they behaved like students. They behaved like, who needs you here?" Samina wished longingly for a classroom of students who would stand up and say "good morning" like her students in India had done; instead, as I witnessed during one classroom observation, she was greeted with students who were running around the classroom, throwing pencils, and dancing in the aisles. They acknowledged that, in the United States, teachers had to "earn" students' respect, while Indian students automatically afforded their teachers respect because of their authority. This acknowledgment, however, did not make it any easier to adjust to this drastic difference.

Teachers were similarly stunned by students' lack of respect for educational resources and spoke of this respect in religious analogies. Samina said, "Teachers are like gods to us [in India]," and Shrusty elaborated, "Schools are like churches; we worship them." She was especially aghast when she saw students kicking their books and tossing their materials into lockers or onto the floor. "In India, we pray the book," she exclaimed, and demonstrated how Indian students are taught to pick up a book and touch it to their foreheads with reverence, should it fall to the floor or be touched by their shoes. Because of their cultural respect for school buildings and property, they were appalled when American students threw paper on the ground, left their materials sprawled across desks, or brought food into the classroom. Shrusty also shared a story of finding a used condom on the school steps on her second day in the United States: "Imagine my horror, on my second day! I just hoped it wasn't normal. How disrespectful."

Lack of self-control. According to the Indian teachers, students who could not or would not self-regulate proved to be distinctly different from students in India who sat through hour-long lectures, diligently taking notes and raising their hands to ask questions only when prompted. Even when U.S. classroom lessons took the form of a group discussion, where students were free to express their opinions, Samina found it difficult to monitor their behavior because they were not able to control themselves, thus forcing her to "control" them instead of teach them:

> The best part about being here is the group discussion. It is not like that in India; we do not go for group discussions. So that one was exciting, but at the same time, it was annoying too because it was really hard for me to just keep them under control. They do not listen. It was really difficult.

Samina's middle school students offered an interesting perspective on the issue of self-control. During one observation, in which the majority of students were talking in small groups and not working on the assignment, I conversed with Stefan, a male student whom Samina described as "smart, but uncontrollable."

Stefan: I'm going to be honest; we give it to her bad because she's Indian.
Alyssa: Why?
Stefan: Why not? She doesn't control the class. She can't control us.
Alyssa: And you think that is because she is Indian?
Stefan: Maybe. We don't do this shit to other teachers.
Alyssa: Is it her job to control you, as you say, or your job to control yourselves?
Stefan: [Thinks quietly for a moment.] I guess I don't know.

Stefan's collapsing of the teacher's identity as an Indian and what he sees as her inability to control the class was an important revelation. To him, only someone who controlled students was worthy of good behavior, of a "shit"-free environment. Yet, he failed to notice or chose to ignore Samina's constant pleas and management strategies. For example, during one observation, Samina moved to each student's desk individually and asked them to get back to work; she worked with small groups of students who were fighting in a corner; and she raised her voice and spoke to the whole class in an attempt to "control" them. She continuously redirected students in small groups or as a whole class for 45 minutes in a 55-minute period, a length of time that seemed interminable to me as an observer. It was a wonder, then, what Stefan thought "control" looked like. It was not only her *effort* to manage, but her *success* at doing so, which was closely linked to his own willingness to be "controlled."

Principals and district officials supported this finding about difficulties with managing the classroom by describing their own observations. One principal stated,

> Mainly it is not knowing how to deal with the kids, not knowing what to do when there was blatant disrespect, not knowing how to motivate a kid that is not motivated. . . . There is chaos in the room and [the teachers] do not know how to have control. When I say chaos, I mean like [what you see on] television: the kids throwing paper, kids talking, turned away from the teacher at the board, kids on their cell phones.

As district official Ms. Muller stated, problems with classroom management, if perpetual, led to other difficulties: "If we do not recommend someone staying, it is usually due to some type of classroom management problem that trickles down to performance. If you can't maintain order, you can't be effective in instructing." The belief that "control" and "order" were necessary for good teaching was clearly conveyed to foreign teachers (and to students, as evidenced in Stefan's quotation above), who emphasized that they did not *want* to be strict, but felt it was necessary, based on what they had seen in other classrooms and heard from the administration. One teacher spoke explicitly about the uncomfortable adversarial relationship she felt was necessary with students:

> *Samina:* The most important issue which I have is just discipline . . . and fear. They do not fear me.
> *Alyssa:* They do not fear you? Do you think they need to fear you?
> *Samina:* At least for respect. I think they do not respect other teachers, they just fear them. . . . "Oh, Ms. Samina? She is not going to do anything."
> *Alyssa:* So they are scared that they are going to be punished by the other teachers and not you?
> *Samina:* It is not just punishment. I also give them punishments. I also give them suspensions. I also give them calls to parents. . . . I do not know, maybe [it is] because of my international status.

I wondered initially if these difficulties have anything to do with the teachers' transient status. That is, not only are they battling the stereotypes and difficulties associated with being an international educator, but also with being a transient employee. However, when I spoke with students, they did not know that the international teachers were only temporary. And, indeed, in urban schools with the high turnover rate, it was not unusual for them to see teachers come and go at a rapid pace.

Resources

A second major difference the teachers identified between Indian and American schools was resources. All of the teachers noted that American schools were better-funded and provided more resources than did Indian schools. They cited three different kinds of resources: materials, money, and technology. Ironically, the schools in which the teachers were placed were four schools that American teachers and administrators might consider underfunded. For example, the schools' textbooks were somewhat outdated; there were no full science labs; and there were no more than two desktop computers per classroom for student use, if any. Compared to the resources available in suburban schools in the same area, these schools lacked critical assets by American standards. However, by Indian standards, a very different story emerged.

First, the teachers noted that there were more materials available in schools in the United States than in India. Evoking her own educational history, Shrusty remembered that "we lacked resources, like there was no copying machine in the school . . . and bringing a globe to the classroom was a big, big thing that the teacher would talk about for a whole month." She saw the difference most drastically in the available accommodations for her special education students. Not only were there no public schools for special education students in Hyderabad, but the private centers that some students attended did not often have enough facilities to support them. Resources like wheelchairs, handicap buses, and tube-feeding systems that were government-supported in the United States were new to Shrusty: "Those profound[ly disabled] students whom I see here might not even be alive in India." In India, parents had to pay for different therapies, such as physical, occupational, and speech, but U.S. schools provided these services free of charge, in addition to augmentation devices that Shrusty said were critical in enabling her nonverbal students to express themselves. Aleeza agreed with Shrusty's assessment, but only by Indian standards. Compared to India, U.S. schools had more materials for her science projects. However, once she "learned" the American system, she realized that resources disappeared quickly and that she had to supply her own because, "if I depend on the school, it is going to take till the end of the year."

Second, the teachers stated that there was more money available for U.S. schools than Indian schools. Not only were the teachers' salaries higher in the United States than in India, but the teachers were also given more discretionary funding for classroom needs. In the United States, Aleeza was given $50 at the start of the school year; in India, she said, teachers had to pay for any materials they used. This was a notable hardship for her especially because, as a high school science teacher, she had to use her own money to buy supplies for experiments. Further, if she did pay for her own classroom resources, she ran the risk of being ostracized by other Indian teachers for being "the initiator" who forced others to start spending their own money, too. Also, her students in the United States had enough money to buy their own supplies for projects, whereas in India, she had to buy her students' supplies "because of their financial condition."

Third, the teachers cited the availability of more technology as evidence that U.S. schools had more resources than Indian schools. Though the teachers had little to no technology in their individual classrooms, other than a personal computer, they saw the technology at the school, like computer labs and a rotating projector, as impressive. Shrusty noted that, in the United States, "If I think of teaching something, we have Internet. I can go on Google, get some good pictures, good lessons, and make a good activity, where the school provides all the information technology. . . . [In India], we do not have resources, even if we have ideas." Aleeza agreed that technology made teachers' lives easier. For example, in India, she had to do all of her grading manually, whereas computer programs in the United States saved her time and energy.

Shrusty and Aleeza, whose children were in elementary school, appreciated the fact that children that age would be able to use technology in school. "I am not saying we do not have that in India; of course we do. But at this [elementary] level of school, they are not being taught practically, they have everything in theory," explained Aleeza. Her children would have to wait until 10th grade to have technology access in India, whereas, even though limited in U.S. classrooms, computers were available at a younger age.

Pedagogical Strategies

All four participants confirmed the need to learn new ways to teach American students, who were not used to lecture-style classes, as noted in the literature (Henry, 2001; "School districts import teachers," 2001). Hutchison (2005) interviewed four international teachers at a private international school in the Southeastern United States. He found that the teachers were challenged by "pedagogical gaps," due to differences in school systems, assessment, philosophy, communication issues, and teaching methods. Foreign teachers also experienced "pedagogical shifts," which forced them to change the way they behaved and taught in U.S. schools. The Indian teachers in this study had previous experience teaching in their home countries, ranging from 2 years to 7. Yet the methods they implemented in India were neither acceptable, because of the structure of the school day and work periods, nor effective in urban schools in the United States.

First, the teachers cited the need to move beyond lecturing. All of the participants in the study were accustomed to lecture-style instruction. In their middle and secondary schools in India, they spent alternating days lecturing. For example, they would lecture on Monday, Wednesday, and Friday, for an entire period, and on Tuesday and Thursday, the students would work independently to review what they had learned on the previous days. Conversely, students in the teachers' classes in the United States did not respond well to lectures. Aleeza claimed that, "other than lecture method, anything is going to work [with U.S. students] . . . because they do not want to listen. They are not good listeners, except for a few. Though I have to lecture sometimes; I cannot do without lecturing." Samina elaborated on why she believed the Indian lecture method was not effective in her new country: "For these students maybe [no lecture] is the right thing. . . . Their retaining power or the time they can sit together in one place, it is just 5 minutes. They can just sit in one place for 5 minutes. They cannot sit altogether for 1 hour. But in India they can, and they do it. If they do not do it, they are out of the school." The teachers said they also appreciated the challenge and enjoyed learning new methods.

Next, the participants cited the need for using hands-on activities with American students. Aleeza surmised, "They [American students] are more for hands-on activities, especially for science." In India, her students were unable to have full-scale labs because of money and resources, so learning how to plan more hands-on activities was new to her. During two observations of her high school science class, I observed students participating in a lab and a group project. Both activities were ones that Aleeza created in co-planning with her department colleagues and were not lessons she typically would have planned in India. She thought (and I would agree) that they were somewhat successful in terms of getting students to participate in their own learning.

In addition to hands-on activities, participants also mentioned the need for group work and class discussions. Samina stated that, "When we work with these kids, they have more freedom, [so] it is really very much necessary to keep them engaged." One method the teachers employed to keep students engaged was discussion, either in small groups or as a whole class. For example, during an observation of Faria's high school math class, students worked in pairs or groups of three to complete a worksheet on algebraic equations. After class, she reflected, "I cannot get to them all at the same time, so they can help each other. Sometimes it helps them focus." Aleeza agreed that students in the United States were more likely to expect and respond to whole-class discussion than students in India, who were accustomed to the teacher speaking most of the time.

Small groups, Samina maintained, could either aid or inhibit classroom learning. At times, students learned from each other. Other times, however, it did not work as planned:

> I always believe[d] in small groups, collaborated groups, instructions like that. Because when they sit together and they discuss it they can explain it to each other and they can have better understanding of whatever is going on. But you know, it is not so easy to put them in groups and leave them on their own to discuss it, because I am sure they are not going to discuss it. They are going to discuss something else and pretend like they are discussing it.

Almost all of the small-group work I observed in Samina's middle school language arts classes followed the pattern she described above. The self-selected groups were divided by gender, with the boys choosing other boys as their partners, and the girls on the other side of the room. In one class, of the nine groups that were formed, only one group managed to stay on task and complete the assignment before the bell rang. The other groups discussed things like basketball, the daily lunch menu, the latest "couple" to break up, an upcoming family vacation, and a new student in their physical education class. Samina circulated among all the groups, encouraging them to work and directing their attention, both verbally and physically, by putting them back in their seats and tapping the worksheet in front of them, but their focus could not be regained once they had been paired with gossiping friends.

Curriculum and Assessment

In addition to differences in teaching methods, there were also contrasts in content. Though Faria pointed out that math anywhere was math everywhere, other teachers who were faced with scripted lesson plans used in the particular school district and standardized testing found the differences between U.S. and Indian curricula to be at once confusing, challenging, and frustrating.

One teacher was required to use a scripted curriculum plan for her middle school English class, which further restricted her, she said, from reaching her students. Samina explained that,

For one persuasive essay, they are asking [us] to teach 22 lessons. It does not make any sense to me. . . . I think 6 to 7 lessons, that would be enough. This is dragging like a rubber band. And because of that, it is really hard to me to just keep them focused. . . . It just restricts me, ties my hands, but I try to give my own resources for them to work.

The curriculum she spoke about, America's Choice, was not actually a choice for her at all. The district required several "failing" schools to adopt the curriculum for middle and high school language arts and math classes. Like other urban teachers compelled to use scripted lessons, Samina found it difficult to integrate what she believed students need to know and useful ways for them to learn into the highly structured curricular units. This was especially ironic because she and other foreign teachers were touted as being content-area experts, yet they were not allowed to use their content expertise to plan their own lessons.

Testing is nothing new to India. Indeed, participants spoke about the numerous exams they had to take for admission to college or their teacher preparation programs. Shrusty explained the process by which she had to be selected to even participate in taking the 3-hour exam for her bachelor's degree in special education:

It was like 2,000 applications came, and they just sent an admission card for 600 people. From that 600, only 20 was [sic] selected [to take the exam]. So I was among those 20. . . . So my dad said, "Just go and write the exams," so I wrote the entrance [examination].

The main difference in testing between India and the United States, according to the teachers, was how testing was used to make decisions at the K–12 level and the over-abundance of multiple-choice questions on such examinations in the United States.

The Glendale School District tested students in almost every grade, in compliance with the No Child Left Behind legislation, with end-of-course tests and with high-stakes graduation exams. The teachers in this study were most concerned with the end-of-course tests because they thought the exams were insignificant if also combined with student classwork. Faria described the testing system in India, whereby students "prepare the whole year" for one final exam and "do not get a grade for their classwork." As a result, they are more focused on "mastering" the content thoroughly and not just preparing to guess at multiple-choice questions.

Aleeza, too, stated that this end-of-course plus classwork grade often back-fired and became more burdensome for the teacher than the students.

I am not saying you [in the United States] have to do exactly what we do [in India]. . . . Some of the students are like, "It is all right if I score a 50 on my [exam] because I am still going to pass your class. I am going to do all the work that you gave." And if she does that, I have to pass the student. The standardized test should count something on the student. . . . So, you know what I feel? It is more pressure on the teacher than on the student, for the exam. It should be the other way. We have to pressurize them.

Aleeza's quotation expands on Faria's notion of competition discussed earlier. For these two teachers, competition bred success, as it forced Indian students to focus more in class and become more "keen learners." The cultural expectation for Indian students of a certain class and caste is that they compete with each other to "get admission into a good college" and "make their career better and better." The highly selective universities in India are overwhelmed by the increasing student population and the rising middle class, according to Najar (2011), and many are turning to education abroad. The teachers saw this phenomenon in stark contrast to the school culture in their American urban schools, where, they said, very few of their students attended 4-year colleges upon graduation.

Additionally, all four participants lamented the use of solely multiple-choice exams, which was something they were never exposed to in India, either as students or as teachers. Samina explained that "here [the United States] is a little bit easier" because Indian exams require students to "write everything we know; the whole book we have to read and learn." Aleeza agreed that Indian exams, which typically consisted of "ten short answers and 30 objective, like multiple choice and [fill in the] blanks, and two or three essays," challenged students to pay more attention in class and study harder:

> [In India] they have to retain the concept because they have essay type of questions on their test. . . . [But in the United States], like 30% of the students, because of the multiple-choice questions they have, they just guess the answers and sometimes their guess is good. . . . I feel sad about that. . . . I do not like the way the test goes here, and students will pay more attention if you challenge their retaining power or understanding capacity.

Although it is possible to create higher-level thinking questions with multiple-choice answers, the teachers were not exposed to these types of questions because they were only drawing from state exams and district benchmarks. Though beyond the scope of this study, the few premade tests that I had the opportunity to examine were, in fact, primarily composed of low-level questions that only asked students to comprehend or recall, not analyze or synthesize.

Students' Lack of Cultural Awareness

A primary purpose of international teacher recruitment, according to recruitment agencies, is to bring cultural knowledge and awareness to American students. This will be discussed in later chapters, but it is important to note here that the lack of cultural awareness discovered by Indian teachers in their American students was surprising and disappointing to the teachers.

Teachers expressed frustration and shock that their U.S. students did not possess much knowledge about the world outside their country's borders. Though they could not attribute this lack of cultural awareness to any one single factor, instead listing the responsible parties as schools, parents, and society, they said that the American students they knew were missing important pieces of information. Aleeza maintained that school had failed students: "The way they talk about their own country, they really do not feel there are a lot of people outside the United States. Maybe because they are not educated in that style, I guess. But I have felt that they do not know anything about the outer world. A lot." As described by Samina, who summarized an interaction with her middle school students: "I'm sorry to say that these kids are not exposed to many things. I asked them 1 day how many continents are there, how many oceans, and only one or two could tell me. In India, they would just [snaps fingers], they would know everything about the whole world."

Samina also told a story about an American student who believed that India and the United States were close enough for her teacher to travel by cruise ship. She bemoaned, "They don't even know the distance between India and America. In an atlas, I showed her where I was in India and where she was. I said, 'I had to take two flights.' She was saying, 'Really? I thought you could take a cruise.'" Students of the same age in India, she emphasized, would never make such a mistake. Aleeza concurred that, "all the Indian students in the 7th grade, they start talking about the outside world, like outside India. . . . They know more than what these [U.S.] students know because, from that age, they are trying to know where it is possible for them to go and earn good." This pressure to get "good jobs" came up frequently in teachers' discussions of Indian schools. They lamented that they did not see this same pressure for U.S. students even though "the economy was failing."

The participants also found their students woefully misinformed or under-informed about Indian culture in particular. Faria believed this lack of knowledge was because "the United States is a very big country, so they do not go out of that world to know about India . . . it is two different corners of the world." In contrast, teachers guessed students saw India as a smaller place. Aleeza explained that "they have a lot of questions like 'so-and-so is living in India, he or she is my friend, do you know him?' I am like, 'What do you think? India is just this much [makes finger gesture signifying a tiny amount]? I know everybody in India?' That is the misconception they had, like most of the students have that." Some students asked about cultural habits and customs, such as arranged marriages and religions, but they believed that all Indian parents "forced" their children to marry someone of the parents' choice or that all Indians were Hindus. "They are curious to know why I don't have a red dot; I tell them I am not a Hindu, I am a Muslim," Samina remembered. "Not everybody in India is the same. I don't think they know about any of it." This is a difficult fact to reconcile with what the teaches knew about U.S. schools and urban students before they arrived—primarily only stereotypes and media-related facts. Both the teachers and their students seem to have been flattening cultural distinctions quite a bit.

The majority of questions asked of international teachers were even more basic, demonstrating considerable lack of awareness about cultures outside the United States. Samina's statement that "they think America is the only world" illustrated that students' ignorance bordered on ethnocentrism. Though the Indian teachers can laugh in retrospect, they were shocked, bewildered, and sometimes offended by questions that showed students viewed all of India as a Third World country, far behind the United States in terms of technology and advancements. Participants remembered a variety of questions that students wondered aloud, sometimes in the middle of a lesson. For example, teachers were asked: Do you have McDonald's over there? Do you have the same kind of houses that we have? Do they have cell phones and computers in your country? Do you know how to use the Internet? Do you use Facebook? Do you know who Michael Jackson is? And, perhaps most shockingly, a student asked her teacher if Indians still rode elephants!

Students themselves recognized that culture had an impact on how their peers related to the teacher. During a classroom observation in which Samina was having difficulty getting students to focus, a young girl approached me, introduced herself, and said, "It's hard to learn in here." When I asked why, she said, "Most students don't respect my teacher because she is from a different culture." This honest expression was troubling for several reasons. First, the student here, like Stefan in the previous section, attributed a lack of respect to something that was completely beyond the teacher's control (recall his comment that "we give it to her bad because she's Indian"); the teacher could not change her cultural background, so how would she improve the learning environment? Second, the student believed that the teacher was at a *disadvantage* because of her different culture, whereas the district, recruitment agency, and media argued that that cultural difference was an *advantage*. They assumed that because the teachers themselves were non-White that they would work well with non-White children. Samina's principal, Mr. Sutherland, agreed with the student's assessment, noting that his students "who had never been outside these blocks" were a "mismatch" with someone from another culture. I will discuss more about the cultural divide and how teachers responded to it in the next chapter.

Policies of School and State

Another difference the teachers noted between U.S. and Indian schools were policies implemented by the district, school, and state. Though education is also top-down in the teachers' home state, the teachers claimed that U.S. schools were more bureaucratic and did not implement changes that helped students. Standardized testing is one such policy; others include disciplinary and academic failure policies and local reform issues.

First, the teachers did not support the district's policies to allow makeup tests or repeated classes or grade levels if students failed. Aleeza stated, "I do understand it is a good thing for those students who have an excused absence . . . but not for everybody." Some students, she divulged, took advantage of the makeup policy by coming to tutorials after school when they had not paid attention in class. Indeed, during one observation, I saw a student, who had slept through the whole class, wake up and turn to a friend, saying, "I'll just come after school. She explains it quicker then anyway." In India, she explained, parents had to pay additional fees for private tutorials, so students were less likely to "abuse" classroom time. Further, the teachers argued that American students were not "pressured" enough to succeed because they had multiple opportunities to repeat classes. "If they are going to take it easy," Samina said of her Indian students, "they are going to land up somewhere [bad]. So it makes sense to keep them under pressure." According to the teachers, Indian students only had one opportunity to succeed, both academically and behaviorally, so the teachers were unfamiliar with the policy of multiple chances.

Disciplinary consequences, the teachers also noted, were nonexistent or unenforced; some asserted that there were more rules and regulations for teachers than for students. Samina explained that, in India, if students "are not performing well, or if they are disrespecting a teacher, or they are involved in any kind of issue, they are not just suspended, they are rusticated [expelled], out of the school with bag and baggage." An added consequence was that "if they misbehave, or if there is bad conduct, then their future is in darkness because other schools, too, will not take that student." Extremely problematic, then, were their American schools' plans of verbal warnings, phone calls to parents, detentions, and in- and out-of-school suspensions. During one observation when Samina's students were especially disruptive, she sent four young men to the principal's office; three returned before the class period was over, calling to their classmates as they came in, "We're back!" Thus, Samina had to stop instruction for an extended time: to ask students to quiet down, to ask several to leave, to refocus that class upon the boys' return, and then again to ask the class to quiet down. The teachers were clearly struggling with reconciling their classroom management practices with the schools' policies and the administrators' support (or lack thereof). However, I would argue that there is a fine but absolutely vital line between enforcing policies that are necessary for productive learning and enforcing zero tolerance policies that negatively impact a large proportion of students of color (e.g., Ayers, 2001b; Skiba, 2008). The Indian zero tolerance policies that the teachers discussed, if implemented whole-scale through the United States, would surely result in larger proportions of suspended and expelled students of color and contribute to the school-to-prison pipeline in tragic ways.

Teachers also commented on school reform policies. Coming from a culture where teachers often do what they are asked to do without questioning, Aleeza's first response when asked about school reform initiatives was to say, "We have to do what we have to do, that is what I say." She said that, despite similar reforms in India, the government is more careful to think of the reforms' effects on children. Just as other teachers said that administrators did not consider the consequences of student behavior, Aleeza conjectured that officials did not always consider the consequences of reforms:

> You cannot blame the teacher if she is not able to handle 50 kids in a class [referring to the possible increase in class size]. If it is affecting their education, then see what you are going to get for America. . . . Before making these big decisions, they really have to look at what is the outcome of that. . . . . It is easy to cut jobs. It is easy to cut down on teachers. That is easy. . . . What about the students? Who is thinking about the students?

I believe that, if given the opportunity, international teachers would also fight for students' rights and argue against policies that negatively impact students' learning. However, they are rarely even given the opportunity to fight for their own rights, let alone the rights of their students. Like many U.S. teachers who find it difficult to balance activism and classroom teaching, international teachers have to choose which battle they will fight. Inevitably, if they fight at all, the first battle they wage is for their own job security and safety.

Relations with Parents and Families

Teachers expressed conflicting views about their interactions with parents and families. Several described trouble garnering parents' support, possibly due to communication problems. Others said they felt very supported by their students' families, which added to their general job satisfaction. Participants found a difference between parents supporting versus challenging teachers' authority. Parents who defended their child if he did something wrong, or parents who went to the administration with complaints, surprised several of the teachers. This was not common in India, where parents trusted teachers and accepted their decisions without question. When discussing this, several teachers used the example of corporal punishment, which was acceptable in India. Shrusty summarized,

> Parenting in the United States is hard . . . because in India, you can whip your child anywhere. In front of the teacher, and the teacher has full right. . . . You are doing the thing for the kids' betterment. Here, there are too many laws, you cannot touch the child, you cannot do this, you cannot do that. The child has this right and that right. What about teachers' rights?

Aleeza agreed that "the basic difference" was that Indian parents "will whup [children] if they come to know that we misbehaved in school for any reason, whether it be right or wrong," but that American parents often questioned teachers' disciplinary decisions. The principals confirmed a struggle between parents and teachers, noting that many parents called the administration to discuss the Indian teachers' classroom practices.

In contrast, Faria said she felt supported by school parents, several of whom attended her class after their children complained that Faria was difficult to understand. She explained, "They observed and said it is their children [who were wrong] because they said, 'The class was so wonderful and your accent was so clear for us to understand. We think they are just playing.' " Shrusty, too, reported that her special education students' parents were quite supportive of her efforts and their children, and frequently visited the school or attended class field trips.

But many teachers in this study saw parents as part of the "problem." When parents challenged the teacher's authority versus supported it, as the teachers reported is more common in India, the teachers argued that parents often enabled or emboldened their children's misbehavior or lack of achievement. They viewed parents, and society at large, as part of the problem. For example, Aleeza explained that, in India,

> When the teacher enters the classroom, they know they need to be quiet and listen to whatever she is teaching. Basically, that is how they are because they know if something goes wrong with them in the school then their parents are going to be upset with them. So we never had any problems with students.

Thus, in the United States, where parents may not be as involved in their children's education for a variety of reasons, Aleeza said that students were more able to do something wrong because they did not fear the wrath of their parents. Further, parents were "demanding" of teachers because they felt that students who came after school for tutorials should be given makeup work, whereas Aleeza said that paying attention during class the first time was significantly more important.

Samina discussed at length why she viewed parents as part of the problem, noting that student misbehavior was not a force of nature, but of nurture.

Samina: I really pity them. I do not know why. . . . They are not like this by birth. Situations are making them like this.
Alyssa: What situations do you think?
Samina: Maybe their surroundings, [the way] they're brought up, their financial status, their parents and their relationships, relationship between the parents. Because we do not have one father and one mother over here; we have stepbrothers and stepfathers and all that. Maybe that

is one more reason, and too much of freedom. They are not responsible for this kind of behavior. [In] some way, others are responsible, because they are not like this by birth.

Alyssa: Was that a surprise to you, or a shock, learning about the different family situations that are very different from . . .

Samina: That was not exactly a surprise; I was aware of it. But the extent was not known to me. I did not know that it was up to this extent that the kids are going nowhere, because of the parents and because of the financial situation.

Alyssa: The kids are going what?

Samina: The kids are going nowhere, they are all landing up in troubles, and they are landing up with no future, because [of] lack of education.

Samina's belief that students are not "like this by birth" shows her willingness to consider the contextual factors in her students' lives. However, her placing blame on the parents is troubling and potentially revealing of a deficit perspective. This too will be explored in depth in the next chapter.

EFFECTS ON RELATIONSHIPS AND PRACTICE

"Who are you?" said the Caterpillar . . .

"I— I hardly know, Sir, just at the present," Alice replied rather shyly, "At least I know who I was when I got up this morning, but I think I must have been changed several times since then."

—Lewis Carroll, 1920

As one would expect, the extensive list of differences just presented had both immediate and long-term effects on international teachers. Their evolving identities as teachers and border-crossers changed, like Alice in Wonderland, on a weekly, if not daily and hourly, basis. In particular, their relationships and practice changed over time. They developed relationships with American allies and with each other, and they tried adapting their pedagogy and classroom management styles to their new contexts.

American Allies

All four of the teachers spoke highly of their colleagues, fellow educators who had "shown them the ropes" and helped them navigate the new culture. "I had a gala time," Aleeza noted, "because as an outsider, I wanted acceptance, not only from my students but my coworkers. It was really lovely because the faculty was very good, very supportive." These American allies helped with planning lessons, managing classrooms, and navigating school rules. For example, Faria described a "friendly" atmosphere where everyone "was so supportive that I have never felt that I was in a different country." She was also able to get assistance with classroom management from the administration, department chair, counseling office, and school intervention officers. Aleeza, too, garnered help from the department chair, whose classroom she "floated" into to teach during her first 2 years. The department chair was instrumental because she heard the way students were talking and instructed them to pay attention and watch their language when Aleeza did not yet know American slang or curses.

American allies also helped with personal adjustments and feelings of belonging. When asked if she felt like part of the school community, Samina hesitated, and then answered, "Part of the community, hmm. . . . When I deal with teachers and my colleagues, I feel like I am part of the school community." Another example is when Shrusty spoke at length about her "American family," the other special education teachers and paraprofessionals with whom she worked. One coworker, her "best buddy," called parents for her if there was a problem with a student, because it was difficult for Shrusty to understand some of the parents over the telephone. Her paraprofessional, Mr. Woods, whom she prefers to call her "coworker" and not her "assistant," gave Shrusty and three other foreign teachers rides to and from school each day. Later, when Shrusty bought a car from a terminated teacher, Mr. Woods became her "car guy" who offered her driving lessons and tips on where and how to fill up her gas tank. And then, not long after Shrusty began driving herself, he became her "hero":

> I was trying to make a turn and I did not anticipate the turn, and my car was in a ditch. The only person I could call was Mr. Woods. I did not know anything about 911. . . . He was a track coach, and there was a track meet going on, but he left everything and he came. He said, "Don't hang up the phone, keep talking to me, here I come, don't panic, here I come." . . . Then he called a tow car. He was like a hero. . . . He had his hands bleeding and everything. Oh my goodness. I can never forget that day. That was May 23. . . . Mr. Woods came to my rescue, and everybody thanked him, my mom, my dad, I had to tell everybody and even my husband. The next day, I brought Indian food for him as a gesture of gratitude, but he didn't like it! Too spicy! [laughs] From that day till here, he never ate Indian food!

This story was especially meaningful because it further demonstrated that Shrusty could trust and rely on Mr. Woods, her American ally. It solidified a working relationship of mutual trust, goodwill, and good humor that lasted throughout their 3 years together and which I witnessed during my classroom observations. Shrusty and Mr. Woods would tease each other and make jokes frequently, and Mr. Woods was eager to share with me what he viewed as Shrusty's strengths and weaknesses: "She is the nicest and most giving person I have ever met. Sometimes she is too nice. She shouldn't be so nice all the time because people walk all over her. But I am trying to get her to toughen up. I'll teach her yet!" Because of the support of colleagues, as well as the community they were able to create with other international teachers, the "veterans" were able to return after their first difficult year. They felt, as Martin Luther King, Jr. put it, "We may all have come on different ships, but we're in the same boat now." I will explore collegial support in more detail in the conclusion, as I see community-building and professional communities as a vital component of ensuring the success of international teachers.

International Community

The Indian teachers were placed as roommates or neighbors in the same apartment complex, and during their first year, frequently got together on Friday nights to watch American teen movies and learn new slang. Because the agencies did not allow them to bring their families during the first year until they received a satisfactory evaluation, the support of fellow Indian teachers was especially important for both their professional growth and their mental health. Professionally, it was helpful for "novice" teachers to hear from "veterans." Faria described a group that formed during her first year. "We used to discuss the problems, advise each other," she recalled. "And we used to talk to the teachers who were from last year. We used to ask them how did they overcome those problems, so they used to give some suggestions." This "generational" passing down of information from one group of teachers to the next eased their culture shock and transition to new environments.

One powerful example of generational community was the relationship that developed between "veteran" teacher, Shrusty, and "novice" teacher, Samina. When Samina arrived, the school year had already been in session for 2 weeks. She received no orientation other than a brief discussion with the recruitment agency administrator. Shrusty took it upon herself to become Samina's friend and confidante because "I was like the only person guiding her, and the person who was staying with her was . . . scaring her with stories about the kids." She provided Samina with rides to and from her school each day, and they would often talk through challenges on their drives. She also helped Samina prepare for parent–teacher conferences by making "visiting cards with her name and email ID" and even printed the cards because Samina did not know where her school's media center was located. "She didn't know the meaning of f-u-c-k," Shrusty remembered about her friend, who found the word written on classroom materials. "I said 'you better call your husband and ask.' But he didn't know what it means. So I tell her, never ever take that word in your mouth, but it was a good learning experience." For a new teacher with no orientation, no prior knowledge of American schools, who was away from her family and did not feel supported at her school, the value of community could be understated.

Shifts in Pedagogy and Management

This research confirms Hutchison's (2005) findings that foreign teachers experienced pedagogical shifts. That is, the teachers here altered the way they taught based on what they perceived their American students needed. Additionally, they also shifted their management strategies based on classroom experiences.

One example of a pedagogical shift is the movement away from lecture, as discussed in the previous section. Aleeza learned new ways to design science labs as an alternative to lectures. She stated that, "now I know like if you have enough to spend, if you can pull some out of your income, then you can surely benefit the students with little things, doing mini-labs or something, or at least a demonstration, which would not cost you a lot. That has helped me a lot. As a teacher, I have grown; that is what I feel." Aleeza also found that, in addition to group work and discussion, it was also necessary to work with students individually for remediation:

> The [chemical] structure I talked about, I taught them 2 weeks ago. Yesterday, when it was one-on-one, it just took them 2 minutes to understand, but they did not understand it in 2 weeks. Though I explained it the same way I did during my lecture, I could make out they were not listening [during the initial lecture].

This one-on-one interaction between Aleeza and her students was where I saw her pedagogical skills at their best. During an observation where the majority of the class was working in small groups, she assisted several individual students at the front of the classroom. She used their notes to remind them of what she had previously discussed, but she also offered new examples and patiently answered students' questions. For instance, she explained chemical bonding to one student four times in four different ways; finally, on the fourth time, it was evident from the student's facial expression that he finally got it. "I like the light bulb moments," Aleeza said later. These personal interactions were often more satisfying for her because it was clear when students had such "light bulb moments."

The teachers learned that they could ask for help, in terms of what they were teaching, how they were teaching, and how they were managing the class. Aleeza and Faria both remembered that, when they first arrived, they assumed that sending a student out of class for a disruption would be "a bad impression" on them. They gradually learned, however, that sending a student out was sometimes necessary for the benefit of the rest of the class and was more a "bad impression on the student" than on the teacher.

Though Samina acknowledged that she had learned some new skills, she also implied that there were things that would be more difficult to teach to American students, in part because of all the differences and challenges noted above. She saw her accent and her students' frustration with it, and her students' low academic skills, as reasons to avoid certain lessons that she would otherwise like to teach:

I would love to teach them poetry, but I do not know. It is going to be again another task for me. [sighs audibly] Because you know, again the accent [will be a problem]. . . . When I am reading two lines from the poetry, they might think, "Okay, she is not reading it the right way," and that is going to be again a challenge. . . . You need a lot of thinking when you go for poetry. They are not so good at it. Imagination. You have to just figure out things in your mind when you go for poetry. It is not so easy for them.

Struggle Between Hopelessness and Resilience

When I began my research, Faria, Aleeza, and Shrusty were in their third year of teaching in the United States. There were times, they said, when they felt helpless, particularly at the beginning of their tenure when their families were still in India, but because of a variety of factors, including their American allies and international teacher community, they were resilient. Shrusty attributed her resilience to her good English skills, her camaraderie with colleagues, and her personal desire to stay in the country for her children's education. Aleeza agreed, adding that "God wanted us to stay here."

Samina, however, was in her first year, was the only one teaching middle school, and was struggling through feelings of hopelessness that I had not observed in the three veteran foreign teachers, most likely because they had adjusted or acclimated in the years prior to my study. During our interviews, she regularly expressed feelings of frustration, anger, confusion, and sadness. With the exception of Shrusty, her veteran companion, she did not feel supported by her agency or the administration and she felt distant from the school community. She expressed unhappiness when she remembered, "When I talk to some of the good students and they really care about me and they give [a] good response, then I think 'okay, I am part of this. I am a professional in this school.' But when I am dealing with bad kids or talking back to me and all that, I feel left out."

As her students' behavior became increasingly erratic and bordered on violent as the semester went on, Samina felt further overwhelmed, both physically and emotionally exhausted. She said, "We do not have any kind of discipline problems like this [in India]. . . . That upsets you when you do not get the due respect. You deserve that respect, and when you do not get it, you feel sad." Samina, though her days were often bleak, was resilient enough to return to school each day for the majority of the school year. This was especially difficult because her family was not allowed to come to the United States after the first semester, as the agency only allowed family members to come if the teachers received satisfactory evaluations. Because Samina was on a professional development plan in which specific areas were targeted for improvement in her practice, she remained alone for the entire year. Her principal, Mr. Sutherland, was especially troubled when he learned about this, as he realized that teachers were more likely to be successful if they had a support system. You would imagine this would put principals in a bind on evaluations. They would want to treat everyone the same, but the consequences are not the same for their international employees. Perhaps this explains why they were never told about the family arrangements. They only learned about it when I asked them for their opinions on the matter. Samina's days were filled with this inner conflict and struggle for resilience. In the end, she thought of her students and explained, "I really want to love them. But they are making me yell sometimes. . . . I am just helpless."

CONCLUSION

This chapter has demonstrated that teachers reported substantial differences between classrooms in the United States and India. Based on their limited previous knowledge of American classrooms (gleaned from media portrayals, friends' accounts, brief orientations, and personal research), the teachers were not prepared for the reality of American schools, students, and policies. Participants reported only two similarities between education in their home country and the United States: They were teaching students of the same age and there existed economic disparities among schools. Differences were much more salient, the teachers reported. With far more differences than similarities identified, I argue that the continental divide between cultural expectations and student and teacher behaviors, coupled with a lack of pedagogical support, exacerbated the challenges for international teachers. Teachers' relationships and practices changed over time in multiple ways, such as the development of American allies and an international community, shifts in pedagogy and management, and a struggle between hopelessness and resilience. Overall, the struggles that teachers experienced were directly linked to the differences between what the teachers believed was of cultural value and what they perceived was of cultural value to the students. An analysis of how teachers understood and taught students of a different culture from their own is the basis of the next chapter.

THREE

Trying to Build Cultural Bridges

Gandhi, MLK, and Culturally Relevant Pedagogy

Caminante, no hay puentes, se hace puentes al andar. [Voyager, there are no bridges, one builds them as one walks.]

—Gloria Anzaldúa, 1983

Education is all a matter of building bridges.

—Ralph Ellison, 1986

As do most major U.S. cities, especially cities in the Southeast, Glendale houses a variety of tributes to Martin Luther King, Jr., including streets and schools. And, as is common in other cities, the neighborhoods that include buildings and boulevards named in his honor are, ironically and frustratingly, some of the most segregated in the district. The struggle for civil rights is something that students in India learned as well, and international teachers had once learned about MLK's quest, especially how closely it was linked with the nonviolent philosophy of Mohandas Gandhi.[1] In this chapter, I highlight to what extent the teachers' cultural knowledge extended beyond a basic understanding of civil rights and how they attempted to build cultural bridges with colleagues and students. This was especially difficult, according to the teachers, because their own colleagues did not know much about Indian customs. "They asked, 'You are from the land of Gandhi?'" Shrusty recalled. "So at least they know Gandhi. They know Martin Luther King [Jr.] was a follower of Gandhi."

A key argument in the recruitment of international teachers is that the teachers work well with students from diverse cultures, because they themselves are from another culture. This line of reasoning appears to make (some) sense when the culture of the teacher matches the cultures of their students, in the case of Filipino teachers hired in Baltimore to work with an increasingly Filipino population, or Mexican teachers hired in Texas to work in immigrant-dense, Spanish-speaking communities. (Yet, of course, it contradicts the other stated goal: to widen cultural and global horizons.) Hiring Indian teachers to work with primarily African American populations is quite different (Axtman, 2004; Neufeld, 2005). In this case, agencies mistakenly equated "diverse" and "multicultural" with "of color" and assumed that Indian teachers, because they were non-White, would implicitly understand and thus, teach well, students of color.

In this chapter, I argue that international teachers exhibited some evidence of effective teaching practice, but they lacked the sociocultural knowledge of African American students to demonstrate true culturally relevant pedagogy (CRP). Thus, their attempts to build cultural bridges often faltered or crumbled. I contextualize my observations by first analyzing the state of multicultural education in India and later by analyzing students' commentary about their international teachers' ability to understand and value their culture. For these four teachers, American education's focus on race and culture was novel. As one participant recalled, unknowingly echoing the prediction of W.E.B. DuBois and the words of Cornel West, "even today, race matters here."

MULTICULTURALISM IN INDIA

There is one crucial difference between multicultural education in India and the United States. In India, where multicultural education is "a term rarely if ever used" (Joshee & Sihra, 2009, p. 425), it means educating students from many cultures, and does not necessarily extend to what or how to teach those cultures, as is typically the case in the United States. I found that international teachers understood multicultural education and culturally relevant pedagogy in light of three factors: national diversity policies, teacher education, and their prior teaching experience.

National Policies on Difference

After India gained independence from Britain in 1947, the Constitution of India provided for freedom and education for all, regardless of religious, linguistic, cultural, or racial origin. Article 45 of the constitution maintains that the state provide free and compulsory education for all children until age 14 (Govinda, 2002), and other sections guarantee autonomy for diverse groups, or the "right to maintain and develop their distinct identities" (Joshee & Sihra, 2009, p. 425). National education and diversity policies purport to practice Gandhi's ideal of participatory pluralism (Madan, 1999). Similar to Banks's (2004) theory of multicultural education, participatory pluralism is "breaking down hierarchy and addressing social injustice . . . bridging the distance between groups . . . celebrat[ing] identities other than one's own . . . recogniz[ing] that cultures are not static . . . and addressing inequality between and within groups" (Joshee & Sihra, 2009, p. 426). Because, under colonial rule, Indian society had been rigidly hierarchical and some groups like the Scheduled Castes (SC) and Scheduled Tribes (ST) had been severely disenfranchised, postcolonial policies attempted to remedy past grievances by guaranteeing these groups equality and respect. Yet there are still rigid divisions between and among Indians. SC groups are those groups formerly called "untouchables" who have been historically disadvantaged. ST groups are aboriginal Indians who resisted the modern caste system.

This national commitment to underrepresented groups evolved into the "three main foci of multicultural education in India: . . . address the disadvantages faced by marginalized groups, encourage the valuing of diversity, and build a strong national identity" (Joshee & Sihra, 2009, p. 429). One can imagine how the third goal to build a strong national identity might often conflict with the first two goals. Unfortunately, much as in the United States, India's commitment to educational ideals of diversity is more often an aspiration than the "current reality of life" (p. 428). Despite these constitutional "guarantees," 60 years after the enactment of compulsory education, traditionally marginalized groups continue to lag behind dominant groups in educational achievement (Chakravarty, 2001; Rustagi, 2009). These marginalized groups include religious or linguistic minorities, women, lower castes, and indigenous tribes.

Scheduled Castes and Scheduled Tribes consistently have the lowest enrollments in school. Less than two-thirds of SC children and only 30% of ST children complete primary school (Consortium for Research on Educational Access, Transitions, and Equity, 2008). Enrollment and dropout in general have been problems for India's educational system. There is a high percentage of students who initially enroll in 1st grade, but about 30% of children do not complete 5th grade, with about 50% dropping out before completing 8th grade, and 60% do not finish 10th grade (Lewin, 2011). The dropout rates are highest for girls in SCs and STs (Consortium for Research on Educational Access, Transitions, and Equity, 2008). Much like in the United States, research has found that participation in school is influenced by household economic factors, sociocultural factors, and school environment, including quality of physical and human infrastructure, and quality of instruction (Rustagi, 2009). For many families in lower castes, it is easy to see how these factors are exacerbated by students' participation in school. Free education is not exactly free because parents have to pay fees, purchase books, and provide transportation.

In a study comparing two similar states, Andrha Pradesh and Rajasthan, Ramachandran (2009) found that SCs and STs mostly live in rural areas and attend school in a one-room, multiage classroom with only one or two teachers. These schools, which sometimes lack running water and proper toilet facilities, also have limited books, teaching and learning materials, academic support, libraries, and other resources (Ramachandran, 2009). These factors influence students' perceptions of schools and the level of interest that they display in attending school. Even if students are able to attend a formal primary school, their educational experience is different from forward-moving caste groups because, in part, they are excluded by the mainstream language use.

In its 2010 "Education for All Global Monitoring Report," the United Nations Educational, Scientific, and Cultural Organization (UNESCO) stated that "marginalization in education is a form of acute and persistent disadvantage rooted in underlying social inequalities" (p. 135). India and more than 130 countries joined together to implement the Right of Children to Free and Compulsory Education.

Although this declaration is no different from numerous polices that India has previously passed to support free and compulsory education, the goal is to continue to work toward closing the gap between poor and wealthy in the school system. Mehrotra (2012) states that there has been a lack of vision on the part of the policymakers when it comes to implementing national policies, causing the poor to be excluded from the "fruits of education." For example, after the National Policy of Education was formulated in 1986, there were efforts to open more schools. From 1986 to 1993, though there was an increase in the number of schools in some areas, the school access for SC and ST children did not improve significantly (Tilak, 2009).

One of the other major diversities in Indian classrooms is language. According to Chakravarty (2001):

> The medium of instruction beyond primary level is required to be one of the 18 regional languages. . . . However, in a country of over 300 dialects, this means that for the children of groups that do not speak any of the 18 languages, education is an alien language that becomes virtually meaningless. (p. 64)

Many students in India are educated in three languages, including English, but the quality of English-medium instruction varies based on the quality of the school, the teachers' education, and the students' home lives. "For those whose home environment does not complement the English conceptual world," writes Chakravarty (2002), "schooling prevents real learning, requiring rote learning instead. . . . English is not merely a skill to be acquired, but rather a symbol of long-term advantages" (p. 65). Further, the inclusion of English as one of the three languages, of which the second is almost always Hindi, "reinforced the supremacy" of these two languages over the other regional languages. In tribes that have a population of more than 100,000, the tribal dialect may be used as a medium of instruction, but this type of instruction is limited because of a lack of feasibility (Govinda, 2002, p. 8). The teachers with whom I worked possessed long-term advantages associated with English learners because they all received some English-medium instruction growing up. It was this proficiency that allowed them to qualify for placement in the United States, an experience they hoped would further increase their competitive advantages.

In sum, education was seen as the great equalizer and a way to address the "complex politics of diversity in India" (Public Report on Basic Education, 1999, quoted in Chakravarty, 2001, p. 65). Especially for groups that were often "unreached," like "child laborers, adolescent girls, tribal children, scheduled caste and scheduled tribe children, street children and children from slum colonies, children of migrant laborers, and physically and mentally handicapped children":

> The goal of multicultural education then becomes to provide high-quality education to all students, so as to equip them to function effectively both in their own "world"

and in the larger multicultural world. . . . The task, however, is herculean, the numbers formidable, and the multicultural complexity overwhelming. (Chakravarty, 2001, p. 66)

Indeed, unequal access stemming from historically rooted discrimination is at the core of the India's educational problems. With such a "herculean" task before national policymakers and teachers themselves, it is not surprising that many schools and classrooms in India have not moved beyond the United Nation's Education for All initiative into a more meaningful implementation of participatory pluralism, or critical multicultural education. Therefore, it is understandable why the Glendale teachers conceptualized multicultural education as "treating all students equally," in the words of one participant, as this was the vision of multicultural education they learned in India.

Teacher Education in India: Curriculum Analysis

In 1978, the Indian National Council of Education Research and Training (NCERT) established a national curriculum for teacher education. Since then, various initiatives have extended the original, including a reissuance of the curriculum framework in 1998 with a focus on "dynamic skills, . . . rigorous training in training institutions, in schools, . . . [and the] professional know-how to handle situations with care, caution, and empathy" (Rajput, Kumar, & Walia, 2002, p. 20). The Indian National Council for Teacher Education (NCTE) was established in 1993 and served to regulate programs and ensure standards, similar to the function of the National Council for the Accreditation of Teacher Education (NCATE) in the United States.

Much like in the United States, teacher education programs in India vary based on location, duration, and content. As a result, Indian education scholars worry that a lack of trained teachers in certain rural areas, short-length programs, and inadequate content contribute to underprepared teachers and undereducated students. According to Rajput et al. (2002), "in certain areas and regions, trained teachers are available in excess . . . while in others, non-trained teachers have to be appointed due to the non-availability of trained persons" (p. 6). Though the situation is worse in India, such a sentiment could also be leveled against many states and urban school districts in the United States, including Glendale, where there is an excess of teachers looking to work in north side schools, but not the south side schools. In India, teacher education programs are, most often, only 2 years in duration. Primary teachers are required to spend even less time than secondary teachers, earning only a certificate or diploma, as opposed to a bachelor of education degree. As Shrusty confirmed in her interviews, researchers assert that "the entire teacher education is still examination-oriented and the major focus of training is on theory papers and not on the practical aspects and practice teaching which is relegated to a secondary position and often gets ignored" (Rajput et al., 2002, p. 12).

For the purposes of my research, the most relevant aspect of teacher education in India is the discussion of multicultural education and diverse student populations. Although Aleeza remembered two particular courses in her preparation program that discussed diversity, the other participants did not recall anything specific. Aleeza recollected,

> There was a subject called psychology for me . . . and culture and education . . . so our professor used to teach us like, you know, you cannot expect all the students to be [the] same. There are different people working differently. Some things may be right at somebody's home, in somebody's country, and the other things may not be, so you have to work according to that.

Though participants remembered little about any diversity preparation, a curriculum handbook from the National Council for Teacher Education (NCTE) that was designed to "sensitize" teachers and teacher educators suggests what preservice teachers in India were taught. This handbook, *Discrimination Based on Sex, Caste, Religion, and Disability: Addressing Through Educational Interventions*, was designed to prepare teachers of all levels to "get broadly familiar with the content associated with the areas of discrimination as well as possible strategies which can be kept at the back of the mind while transacting curricular and co-curricular activities" (NCTE, 2003, n.p.). The handbook was divided into modules, one for each type of discrimination listed in the title. Modules included objectives for learning, definitions of important terms, explanations of relevant laws related to discrimination, graphs and tables with related descriptive statistics, and questions and activities.

For example, the module on sex/gender discrimination included an activity in which teacher candidates were to complete a worksheet stating whether they agreed or disagreed with a list of statements about equal educational opportunities for boys and girls, and then discuss with the group. Sample statements for discussion included:

> Girls and boys need equal education; Both need to be given equal health care and medical attention when needed; Both can be assigned some duties/responsibilities; Both should be given the same freedom; Both can have similar occupations; Both have the same intelligence and abilities; Men and women should be paid equal wages for equal work; Husband and wife should take all decisions jointly; Equal share for daughters and sons in family properly [property]/assets. (NCTE, 2003, p. 39)

The module then went on to ask teachers to (1) compare "traditional" male and female tasks, like sweeping the floor, grazing the cattle, and fetching water from the well; (2) compare "traditional" male and female occupations, such as lawyer, doctor, tailor, pilot, cricketer, and teacher; and (3) compare "traditional" male and female characteristics, like self-reliance, flexibility, playfulness, aggressiveness, neatness, and tenderness (p. 40). These tasks led to a reflection activity in which teachers were asked to consider how they planned lessons and behaved toward boys and girls in their own classrooms. Recommendations were then offered for ways to promote gender equality in the classroom.

This module is revealing because it highlights a continuing aspect of Indian culture that many American schools no longer even discuss. Though, in the United States, attention continues to be paid to the "gender gap" in math and science, and recently to the gap in graduation rates for young men, a discussion of gender access to education is not one that dominates educational policy in the contemporary United States. That is, though research continues on gender-based *success* in school, there is little contemporary research in gender-based *access* to schools in the first place.

To address needs in India, some scholars call for reforms in Indian teacher education. As Rajput et al. (2002) argue,

> Over the last 5 decades efforts to indigenise the Indian teacher education system and make it responsive to the needs of communities, regions, and socio-cultural realities have either been inadequate or have remained only at the policy level. The teacher education system and the teacher preparation programmes continue to function in the same manner and with the same approach inherited at the time of Independence. (p. 1)

Srivastava (2006) suggests a multitude of reforms for teacher education in India because of 21st-century changes like technology and globalization. He notes, "Due to modernization and globalization, tremendous changed [*sic*] has taken place is [*sic*] the society. The mode of teaching has also been modified. The duty of the teacher is to provide facilities and channelise [*sic*] the knowledge instead of teaching in the class" (p. 168). He recommends improvements to admissions policies, curriculum, duration, academic programs, teaching methodology, integration with other disciplines, communication skills of professors, and evaluations of programs.

Teachers' Prior Experience with Diversity

So, then, given the emphasis on welcoming diversity, but not necessarily providing teachers with the support for *being* welcoming, what experiences did my participants have working with a diverse array of students? All their prior teaching was in Indian schools. They acknowledged that they had no experience with students from different races or ethnicities because their previous environments had been "all Indian." Further, the English-medium schools in which they taught served primarily middle-class students.

Aleeza, however, did expand upon the notion of interstate linguistic and religious differences, as noted in the previous section on national policies. She explained that her students were "all Indians, but not from the same state." Because she lived in Hyderabad, one of the economic centers of India, there were transient students from families who were "working for government services, [and] they used to shift, have transfers." She continued,

> There is a large difference between each state because in each state they speak different languages. . . . I myself know four languages including English; one is my state language, the other one is the national language [Hindi], and the other one is my mother tongue. . . . But in your classroom, you can expect at least ten languages.

Her experience working with students of different abilities stemmed from this linguistic diversity and internal migration. Based on their previous educational experiences and their parents' level of education, her students had varying levels of English ability when they reached her classroom. "If they have educated parents, then their English level will be good," she recalled. Aleeza may have experienced similar linguistic diversity had she been placed in another of Glendale's schools, where there were large groups of English language learners; at her school, however, it was very rare to meet a non–African American student whose first language was not English. In this sense, then, her Indian school was more linguistically diverse.

Aleeza also talked about religious diversity in Indian schools, which she noted could be as divisive in India as racial diversity can be in the United States, and which the NCTE (2003) noted was "the nearest equivalent [to] the factor of race in the West" (p. 13). To understand the current religious division in India, it is important to step back for a moment to examine the historical legacy of Hindu–Muslim relations in India. The tension arises from the legacy of "partition," which has been an open wound in India's history. In 1947, when the Independent Act of India ended Britain's rule, the subcontinent was divided into the two states of India and Pakistan. This divide was based on partitioning the Indian Empire along religious lines (Mishra, 2007). The dominant political party, the Congress Party, took inspiration from Gandhi in claiming a secular organization and sought a mandate to keep India united, while the Muslim League stood for a separate Pakistan (Ahmed, 2002; Mishra, 2007). Many Muslim politicians saw the Congress Party as upper-caste Hindus and demanded a separate homeland for Muslims. With Britain wanting to relinquish its control over India after World War II, they saw partitioning along religions lines as the quickest way to withdraw.

A British official, given only 40 days to define precisely the political geography of India, did so by simply drawing lines on paper without visiting the villages, communities, rivers, or forests. Mishra (2007) states that "Hindus, Muslims, and Sikhs on either side of the new border suddenly found themselves reduced to a religious minority, the tensions of the preceding months exploded into the violence of ethnic cleansing" (p.4). The anger and violence led to the deaths of approximately 2 million people, and an estimated 12 to 15 million people were forcibly transferred between India and Pakistan in what Ahmed (2002) calls "one of the cruelest and bloodiest migrations and ethnic cleansings in history" (p. 9). Many believe that the division and subsequent bloodshed played a major role in the educational poverty of Muslims. Most of the high-service class and higher-income groups of Muslims migrated to Pakistan, and those who stayed in India were mostly laborers, marginal farmers, and other low-wage workers. Community violence forced Muslims to live in slums and ghettos, which did not have educational facilities, thus limiting Muslims' access to education. Today, Muslim children are the largest group of out-of-school children in India (Qureshi, 2010).

Hyderabad, though predominantly Hindu, is also home to the largest Muslim population in the state of Andhra Pradesh. Shrusty was Hindu; the other three teachers were Muslim. However, according to my participants, the majority of the time, religion was not an issue for either teachers or students, as long as teachers were vigilant in implementing fair classroom procedures. Aleeza stated:

> Inside the classroom they [students of all religions] are sitting together. . . .
> They are named differently, according to their religion, so the teacher does
> know to what religion they belong. So the other students know as well, but
> they don't care. You know, I think that comes from home, like you know, if
> your parents are practicing that [discrimination], then definitely the kids
> are going to practice that. . . . But of course we do have different religions
> and the teacher needs to be on her toes. . . . We don't want anybody to
> think we could do injustice to any of our students just because they are
> from [a] different religion. We cannot have pets [because they are the
> same religion]. . . . As soon as the kid fails, the parent asks "Is your teacher
> a Muslim or a Hindu?" So that is how I learned that it never gets to my
> religion when I am teaching.

Aleeza's solution to dealing with different religions is to ignore them. When I pressed her about what she did if she was teaching issues that were religiously influenced, she and other teachers said they did not teach anything like that. Given the trauma and subsequent instability that occurred less than 50 years ago during the Partition, this seems unlikely.

The combination of national identity politics, teacher education, and previous multicultural experience with different languages and religions may have prepared my participants to work with diverse groups in India. However, the recruitment agencies' assumption that diverse groups could be instructed the same way across cultures—and Glendale's unquestioning acceptance of this assumption—left the teachers unprepared for the climate of the U.S. urban schools where they were placed. Though the participants in my study expressed confidence in their prior education, a lack of focus on, or sometimes even a consideration of, multiculturalism left them further unprepared for urban U.S. classrooms in which multiculturalism was a salient feature. For foreign teacher recruitment agencies to be truly effective, they need to conduct additional interventions to prepare teachers for the U.S. context. In the next section, I discuss the teachers' practices with respect to culturally relevant pedagogy (CRP).

CULTURALLY RELEVANT PEDAGOGY

In her examination of what makes teachers successful when teaching African American students, Ladson-Billings (1997) posits a list of characteristics common among successful teachers she observed, an approach that has come to be known as culturally relevant pedagogy (CRP). The ability to teach students using methods that validate their cultural identities has been labeled in a variety of ways, such as "culturally relevant, sensitive, [student] centered, congruent, reflective, mediated, contextualized, synchronized, and responsive" (Gay, 2000, p. 29). But a common finding of all this research is that "students' cultures need to be validated in both what they are taught and how they are taught, combined with a wider transformative purpose to empower students" (Stairs, Donnell, & Dunn, 2011). Culturally relevant teachers exhibit certain beliefs and behaviors related to how they see themselves and others, the way they structure their social interactions, and the way they view knowledge in their classrooms (Ladson-Billings, 1997). Teachers who use CRP combat traditional assimilationist pedagogy that ignores students' histories and cultures and instead view their practice with a cultural eye (Irvine, 2003; Ladson-Billings, 1997). They also refuse to accept the deficit-focused master narrative that has been painted about the children they teach, instead focusing their high expectations on teaching students how to speak truth to power (Delpit, 1995; Irvine & Armento, 2001; Ladson-Billings, 1997). Table 3.1 illustrates some common practices of true culturally relevant teachers in contrast with the "watered-down" version of CRP that is too often passed off as the best way to work with urban students.

It is important to remember, however, that simply because a teacher is the same race or culture as her students does not mean she is automatically culturally relevant or a better teacher than someone of a different race who has been educated to use culturally relevant pedagogy. As Nieto (2003) explains:

> We cannot assume that, simply because of their marginal status in society, African American, Latino, Asian, and American Indian prospective and practicing teachers and others different from the majority can teach students from other backgrounds.... It does not necessarily give them an added advantage in confronting actual differences in the classroom and helping them address these differences effectively. (p. 231)

Table 3.1. Characteristics and Examples of Culturally Relevant Pedagogy

What Culturally Relevant Pedagogy IS	What Culturally Relevant Pedagogy IS NOT
Having high expectations for students of all backgrounds to achieve their "highest potential" *For example:* A teacher of English Language Learners (ELLs) believes that her first-generation immigrant students are capable of attending college if they desire.	Lowering expectations because of a belief that students of some backgrounds are not capable of high achievement *For example:* An ELL teacher creates lessons that help prepare her first-generation immigrant students for menial labor positions because she does not think them capable of attending college.
Using high-level teaching strategies and encouraging intellectual rigor *For example:* A language arts teacher uses similar teaching strategies, like a Socratic Seminar or literature circles, for her students in a gifted class and a general-level class.	Using low-level teaching strategies and teaching only basic skills *For example:* A language arts teacher uses project-based learning for her gifted class but uses only test-prep and rote memorization lessons with her general-level class.
Making explicit issues of power and privilege *For example:* A social studies teacher discusses residential segregation and gentrification with her history class and provides the historical context for such inequality.	Pretending that issues of power and privilege do not exist or are too "uncomfortable" to discuss *For example:* When discussing the history of their city, a social studies teacher does not cover the history of residential segregation or racism.
Incorporating students' cultures into the curriculum *For example:* A math teacher discusses the evolution of mathematics from Egypt and Babylon, instead of focusing only on Greek math systems.	Teaching curricular content that does not relate to and respect students' funds of knowledge *For example:* A math teacher uses a classic example of a standardized test question about the speed of a boat in a regatta. For urban students who have no cultural knowledge of sailing, this example is not relevant or responsive.

(continued)

Table 3.1. (continued)

What Culturally Relevant Pedagogy IS	What Culturally Relevant Pedagogy IS NOT
Providing opportunities for students to engage, cooperate, and collaborate with each other *For example:* A science teacher allows groups of students to develop their own experiment and demonstrate the process and results to the class.	Focusing on teacher-centered instruction that replicates the "banking model" of education (Freire, 2000) *For example:* During a science class, the teacher puts a cell diagram on the board and lectures about each part's function, then requires students to memorize the information for a multiple-choice exam.
Demonstrating that all cultures have value *For example:* An elementary teacher discusses the conflict between Israel and Palestine during a current events unit, presenting both sides of the story and challenging students to form their own opinions.	Valuing some cultural beliefs or practices above others *For example:* During a lesson on the Israeli–Palestinian conflict, an elementary teacher presents only the portion of the story with which she agrees.
Sustaining a commitment to multicultural education throughout the year and throughout curricula *For example:* A Spanish teacher discusses the political movements behind and social implications of Cinco de Mayo, instead of having only a food-centered celebration.	Celebrating only "heroes and holidays" or discussing only "food and festivals," thus encouraging a cursory approach to multicultural education *For example:* A Spanish teacher asks students to bring in tacos and piñatas to celebrate Cinco de Mayo without discussing any historical or cultural facts.

Source: Stairs, Donnell, and Dunn (2011)

Thus, we cannot assume *a priori* that teachers from another country will be more or less effective at culturally relevant pedagogy, and we must investigate how, if at all, international teachers serve as "cultural ambassadors" who are able to bring their culture into the classroom.

Based on the culturally relevant pedagogical practices outlined by Gay (2000), Irvine and Armento (2001), and Ladson-Billings (1997), I interviewed my participants and observed their teaching to discover if and how they implemented CRP in their classrooms. Though none of the teachers I interviewed had ever heard of the term or any of its variations before, there were some culturally relevant behaviors and beliefs that they demonstrated without defining them as such. They demonstrated some evidence of effective teaching. Other times, they espoused culturally relevant beliefs, but I did not see these practices manifest themselves in classroom practice. Finally, there were multiple components of CRP that were neither espoused nor implemented in my participants' classrooms. The areas where teachers were least effective were those in which they had to know their students' culture. Hence, the very limited preparation and support these teachers received was the most damaging to their success in relation to culturally embedded practices. Table 3.2 summarized which aspects of CRP were exhibited at which frequencies.

TRANSLATABLE SKILLS: COMMON CRP OF INTERNATIONAL TEACHERS

"Teaching begins in challenge and is never far from mystery," according to Ayers (2001a, p. 122). For international educators, teaching begins, continues, and ends in a challenge and is consistently a mystery. Despite these consistent challenges and mysteries, there were some practices that teachers were able to bring across the border, some habits that translated into effective teaching in any context. International teachers were able to translate: (1) their ability to teach skills and content and their passion for doing do; (2) a commitment to implementing a variety of pedagogical strategies, with varying levels of success; (3) a willingness to make accommodations for students with special needs; and (4) their desire to care for their students.

Teaching Content and Skills

Ask any American-born teacher how she first became interested in teaching and you are bound to get a story. Perhaps it was an inspirational teacher, a passion for a particular content area, or even a negative experience with schooling that made her want to be a "different kind" of educator. The same is true for foreign-born educators. Aleeza, Shrusty, Faria, and Samina were interested in and excited by the subject areas they taught. They openly discussed their own education and how

Table 3.2. Frequency of International Teachers' Culturally Relevant Pedagogy

Translatable Skills: Frequently Exhibited CRP	Trying to Speak the Same Language: Occasionally Exhibited CRP	Lost in Translation: Claimed, but Not Exhibited CRP	All Greek to Me: Not Evident CRP
Is passionate about content	Encourages a community of learners	Believes all students can succeed	Makes connections between students' levels of identities
Teaches necessary skills	Encourages collaborative learning	Nurtures fluid and equitable teacher–student relationship	Views knowledge critically
Makes accommodations for special learners	Structures ongoing and varied assessment	Makes meaningful home–school connections	Acknowledges students' culture and heritage as part of the curriculum
Uses a variety of strategies			Demonstrates a connectedness with all students
Demonstrates care for her students			Teaches students to know and praise their own and others' cultural heritage
			Incorporates multicultural resources into existing curricula
			Ensures that knowledge is shared, created, and recycled
			Sees herself as part of the community

they entered teaching, and each demonstrated a desire to work with children and a desire to continue learning in their content area. For example, Aleeza explained that she began tutoring other students at her home as an adolescent, especially in her favorite subject, science:

> You know in the beginning, when I was teaching when I was in the 11th [grade], that was just basically to earn something, and then when I got into it, it became my passion. . . . When somebody is asking me some question, I want to answer, so that drove me towards this. . . . I was always the science student, investigating things, finding out new things, especially that are connected to you as a human, so that is what makes me like science more.

Samina, too, showed commitment to her content when she expressed frustration over the scripted curriculum provided for her middle school language arts class in Glendale. She said she did not believe that the curriculum focused on anything other than preparation for the high-stakes state exams, and as a result, her students were not exposed to some important parts of English. She commented, "I would love to teach them tenses, which they are really bad at; how to use perfect tenses, how to easily identify and analyze perfect tenses and what are the easy methods to do them, [the] simple way to find it out. . . . For reading, I could teach them poetry. . . . I would love to teach them poetry."

Observations of Samina's classroom attested to her passion; despite classroom management difficulties, she often persisted in trying to teach small groups of students who would pay attention for longer than 5 minutes. She clearly knew the content and tried to find ways to make grammar exciting for her class. For example, with the help of the school's language arts coach, Samina attempted to teach her students about coordinating conjunctions. She took three sentences from age-appropriate books, wrote them on a small board at the front of the room, and then wrote "FANBOYS" above it. "FANBOYS stands for coordinating conjunctions," she said excitedly. "It is an easy way to remember all of them. It's easy, see? What words in these example sentences do you see that are conjunctions that could be part of the FANBOYS list?" (FANBOYS was a pneumonic device commonly used to teach the coordinating conjunctions: for, and, nor, but, or, yet, so). She invited students to call out answers, but it was difficult to hear their responses because the majority of the class was talking to each other and not paying attention. Samina tried to create new sentences using the conjunctions and students' names. When she used a student's name, the student would look up from his side conversation for a moment, but then went back to his distractions. The activity took almost an hour, and according to the language arts coach, it should only have been the 10-minute lesson opener. The coach told me, "It is like this every day. They take advantage of her because she is new and because of the cultural misunderstandings. In the other room, they are quiet as field mice." Despite these difficulties, Samina remained fervent about teaching language arts and grammar.

Similar classroom management problems occurred in Faria's high school mathematics classroom, but she, too, demonstrated passion about her content despite difficulties managing her students' behavior. For example, Faria discussed multiple ways to solve one algebraic equation and charged her students with using these multiple methods with increased frequency so that, as she had done when she was a student, "you will learn through practice." Shrusty's passion for her content—special education and life skills—was literally written all over her classroom. Colorful posters about student safety, numeracy, and public servants such as policemen, firemen, and teachers lined the boards and walls, and she frequently referenced these posters when talking to her students.

In addition to teaching content itself, teachers were able to teach related skills. Principal comments provided a good gauge of how teachers taught necessary skills, as the principals were able to reflect on how prepared students were for final exams and subsequent courses. For example, Mr. Norman and Mr. Clark, who worked with Aleeza and Faria respectively, expressed confidence that their teachers were teaching important content-area knowledge and skills because their students were succeeding on end-of-course exams. Both principals reported that they saw this in practice when observing Aleeza and Faria's classrooms. During one observation, I saw Aleeza's students reviewing for a test on types of energy. All of the questions in the discussion-based review were related to skills noted in Glendale's pacing guide and the state standards, including a focus on using formulas to understand energy conversion and heat transfer. Faria's students also followed the pacing guide and state standards closely. During an observation of her class, students reviewed the slope-intercept formula and learned several ways to solve linear equations, including graphing by hand, all skills that would be needed on the end-of-course exam in algebra.

Special Accommodations and Strategies

Shrusty's class provided the best example of accommodations for special learners, and not merely because she taught special education. In a class of eight students, Shrusty was responsible for learning about each students' abilities and challenges, teaching "academic skills" as mandated by the Glendale standards, and managing personal care for individual students, including feeding and changing. Though she was assisted by at least one or two paraprofessionals, there were times during my observations when her assistants were out of the room for various other responsibilities and Shrusty herself was responsible for the very individualized needs of all her students. According to a daily schedule posted on the wall, Shrusty led her students in: daily living skills, breakfast, adaptive physical education, academics according to state standards, lunch, a second academic session, vocational skills, individual activity, leisure activity, and living skills.

Within each of these periods, however, Shrusty made accommodations based on students' specific needs. For example, she knew that Julian liked to listen to Michael Jackson on his headphones while practicing his alphabet on a worksheet. She knew that Tatiana especially liked to color with the red crayon, but she could only do so if Shrusty guided her hand. She knew that Deaunte needed extra help recognizing and reading key written phrases like, "Where is the bathroom?" and "Nice to meet you," but that he was very confident about "My name is Deaunte" and "Thank you very much." Shrusty acknowledged that some people who did not understand special education would not view her as a "real" teacher, but the amount of individualized and differentiated instruction that she was able to provide on a daily basis was an incredible testimony to her teaching abilities and personal dedication.

Other participants also said they provided accommodations in their regular education classrooms, as they realized that students possessed multiple intelligences and diverse abilities. Samina emphasized that "all the students are not [the] same all the time. . . . Their mentalities are different. . . . You need art; you must be talented enough to deal with them." Aleeza's understanding of learning differences influenced how she structured instruction: "I really don't want to give them worksheets. . . . I want them to talk, come out with the examples so that they understand what is the concept, and sometimes kids are good when they listen. . . . [Other times] some students can learn when they see it, when they visualize it, basically differentiated instruction." Samina and Faria also demonstrated a concern for special learners by paying attention to those students who benefited from individualized instruction. Though they were not able to do this as frequently as they wished, they made consistent efforts to provide for their students' needs.

During interviews and observations, I witnessed and heard about a variety of pedagogical strategies that each teacher implemented in her classroom. Shrusty frequently used multimedia, including computer games, music, movies, and technological aids, to teach students basic life skills. For example, during a classroom observation, one student played a computer game on the alphabet while another practiced counting with pegs and blocks. Samina and Faria used teacher-centered and student-centered methodologies, such as mini-lectures, group work, or individual reading and/or writing time. Faria described the projects she conducted with her students each semester, including one on mathematicians that required them to work with a partner, present to the class, use technology and library resources to conduct outside research, and evaluate their classmates. Aleeza used similar strategies and also added individual and group lab work in her physical science and chemistry classes.

Teacher Care

Though not always included in lists of culturally relevant pedagogical practices, researchers have found caring to be important for working with all students, especially African American students (Noddings, 2005a; Roberts, 2010; Siddle Walker & Snarey, 2004). Teachers in this study saw caring about students to be as important as their content knowledge and classroom management. According to Noddings (2005a), "To care means to respond to needs, and needs do not stop (or start) at the schoolroom door" (p. xxii). Aleeza expressed a similar sentiment when describing the ways she cared for her students:

> I think some of the kids have some issues at home or some personal issues because of which they cannot concentrate. When I see that it is affecting their grade, . . . I go to them personally and [they] talk to me about what is going on. If they don't want to disclose anything, keep that confidential and let me know what I can do to help them get through the subject. . . . I think the biggest thing we need is to be patient. You cannot give up with the kids. . . . I just let them know that I will be ready for whatever they need.

Students in Aleeza's class saw evidence of care in her classroom behavior. "She pushes us," said one female student. "She wants us to do better because she knows we can." A male student concurred, "Yeah, she does care about us. She may not always get it 'cause she ain't from here, but she tries to get it, ya know, and she cares about us."

In most circumstances, I saw teachers connecting to and caring about students individually. For example, Aleeza spoke quietly to a student who had joined her class 3 days earlier. She reminded him that he needed a notebook for her class, inquired about his weekend and previous courses, and joked with him a bit. It was clear that the student and teacher were comfortable with each other, even though he was a relatively new addition to Aleeza's roster, and that she was trying to establish a rapport with him. Samina shared a story with two female students about the henna on her hands, which they thought was a tattoo. She explained that it was an ink design that did not hurt, and they eagerly asked her to draw one on their hands on the last day of school.

Noddings (2005b) wrote, "the caring relation is essential as a starting point and a continuous framework of support, but it is not enough by itself to ensure competent teaching" (p. 1). Though caring was not enough to make them entirely effective educators of students in their new settings, participants frequently demonstrated some of the ways they attempted to care for their students, through use of skills preparation, accommodations, and varied strategies.

"TRYING TO SPEAK THE SAME LANGUAGE": OCCASIONAL CRP OF INTERNATIONAL TEACHERS

There were several components of CRP found in other studies that I observed only occasionally with my four teachers, or that only one or two teachers demonstrated throughout the course of my research. As opposed to "translatable skills," these were examples of teachers metaphorically trying to speak the same language. Their practices—including encouraging collaborative learning and a community of learners and using varied types of assessments—were attempted but not always implemented successfully or systematically.

Collaboration and Community

Each of the teachers stated that she believed in and encouraged students to work collaboratively. What this collaboration looked like in practice varied among classrooms. Samina stated,

> I always believe in small groups, collaborated groups. . . . Sometimes what happens is teachers try to say something and they [students] cannot understand. They can understand the same thing when they are talking to each other. They can make it more simple . . . and they can resolve if they have any problems.

In her class, during one observation, students were allowed to work together to complete a grammar handout with a "scramble" of transition words in different shapes and fonts. They were supposed to be classifying them based on the word's function, which Samina had labeled as: "sequence, time, contrast, adverb, and addition." After Samina distributed the handouts and read the directions aloud to the students, the collaborative groups descended into chaos. "You should be helping each other," she yelled over the din. "You can work together and help your partner on this, too!" The following is an excerpt from my field notes, written during this episode:

> The young girl (who pays attention with her twin sister) has her hand raised in the front row; she appears to need help on one of the questions and is eager to find an answer. But Samina can't pay attention to her because she is "putting out fires." Two boys go back and forth yelling, "Shut up. Shut up! SHUT UP! Shut Uuuuup!" She tries to intervene by yelling their names. At this point, only 2 boys (out of 10) are seated. Others are in and out of the open door. The chaos continues. One boy is kicked out after Samina threatens to call his mom. He says he'd rather be in detention than in the classroom. Three girls "sneak" out of the classroom without asking permission. One boy runs around the classroom, and she says, "This is a classroom; this is not a zoo." In order for the collaborative groups (the three that are actually working) to talk to each other now, they have to talk even louder. I am not sure how she doesn't have a headache. There is a lot of pushing, shoving, grabbing between the boys. They are very physical with each other. The boy on crutches holds it up like a gun and points it at the

teacher, pretending it is an AK-47. He does it again so more boys will notice; they laugh. One says, "I wish I was in a gang so I could get a good gun." Does she notice? I don't think so because she is now helping the twin girls' collaborative group. Amazingly, as if it knew we were waiting for it, the bell rings and the students stream out. It is eerily quiet.

This anecdote was typical of the daily interactions in Samina's classroom. Though she tried to implement the collaborative group aspect of CRP, the group's function was lost in the chaos of the lessons I observed.

Collaboration in Faria's class served both a pedagogical and logistical purpose. For instance, as students worked collaboratively in groups of two or three on a worksheet on algebraic equations, Faria and her co-teacher circulated amongst the groups to provide additional support. Some groups required more assistance than others, and in our post-observation discussion, Faria revealed that collaborative activities like that one I had just witnessed allowed her to give individual attention to students who needed it most, because "I cannot get to them all at once, so pairs help because they can help each other if I am not able to get to them fast." Collaboration was evident, too, in Aleeza and Shrusty's classrooms; students worked together to complete assigned tasks. In Aleeza's science classroom, this meant completing a project, study guide, lab assignment, or homework. In Shrusty's special education classroom, this meant students helped each other prepare to eat lunch, get ready to board the bus at the end of the day, or color a worksheet.

In these instances, collaboration was viewed as an activity, or a specific, time-bound strategy. Though it may have been used on multiple days and in various ways, it was not necessarily a foundational commitment that extended beyond single activities into the fabric of the classroom environment. That is, though there were collaborative *activities*, there was not a *culture* of collaboration. This was partially affected by the way teachers did or did not structure their classrooms as communities of learners.

All of the teachers stated that they believed establishing a community focused on learning in their classroom was important. However, their success in implementing this goal varied widely. For instance, it could have been a particular challenge to initially establish a community in Shrusty's classroom. With only eight students, most of whom were nonverbal and all of whom had very different abilities and disabilities, there seemed to be little that all the students had in common or that they could do together. Yet Shrusty found ways for individual students to aid others in the learning process, as when one student assisted another with counting pegs and moving the pegs between boxes, or when one student chose the appropriate crayons for another student to use when coloring a picture.

Aleeza also worked to create a community of learners through her use of science labs. During two observations of Aleeza's classroom, I saw students working together to complete a task. First, they were engaged in a lab on types of waves using springs. In small teams, students examined the coils of springs when compact and when stretched out in order to make transverse and longitudinal waves; some springs were so long that students had to take them into the hallway for closer examination. In another observation, I saw the students completing a summative assessment on chemical bonding. Students were each creating their own poster that illustrated the chemical reaction of two assigned elements, including the elements' chemical formula and structure. Students were sharing materials, and more important, were sharing ideas for improving each other's posters or reminding each other of what they had learned in class. In both activities, there were students who stayed in a group with their friends, but there were others who "branched out" and worked with peers as part of the community. They were able to answer many questions within or among groups so that Aleeza was able to play a minimal supervisory role.

Samina, on the other hand, found it difficult to create a community of learners in her language arts classroom, perhaps because, as she explained, she believed that many of her students did not want to learn, and their disruptions negatively impacted the other students. She stated,

> All of them need attention; individual attention [is] impossible for me. What I think is, because of the attention we are giving to the disruptive kids, the deserving kids are not getting the attention. . . . I feel really sorry for the kids who deserve real love and care, and they are not getting it because of the [other] kids. Whatever I can do, I always try to make them understand it. They are slowly becoming bad because of the bad kids; oh, he's doing it, why can't I do it? The bad kids are motivating them.

Whether it was the students' actions that caused Samina to feel this way, or Samina's feelings that further incited students to act out, it was nearly impossible to create a learning community with such feelings of disappointment from teacher and students alike. Imagine the sense of frustration Samina must have felt to claim that some students were deserving of "real love and care" while others were not.

Assessment Variation

The teachers occasionally used a variety of assessments. I saw evidence of multiple-choice tests, essay tests, performance assessments like projects and labs, and ongoing assessments like class notebooks. Aleeza required her students to maintain a class notebook in which they kept class notes, lab reports, diagrams and other pictures, questions and answers from textbook activities, and review materials. She collected this notebook every 2 weeks to check for completion, to ensure that students were keeping up with the subject. The notebook, then, became preparation for a final assessment and an assessment in and of itself:

I am very particular about the notebook because especially when we are reviewing, they have something in hand and I really don't want them to give study-guide-like notes. I don't believe that students read those big study guides that we give. I am more like, you know, draw the picture for this concept so at least when they are reviewing, they can at least look at the picture and they can figure out, okay this is what we did in class. So that is why I keep up with that notebook.

One example of a variation on traditional math curriculum occurred in Faria's math class. She assigned her students a project on cell phones where they had to collect data from different companies and compare using algebraic equations. Additionally, she explained:

We did a project [where] they have to select a mathematician of their choice. I gave them a list of mathematicians, and they did that project . . . in pairs. And they have to do a presentation and they have to get a picture, they have to make a timeline and all kind of stuff. They had to get the history of that mathematician and the mathematical contributions. . . . That was really wonderful, I mean like, they were really enthusiastic. . . . It was great; I mean, it was more than what I expected.

Though teachers did include periodic projects and labs, the majority of assessments in Faria, Aleeza, and Samina's classrooms were traditional pencil-and-paper assignments. I did not see evidence of any portfolio or other alternative assessments. The international teachers, like many U.S.-born teachers, may have felt restricted by the curriculum and/or may not have been shown how to diversify assessments while still following the state standards and district's curriculum pacing guides.

"LOST IN TRANSLATION":
STATED BUT NOT EVIDENT CRP OF INTERNATIONAL TEACHERS

There were several culturally relevant pedagogical practices that teachers espoused but that I did not see evident in practice during my classroom observations. These practices were part of teachers' philosophies but not their everyday practice; somehow, then, they were lost in translation. Aspects of CRP that were present in word but not in deed were their statements that all students could succeed, that they tried to build equitable teacher–student relationships, and that they connected students' interests to school lessons.

Attitudes about Student Success

A recurring debate in education is whether all students can learn. One would think this would be self-evident by now, as research has proven that students of all races, backgrounds, and genders can and want to learn, yet racist and classist arguments continue to contend that some groups (read: White, upper-middle-class) are better able to learn than others. Students may not always want to learn exactly how teachers want to teach, but it is abundantly clear that any student has the ability to acquire new skills, habits, and knowledge. Yet, as in the education community, the international teachers were divided on this issue. Shrusty and Faria stated that they believed all students, regardless of previous background or ability, could succeed in some way in a classroom setting. Shrusty was especially adamant about this belief because she said that outsiders did not always see her special education students as successful or capable of learning; being with them on a daily basis, however, showed her the little ways that her students learned and improved. Observations of her classroom showed that she rejoiced, and encouraged her students to rejoice, in small victories. What other teachers may not see as student success, such as when I observed a student stay on task counting pegs for 3 minutes, Shrusty praised as an improvement.

Samina held a different opinion. When I asked if she believed all students could learn and succeed, she replied, "Yes, but if they want to. It is a mutual thing. Someone should be ready to teach and someone should be ready to learn." Aleeza argued, "No, because their basics are not good, one. Second is because they are not interested to learn." In these two statements, the teachers were collapsing their students' *ability* to learn and their students' *desire* to learn. Samina and Aleeza said they thought the reason students were not successful was because students didn't care or were not "interested to learn." This belief was contrasted with Ladson-Billings's finding that culturally relevant teachers were those who believed all students wanted to and could learn.

Equitable Relationships

Though the four teachers all verbally agreed that it was necessary for teacher–student relationships to be fluid, it appeared difficult for them to practice this belief because of their previous experiences with predominantly teacher-centered instruction. Aleeza commented, "For me, education is learning all the time, while you are teaching, while you are studying yourself. And be ready to learn from your students, too. . . . [The] teacher is ever learning." When asked what they could learn from students, the teachers said their students sometimes gave examples or answers that they had not previously imagined. However, giving answers to specific problems is still quite different from teachers who strive to learn new skills, cultural histories, ways of thinking and being, and interpersonal knowledge through a fluid, Freirian teacher–student relationship.

Much classroom interaction was still teacher-focused and strictly didactic, such as reminding students of classroom rules when they were not paying attention, or leading recitations where students raised their hands to answer teacher questions one at a time and the teacher then told them if they were correct or incorrect. It was unclear, though, how much of the teacher-centered classroom was the *choosing* of my participants and how much was a *response* to school policies that mandated strict "control" and "discipline." As I noted in Chapter 2, several principals said that teachers needed to be stringent in their classroom management in order for students to learn. For example, Mr. Sutherland encouraged his teachers to "be very stern; you have to be very, very stern and you have to say what you mean and do what you say because if you don't do what you say you are going to do, then they will take that as a weakness." Thus, the didactic, discipline- and teacher-focused classroom environment that I observed may have reflected the teachers' interpretations of administrative expectations.

Meaningful Home–School Connections

Teachers expressed strong desires to connect academic learning with students' lives outside school. One example of a potentially successful connection between home and school life was an essay assignment in Samina's English class. Samina wanted her students to be motivated writers, so she allowed them to write persuasive essays on topics of their choice, which she gleaned from a class discussion and then posted on a large paper on the classroom wall. The results of their discussion, which began with the question, "What are some issues facing our community?", included a variety of problems, from teen pregnancy and gangs to gas prices and "indiscipline in school." She said the lesson went "fine," and when asked what she learned about students' culture or community as a result, she remembered, "Most of the girls took teen pregnancy [for their paper topic]. It was a shock for me. That was a shock. At the age of 12 they get pregnant and they get babies; when they are a baby and they have a baby."

However, this was an isolated lesson in Samina's curriculum. She and other teachers did not always make *meaningful* connections between home and school, as multicultural education scholars recommend (Gay, 2000; Irvine & Armento, 2001; Ladson-Billings, 1997). Two examples of the ways in which teachers explained connecting to students' lives illustrate how their interpretation of a home–school connection diverged from a more nuanced, sociopolitical connection to students' lived realties. First, as mentioned in the previous section, Faria planned a project on cell phones to make math seem applicable to real life. She stated,

That is a motivation for my students, because when they do not see anything related to their real life, they do not feel motivated. I mean some of them they just do it because they have to do it . . . but most of them they want [a] connection between the subject and their real life and so I need to think about the real-life situations whenever I am teaching a particular lesson.

Second, Aleeza concurred that real-life examples were necessary to help students understand a concept and keep them interested in the subject matter, and she spoke at length about how this belief influenced her teaching practice:

I try to give examples everybody can relate to. Today, like when I used the roller coaster [as an example for a chemistry problem]. I was sure that everybody had at least seen a roller coaster. . . . I use lot of Internet [examples] to get students, like you know, what is interesting for them to understand and they really want to know. They want to relate, and science is more like, I want them to relate to it, to understand, okay this is what is going on with us, we know this already. . . . I want to motivate the students towards learning to understand in a better way rather than just retaining the information like just to, you know, memorize the thing. I don't want them to memorize. I want them to learn the concept, understand the concept, so that is why I try my best to give real-life examples to my teaching.

These two assignments were based on real-life examples to appeal to student interest, but did not connect to students' home cultures in a meaningful way. That is, with these isolated examples, there was no attempt to bring students' values, histories, or voices into the classroom in a more extensive and comprehensive way, as was found by earlier researchers who studied CRP in African American schools.

Teachers may have felt limited by the curriculum and their own knowledge of African American communities, and because they were given no preparation or professional development to show them how to weave students' cultures into existing curricula, they were left with seeing it as an "add-on" and not a central part of the class. For example, I observed a typical 6th-grade lesson in accordance with America's Choice. Samina's board exemplified the rigid structure of a prescribed lesson on transition words, including the relevant state standard, a 10-minute opening period, 30-minute work period, and 10-minute closing-period. Students were charged with brainstorming transition words as a class and then sorting the words by purpose into a chart in their notebooks. To find a way to incorporate students' home cultures into this basic lesson on transitions would have taken time and background knowledge on both students' cultures and culturally relevant pedagogy, none of which were afforded to Samina.

"IT'S ALL GREEK TO ME":
MISSING CRP IN INTERNATIONAL TEACHERS' CLASSROOMS

For international teachers, behaviors requiring cultural knowledge were the least evident in practice. These behaviors were some of the most complex, yet also, according to earlier studies conducted in African American schools, the most important for maintaining a culturally relevant classroom. As the teachers rarely, if ever, demonstrated these behaviors, it is somewhat difficult to discuss their absence because it was unclear whether: (1) teachers exhibited these behaviors on days I did not visit, but did not think to mention them in interviews; (2) they exhibited these behaviors in their home countries; (3) they would and could have demonstrated the behaviors had they been properly prepared and supported; or (4) they thought they were implementing the behaviors, but they were not evident to me. These culturally relevant pedagogical practices included making connections between students' levels of identities; viewing knowledge critically; incorporating multicultural information, resources, and materials into routinely taught skills and subjects; ensuring that knowledge is continuously re-created, recycled, and shared by teachers and students; and seeing herself as part of the community and encouraging her students to do the same.

In addition, several aspects of CRP were contradicted by the teachers' interviews or observations and are discussed here. This discussion of the ways my participants are not culturally relevant is not meant to indicate that they are "bad" teachers or that they did not care about their students overall, nor is it meant to indicate that they could not demonstrate these behaviors if given the proper preparation and professional development. Rather, I argue that knowing where the gaps exist should compel administrators, recruiters, teacher educators, researchers, and policymakers to find and address the specific pedagogical needs of international teachers in urban schools. These areas for improvement can, as with U.S.-born teachers, be alleviated with the right amount of attention and commitment and transformed into spaces of possibility.

Meaningful Cultural Connections and Curriculum

I did not see evidence that my participants taught students to know and praise their own or others' cultural heritage. Even if a teacher is not of the same culture as her students, it is possible for her to nurture in them a desire to know more about and celebrate their culture and that of others (Derman-Sparks & Ramsey, 2006). Indian teachers were coming from a society where they said heritage was an important feature of life, yet as discussed earlier, cultural heritage could also create division in classrooms and society. But once in the United States, the teachers first had to learn about the students' cultures before they would be able to teach the students about these cultures. Aleeza said that she sometimes attempted to learn about her students' lives by asking them questions like, "How do you celebrate things here? You live together, who cooks at home? And how is their relationship with their parents? Can their parents make decisions for them?" Yet, none of the teachers could articulate specific things they had learned about African American culture.

Faria seemed to believe that learning about her African American students' culture was not important or necessary because "there was not really much difference" between their culture and her own. She continued, "We do not need to know about their personal life," because their life in the classroom was more important than their life outside the classroom. Samina, too, apparently did not learn much about her students' backgrounds and cultures, and when asked if she had learned any "positive things" about their culture, she replied:

> Unfortunately, I should say that the impact or the image of these kids was no good in my mind, because you know, how they behave and all that. So all negative things came to my mind whenever I thought of them. . . . But all these kids are not like this by birth. . . . Situations only can be behind this. They are not responsible for what they are now. They were not like that. God did not send them down to the earth with all these bad qualities. So as a teacher, it is my responsibility to do as far as possible, whatever is possible for them.

In this sentiment, Samina collapsed students' behavior, culture, and upbringing in a way that prevented her from seeing the positive aspects of students' cultures because she was unable to get past what she saw as inappropriate classroom behavior. Though she wanted to do "whatever is possible for them," her own situation was so tenuous that she was unable to give her students what they needed, which may have been culturally relevant instruction that praised their inherent funds of knowledge (Moll, Amanti, Neff, & Gonzalez, 1992).

Next, there was no evidence that teachers in this study acknowledged students' culture and heritage as part of the curriculum or that they discussed culture in light of historical lenses of dominance and oppression. I did not observe any discussions of race, power, privilege, or oppression, nor discussions of the different cultures that informed their subject areas. Admittedly, these final culturally relevant practices are difficult for many American-born teachers of all backgrounds to implement in the classroom because of increasingly scripted curricula and test-prep pedagogy. Interestingly, Faria noted that her project on mathematicians led many students to choose to study Indian mathematicians to "impress her" and "get a good grade," but she did not mention any students who chose African American mathematicians.

One potential reason for a lack of students' heritage in the curriculum was because the Indian teachers had been educated in a country where, according to the teachers, cultural difference was "not an issue" in the ways it can be in U.S.

classrooms. More likely, however, was that it was not *made* an issue. In the teachers' Indian classrooms, students had different linguistic and socioeconomic backgrounds, but these differences were not commonly made part of the standard curriculum. Teachers were taught that, to be fair, one must treat all students the same, which is a different notion of "fairness" from what is promoted by critical education scholars in the United States today. If the teachers' behaviors and comments were evaluated from a strictly U.S. standpoint, they would be seen as "colorblind," where someone claims that they do not "see" race. Because the teachers did not "see" race, or see it as important, it was rarely acknowledged in classroom discussions or curricula. For example, Aleeza argued, "You know actually, in India, we don't have this culture division you know. . . . Whatever the race is, when I am in class, I am [a] teacher to everybody." She elaborated that, although she had taken time to learn about her students' cultures because she had "no idea" about their history or culture, race was not significant for how she interacted with her students or how she expected them to perform:

> *Aleeza:* All I did was, I made up my mind, whoever they are, whatever they are, they are students, they are young kids and I have to know how to handle them.
> *Alyssa:* Have you learned anything about their history since you have been here?
> *Aleeza:* Yes, a lot of things, like what did they went through, and then how did they come up, and how did they fight for their rights. . . . You know ups and downs that they had to go to have their rights. So I have learned a lot about those things.

Aleeza was unable to elaborate, during this particular interview or later interviews, what exactly she meant by "what they went through" or what exactly she had learned about struggles for their rights. We later discussed:

> *Alyssa:* You were saying that you have learned a lot since you have been here about African American history. How do you think that affects the way that you interact with African American students?
> *Aleeza:* I do not think that there is any difference that I interact with them, different because of that. No, because some of them do have this misconception that we cannot do anything because we are Black, or you know, they give me answers like that. When I give them a low grade, they say "You are doing that to us because we are Black?" I was like, "Why do you think that you will not be able to do something because you are Black? You have a Black president." And they are like "Oh, [Ms. Aleeza], you catch us like that." . . . I did not know how to answer that

for the first time when I heard that. Then, later on, I understood they are just talking, you know how youngsters talk. They are just talking because they want to say something.

Samina indicated that she had heard similar statements from her students about teachers treating them unfairly because they were Black. Like Aleeza, Samina found these comments unsettling and confusing because she did not see evidence of racism in teacher–student interactions. Samina explained:

They have some kind of fear, or they have some kind of insecurity, something is going on in their hearts. They call names to each other also. Like "nigger" and all that. I do not know why they want to discriminate themselves. Sometimes they call other teachers and other people racist. Why do they call them [that]? . . . Maybe they are brought up, I do not know, I am not aware of it. But they cannot say that to me, but say that to me "You're doing that to me because I am a Black?" What? I don't have anything to do with that. You're a human being, I am a human being. That is more important for me other than skin color. . . . Something is going on wrong in their minds about their race.

As a researcher (and as a White researcher at that), what does one do with comments like Samina's above? One thing I find interesting about her comment is that she shows both ignorance of racial dynamics and also a sort of profound sadness about them. Beyond that, there are so many layers to her understanding of Black children, many of which are informed by her own cultural context. Yet, regardless of her previous context, attitudes like this have dangerous implications for her as an educator, especially of Black students. Nothing I overlay onto Samina's statements will be nearly as significant as her statement itself, especially the words she chose, which she used without a clear understanding of why the terms and ideas were so problematic and wrought with historical anguish. To be sure, there are American-born teachers of all races who may express similar sentiments as this one, but this does not mean that I can ignore Samina's statement, either. Was it her Indian background that compelled her beliefs? Was it more influenced by her religion, which has a tradition of being racially inclusive? I cannot attribute motivations to her, but if either or both are the case, then we have to be especially vigilant about preparing international teachers who come from cultures where they do not see race as important if we are going to trust them with students in a U.S. culture where race is prominent. Research has continuously shown that a refusal to acknowledge racism as a persistent and insidious facet of society (in any national context) contributes to its far-reaching and dangerous perpetuation. Thus, as a researcher, despite the many conflicting feelings I had about including her statement, including the racial slur, I feel it is important to let her voice be heard in all its staggering complexity.

Connections to Students and the Wider Community

There was also little evidence that teachers demonstrated a connectedness with all students. This behavior was closely related to the previous one; if teachers were unable to value and praise students' cultures, it was also difficult for them to truly connect to all students. However, recruitment agency materials touted this connection as one of the positive results of international teacher recruitment. Because international teachers were from another culture, they were presumed to work well with—and thus be able to inherently connect with—students from non-White cultures in the United States. Ms. Muller of Glendale agreed: "They probably work better in those schools [with majority-Black populations] than those environments that are White. They seem to have less adjustment problems, not speaking of performance issues." (It was unclear how she knew this, however, since none of the schools in which they were placed were majority-White.) Ms. Jefferson said the teachers were "average" when working with diverse populations.

The principals I interviewed also had varied, but strong opinions on if and how teachers connected with students of all backgrounds. Mr. Clark agreed that they worked well with diverse students because "they do not get rattled, even when kids were being disrespectful with them, they maintain a level of professionalism. . . . It does not matter, nationality, race, color, creed, or religion. If they can teach, I want them." Mr. Norman said, "They work well with any student. Their discipline is just different." In contrast, Mr. Scott said, "I do not think they come with prejudice," but he did not believe they "worked well with" his student population. "Work well with to me would mean I could handle them, discipline-wise, I understand them," he elaborated, "and I do not think they understand our kids." Similarly, Mr. Sutherland said, "Well, I just do not think that they understand the culture here. . . . I mean even when we had conversations, [Samina] said 'I do not understand that culture.'" The variety of principal comments showed not only the various ways in which foreign teachers were or were not able to connect to their students, but also the difficulty of defining what exactly "connectedness" meant. In the principals' responses, it was evident that they defined a teacher–student connection in ways that ranged from control and professionalism to understanding.

The majority of students in Samina, Aleeza, and Faria's classes, however, did not exhibit a strong connection with their teachers. Many conversed with peers when the teachers were talking. They did not seem bothered by or willing to change their behavior when their teachers asked them to focus. There was not a lot of laughter or good humor between teacher and students. Unsolicited, students approached me and offered their opinions about their teachers, indicating a lack of connection between teacher and student perspectives. Some students' comments were:

- *Middle school student:* Our class is, like, really, really crazy all the time, 'cause she is Indian, ya know, so she is like, really confused by us a lot of the time. We do things and say things that she is like, what are you doing, what are you saying? And it's funny 'cause it's normal for us, but she can't connect to it.
- *High school student:* She doesn't understand us at all, not just like what we say, but like what we do. I think she tries to sometimes, but it's like, it's way different and she just doesn't get it.
- *High school student:* There's a whole bunch of Indian teachers here, did you know that? Are you writing about them, too? 'Cause that would be tight for someone to tell [the principal] about what they are like. You know, they like want to be good teachers and I think they are nice people. But they are like way too nice. They don't relate to us so much.
- *High school student:* I think it's like, there's American kids that she thought she was going to come and teach, and then there's Black kids. And maybe she didn't know she was gonna come to teach a bunch of Black kids 'cause she still seems surprised by it, by us every day. [laughing] I get it, though; I'd be surprised too by some of the shit that comes out of our mouths. Oops, I mean, like, she's a young teacher, and usually our younger teachers can relate to us better 'cause they remember like what it was like to be teenagers. But she must have been a different kind of teenager. It must have been a different world. She has no idea what we're about.

A cultural disconnection, or a lack of cultural synchronization (Irvine, 1990, 2003), is explicit and challenging in the students' responses. Perhaps the sense of "foreignness"—felt by students as they presumed how their teachers felt about them—is no more evident than in this conversation I had with two male high school students.

Student 1: Do you think we're like aliens or something?
Alyssa: Um, no, why would I think you are like aliens?
Student 1: [Laughing.] Sometimes I think our teacher thinks we're aliens.
Alyssa: Why?
Student 1: It's like we're both from different planets. Like nothing is the same as where she is from, so she can't connect to any of us.
Student 2: [Laughing.] Dude, we're worse than aliens. We're Black.

Ironically then, both the teachers and the students feel "foreign." The comments are not included here to serve as evidence that the teachers were ineffective, but merely to raise the questions "What would make a student say something like that?" and "Could anything have been done to help teachers and students better connect to each other?" Further, I would argue that it is difficult to view the teachers as cultural brokers, as the agencies and districts claim them to be, if they have no understanding of the culture in which they are placed.

BUILDING FOUNDATION-LESS BRIDGES

I began this chapter by asserting that international teachers and their recruitment process is an attempt to build cultural bridges. Yet the stories of international teachers, observations of their classrooms, and commentary from their students show that any cultural bridges that are being built are built without a foundation. They are tenuous, like when teachers say they want equity in the classroom and care deeply about their students' success but find it difficult to implement these beliefs in their U.S. contexts. In the current climate of accountability regimes and attacks on teachers and the profession, these cultural bridges need to be stronger than ever to withstand the strong winds of high-stakes testing and increased pressure on teachers. However, international teachers struggled to build these cultural bridges.

Their different backgrounds, both personally and professionally, made it difficult for them to translate their stated beliefs into practice in another cultural context from the one in which they were socialized. Their home culture encouraged teachers to see everyone as the same. Though this same attitude may be encouraged in popular culture in the United States, in education today, to deny a student's culture as different or unique is to ignore a central part of his or her identity. Agencies that encourage teachers to believe that "students are students everywhere," as the owner of IRI plainly stated, further advance a color-blind approach to multicultural education, and without the proper preparation and support, international teachers are left to maneuver their way through a new country's education system where "race matters." Through little to no fault of their own, they found it difficult to practice culturally relevant pedagogy because their previous education in India had prepared them for an entirely different cultural context than the one in which they were now teaching. Other features of culture may have mattered more in India, like religion or socioeconomic status, though the teachers did not acknowledge this themselves, but race was not one of those salient features. Additionally, their agencies and communities in the United States did not provide appropriate, contextualized, and continuous education for them. Thus, the spectacle of constructing bridges was, in reality, the building of barriers.

FOUR

Barriers to Success

Stymied Goals for International Teacher Recruitment

What people say, what people do, and what people say they
do are entirely different things.

—Margaret Mead

Shrusty and I spent a lot of time laughing together. She liked to talk about her experiences and had the philosophy that it was better to laugh than cry about her problems. During one interview, Shrusty became very serious when I asked her if she achieved all of her goals for her U.S. experience. Taking a deep breath and fidgeting with her school ID badge, she began thoughtfully,

> Did I meet my goals? That is hard to say. Three years is such a short time, you know? There is still so much left to do. . . . I have changed as a person. I wasn't this patient before; this profession taught me to be patient and be organized. I see I'm more mature because of traveling, in money matters, relations with coworkers, and with other people around. So yes, my achievement goals I met because I wanted something different and I did it. But there is a lot more to do, you know? There is a lot more I have to do to for my daughter to get into a good American college.

As in Shrusty's case, there are obstructions in the way for other teachers, as well as for schools and districts. The goals of international teacher recruitment are not met because of systemic barriers embedded in educational policies and school organization. This chapter uses data from classroom observations and interviews with teachers, principals, and officials to analyze how—if at all—the goals of the supposed beneficiaries of recruitment—teachers, students, schools, and districts—are achieved.

There are a multitude of stated purposes and goals for international teacher recruitment. First, as mentioned in Chapter 1, international teachers come with personal goals, including the desire to experience the "American Dream," earn more money for their families, expand their children's educational opportunities, and improve their teaching backgrounds. Second, recruitment agency officials and district administrators claim they wanted to increase urban students' exposure to world cultures and improve students' global competitiveness. Third, school administrators hope to hire high-quality educators for urban schools. Finally, district leaders hope international recruitment solves the problem of filling positions in urban areas. The case in Glendale illuminates the many barriers that kept all stakeholders from achieving their goals.

MEETING TEACHERS' GOALS

International teachers expressed mostly positive feelings about their experience working in U.S. urban schools. Despite the challenges explained in the previous chapters, most showed high levels of personal satisfaction when discussing their schools, students, and colleagues. How was this possible, I wondered repeatedly, as they told me that "overall, I'm pretty happy"? In a similar situation, I assumed I would have been remarkably dissatisfied. Shrusty, Samina, Faria, and Aleeza's goals were related to the "pull factors" commonly associated with international migration (American Federation of Teachers, 2009) and those revealed in popular press articles. Though they did not identify it as a primary goal upon first entering the recruitment program, all the teachers indicated that much of their satisfaction came after developing close relationships with individual students or seeing students succeed. Not all of their goals were realized, however, in part because of programmatic constraints and lack of institutional support. The differences in their feelings came when discussing the agency's and administrators' actions and inactions; that was where there high levels of satisfaction took a sharp nosedive.

In Search of the "American Dream"

According to Neufeld (2005), a Filipino teacher wanted to discover what made the United States alluring to many international citizens because she said she "wouldn't have peace" until she discovered what made "everybody want to go there" (p. 3). My participants expressed a similar desire to "live the opportunity of America," "find the American Dream," and "see if the United States was really so special."

As Shrusty explained while reflecting on her goals, part of her American Dream was to make it possible for her daughter to attend a "good American college," a hope she mentioned during several interviews. "Then she could really have the dream," Shrusty explained, noting that if her daughter had a college education from a U.S. university, she could go anywhere and do anything and "be too [very] successful." Shrusty did not feel that 3 years gave her family enough time to achieve the dream, but did think her daughter had received a quality education while she was here. "Education is fun for her here," she said about her daughter. "She will miss it."

The difficulty with such high expectations was that they were often not real-ized. Though she felt successful and satisfied herself, Shrusty had seen several col-leagues, including her own sister, return to India before their 3-year contract was completed. She attributed this to a lack of support from agency and school offi-cials, which will be discussed in more detail in the subsequent chapter. She also explained that leaving before their "time was up" kept them from achieving their potential American Dream. Overall, Shrusty succinctly and powerfully encapsu-lated international teachers' experiences: "So many international teachers like us come to America, the land of opportunity, with these big American dreams, and then our dreams are shattered by reality." The American Dream and the lived reali-ties of these migrant educators had little in common.

Pedagogical Knowledge

In contrast to the traditional lecture-style instruction to which the Indian teachers had been exposed, they hoped their brief tenures in the United States would show them new pedagogy and technology. Aleeza, Samina, and Shrusty agreed that they learned new ways of teaching, particularly using more hands-on activities and group discussion than they had in the past. Even more, though, they learned classroom management techniques that they had never had to use in India and, if they returned to similar Indian classrooms after they left the United States, would presumably not have to use again. When I asked if and how they would use these new classroom management techniques, they acknowledged that, "well, we prob-ably will not." Faria, however, did not believe that her pedagogical goals were met while teaching high school mathematics:

> I will say 3 years was a very short period to meet the goals that I have. . . .
> The first year, you are just learning things, and second year is okay with you,
> I mean like you [are] going. But the last year, you know that you are going
> back. So I would say if it would have been another 2 years or so, I mean
> like there are a lot things that I wanted to learn and I could not. I did not
> get a lot more exposure, especially me I would say, I did not get a lot more
> exposure to things that I expected. I had expected some more exposure
> to technology in here. I wanted to teach the gifted students before I leave,
> which I could not do. . . . Now that I got certified to teach the gifted students,
> I am leaving.

In this example, Faria referred to two factors that impeded achievement of her goals. She listed exposure to technology as one of her primary goals during our first interview. Though the availability of technology was one of the advantages of U.S. schools (when compared with those in India), Faria had little access to it. During her 3 years, she had no student computers available for classroom use, she shared use of a media center and computer lab, and she had no LCD projector to share videos or computer programs. In her last year, she was moved to a new classroom and when she arrived, after a delay of several months, there was an open space on the wall where the Smartboard should have been. Thus, for the last months of school, she had no Smartboard or even a blackboard on the wall. This promise without fulfillment confused Faria. When I told her about my own experience as a teacher, in which a Smartboard was installed over a whiteboard, but I was not allowed to turn it on for 2 months, leaving me without any writing space for the classroom, she giggled and said, "At least it is not just me, then. Maybe it happens to American people, too!"

Faria's desire to teach gifted students also remained unfulfilled. She participated in the gifted endorsement process—at her own expense—but did not complete the endorsement requirements until her final year, by which point all of the gifted courses (of which there were only a very small number) were already assigned. Though Faria had been promised by the recruiter (and the administrator upon her pursuit of gifted certification) the opportunity to work with "the smartest kids" in U.S. schools, this, like many other goals, was not met.

Monetary Incentives

One would have to search very far to find American-born educators who would say they went into teaching for the money. Even though some conservative think tanks would have the public believe that teachers are overpaid since they have summers "off," get "out of work" before 5:00 p.m., and are supposedly making more than they would in the private sector (Biggs & Richwine, 2011), teachers in the United States have notoriously low salaries and benefits. However, because United States teachers are paid more in absolute dollars than teachers in the countries from which international teachers are commonly recruited, the possibilities of increasing one's salary were a huge motivating factor for international teachers. For example, the average salary for teachers in Hyderabad, India, in the 2009–2010 school year was approximately 142,372 rupees, or $3,408 in U.S. dollars (Payscale. com, 2010). In the Glendale School District, the average salary for a new teacher was $40,000 in U.S. dollars. However, given the much lower cost of living in India, the U.S. dollar's purchasing power in India is roughly five times its purchasing power in the United States. Thus, if the teachers had returned to India with every bit of their $40,000, their buying power would have been the same as that of a U.S. teacher taking home $200,000 (Organisation for Economic Co-operation and Development, 2005). Furthermore, teachers in India are paid 8.47 times more than the per capita gross domestic product (GDP) of the country (thus reflecting that they are paid significantly more than the average Indian worker). The much higher salary Indian teachers could earn in the United States combined with the lower standard of living in India meant that teachers who were able to save their pay or send remittances home could be assured of financial security and a comfortable living for themselves and their families. But what was the likelihood that the teachers could have saved every bit of their salaries? They were, after all, living in a country where the cost of living was higher and, for some like Shrusty and Aleeza, were supporting entire families on one relatively low salary.

In addition to the "expected" fees that were disclosed before their departure from India, such as rent and health insurance, there were also additional fees associated with the cost of living. These costs started adding up immediately upon arrival. For example, Ms. Jain, the head of IRI, claimed:

> They get free rides from the airport when they get here; we bring them to their apartment and help them get settled near an Indian grocery store and a place of worship, so they feel comfortable. And then we pay for their security deposit and their first month's rent. And we give them meals for the first 3 days, free of charge.

The teachers, however, argued that Ms. Jain did not fulfill these promises. Upon arrival, they were picked up at the airport, but they were asked to contribute to the price of gasoline. They were also given meals for the first 3 days, prepared by a previous cohort of international teachers, but they were asked to contribute to the cost of food, as well. And their rent and security deposit came from fees already paid to Ms. Jain prior to their departure.

One personal expense that reduced the teachers' net income was transportation. Upon arrival, none of the teachers had cars or American driver's licenses. They were not given information about public transportation, but even if they had used this option, the bus system was such that they would have spent a large amount of time switching buses and walking to their schools. Ms. Jain stated that the teachers were given free transportation for the first 2 weeks of the year, until they made other arrangements with American teachers. However, the teachers disputed this and said they were almost immediately left to their own devices. Because they were not provided with an alternative by IRI, they paid an older Indian man from the same apartment complex to drive them to and from school each day. This was not an ideal situation, but they had no other options. Shrusty explained:

> We didn't know anybody, that was the thing. This was before we knew our American friends in school, like when we first got here and we had to be at [our schools] the next day. This old man, he made us wait for a long time and he was not on time a lot. He couldn't drive in the dark. Oh, it was scary, him jumping on the curbs! He would sometimes say he can't come today so to book a taxi. He charged us $40, but then after a month, it went to $50, $60, $75. And this was $75 weekly, not for a month! It was so much money!

Although some of the teachers did manage to save money, they were not able to save as much as they initially expected or were promised because of the high cost of living and other fees associated with recruitment. The high cost of paying for their own benefits will be discussed in more depth in the next chapter. For several teachers, nearly all of what they saved while in the United States would have to be used to repay their "relocation loans" or other debts to family, friends, or agencies upon their return to India.

International Competitiveness

Participants said they felt that their teaching experience in the United States would make them more "hirable" in India or beyond. Though all of the teachers eventually wanted to return to India, they all mentioned the possibility of teaching in other countries. Shrusty said she would like to begin a part-time Ph.D. program in global labor issues (though she had not yet decided in which country she would like to study). She anticipated that her U.S. experience would make her more likely to be accepted into this program and would also help her research, as she planned on studying teacher layoffs in countries like the United States. Both Faria and Aleeza expressed a desire to teach in Australia because they had family or business opportunities there and it was another English-speaking country. Samina claimed, "My confidence level is up here [gestures with hand near head]. I could go anywhere in the world, any country I want. If I could do this, I could do anything." Interestingly, Samina was more optimistic about her *future* possibilities for success than about her success in her current situation, and it appeared that her confidence was not just in spite of her current difficulties but *because* of her current difficulties.

I find the discussion about international competitiveness to be especially ironic. The teachers are coming to the United States to have a more "worldly" experience that makes them more globally hirable, yet the people recruiting them presume they are *already* worldly and want this worldliness to rub off on urban students. The rhetoric of international competition has become so hegemonic that both the teachers and the recruiters believe it—and they are using each other for a common purpose.

Student Success Stories

International teachers did not identify relationship-building, either with students or colleagues, as one of their initial goals. However, after reflecting on their experiences, they all shared stories of individual students who affected them and made them feel "successful." And what teacher has not had individual students or groups of students who similarly lived on, becoming legends over the years, as their stories of achievement (often despite the odds) were retold to family, friends, and peers?

Not only do these students themselves help shape who we as educators become, but the actual *act* of telling the stories informs who we are as teachers, how we see ourselves, and why we remain committed to the profession.

Achieving these relationships and connections with students made international teachers feel successful, even if they were not successful in reaching their other goals. For example, Faria shared the story of a young woman whom she taught three times in the course of her 3 years at Woodson High, in Geometry, Algebra II, and Algebra III.

> When I saw her [the] first time in my Geometry B class, . . . she did not pass most of my tests, but she was a hard worker, and I think she barely passed with a 71 or 72. . . . When she came to my Algebra II class, I think she passed with a 77 or 78, but I still remember she ended up learning a lot of algebra. She really tried to get the subject in algebra, I still remember, she tried to participate every time I asked a question. She was kind of shy because she thought her answer might not be correct but she did try. . . . She did learn, she did ask for extra help, and I still remember the days when she cannot even figure out how to solve a simple linear equation, but now she is able to do [it all]. Every day I see that she is getting almost over 90% of what I am teaching. She is an A student in my [Algebra III] class right now. She does everything in the class and she is passing all my tests with an A. . . . I really feel happy because . . . I saw that gradual improvement in that particular student, so that is something really that is motivating for me.

Aleeza also recalled an individual student who was a senior in her science class. He had already failed the course once, and he was in danger of failing again. She was able to work with him individually to help him succeed, and as a result, felt successful herself.

> He used to keep his head down in my class, and I was like, "See, you have to work in class. You cannot put your head down and if you keep doing that then I have to call your parents, and if that doesn't work, then I have to write you up. I have to follow up with that. So just let me know what is the reason you put your head down every day. You don't like the subject or you want me to give you a different style of worksheet, what is it?" That boy was so straight, he said, "See, I work whole night and I am tired and I am hungry because I don't eat my breakfast." That disturbed me so badly. . . . He was like, "As soon as I get something to eat, I am fine," and then I told him, "Okay, now I cannot do anything about your lunch. I cannot change the time for you, so just come to me 2 days after school every week." He said, "It is difficult, but I will try to." And he did, and he passed his end-of-course test with a 90. That was big [for him to come to tutorial]. . . . But it showed me,

like you know, sometimes there are some reasons behind it which we as an individual need to understand, so I was really happy at that time. . . . I at least achieved for one person . . . you know, like I could transfer my knowledge to him.

Overall, I would argue that participants' goals were only partially met during their stay in the United States. Though they experienced a new culture, made connections with a few students, and learned new teaching techniques, thus hopefully making them more internationally competitive, they were not able to achieve the conventional "American Dream." Their short stays and only incidental monetary savings meant that the teachers returned to India before they were able to completely fulfill all of their goals.

MEETING GOALS FOR STUDENTS

The students were not involved in the decision to hire international teachers just as, of course, they would not be involved in the decision of which American teachers a school should employ. However, there were many actors making decisions on behalf of students—those claiming to understand what students need and why international teachers can fill those needs. This section expands upon the various stakeholders' goals for students, not the students' goals for themselves. I would argue that part of the reason for the failure of international teacher recruitment is because decisions are being made about what and how students should learn without consulting them and based on faulty educational policies.

The Glendale school system's mission, as displayed on plaques in schools around the district, was to "maximize students' social and academic potential, preparing them to compete in a global society." Recruitment agencies capitalized on this desire for international competition when they realized many urban students had limited exposure to the "global society." According to the principals, many of the students, 99% of whom were African American, had never traveled internationally—or even within the United States—and had little experience with other cultures. Thus, a goal of international teacher recruitment for urban students was to bring cultural awareness, thus increasing their ability to "compete" in the global marketplace.

Connecting the "Global Village" Through "Cultural Ambassadors"

Globalization, or the theory that world economies are integrated through a flow of trade, capital, and migration (Bhagwati, 2004), was encouraged and furthered by international teacher recruitment agencies. Agencies crafted slogans, missions, and materials designed to capitalize on schools' desire to prepare students for an increasingly globalized marketplace. This symbolic language of globalization will be discussed in more detail in the next chapter. School districts were told that international teachers would bring cultural experiences and knowledge to the classrooms, which was an added bonus for district personnel who were primarily concerned with desperately filling open positions. And although the teachers did sometimes discuss their home culture with the students, such as describing marriage rituals, technology, and education, several stated that they did not see it as part of their jobs to teach students about their cultures and only responded when asked directly. Others said they would be willing to discuss culture, but time constraints and an intense curricular focus did not allow time for outside discussions. Yet, the agencies' materials—and the media articles that covered stories of international teachers—made explicit use of language about "globalized citizens," "multicultural awareness," and "cultural diversity." According to the agencies, being a cultural ambassador is part of the teachers' jobs—maybe the most important part—but somehow the teachers did not know this or did not seem to agree. So where was the gap between the rhetoric that the agencies used when marketing and the actual discussions they had with their teachers?

Of the agencies highlighted in Barber's (2003) and the AFT's (2009) reports, the majority linked their mission explicitly to globalization. Because school districts like Glendale were concerned with preparing their students for what they viewed as a workforce subject to international competition, it is no surprise that the agencies' missions would have been appealing. Agencies were also able to build upon the increasing fear that the United States was falling behind other countries in international test rankings (though, unsurprisingly, the countries from which foreign teachers hailed were not the countries that had higher scores than the United States). Despite the fact that education scholars like Darling-Hammond (2010) have seen this failure as an indictment of society's lack of concern for school inequalities and the perpetuation of racist educational practices, many in the general public and some school administrators claimed that incompetent teachers or poorly structured curricula were at fault. In Table 4.1, I have included excerpts from agency mission statements.[1]

As the mission statements illustrate, agencies used language that reflects globalization and internationalism. Statements like VIF's "21st-century skills necessary to succeed in the global marketplace" and GTRR's "the world is growing smaller every day" echoed Friedman's (2005) notion that the most valued skills are those that enable transnational knowledge and people. Further, the repetition of words like *culture*, *global*, *world*, and *world-class*, while emphasizing the agencies' exchange value, added to the sentiment that global knowledge is a desirable and achievable goal.

Table 4.1. International Teacher Recruitment Agency Mission Statements

Agency	Mission Statement
Avenida International Consultants (AIC)	"The current demand and shortage for teachers in critical areas has resulted in alternative and aggressive recruitment programs for many school systems in the United States. The International Teacher Placement Program was designed to address this need by establishing an efficient mechanism for recruiting highly qualified teachers from the Philippines to work in various school districts in the United States, at no cost to the district" (Avenida International Consultants, 2010).
Amity Institute	"Amity Institute is a nonprofit organization dedicated to building international friendship and cultural understanding through teaching exchange. Based on the belief that cross-cultural interaction creates an effective, dynamic learning environment, Amity Institute sponsors international educators to teach . . . in U.S. schools. Amity provides opportunities for global educators to share their knowledge with students, schools and communities" (Amity Institute, 2012).
Global Teacher Recruitment and Resources (GTRR)	"GTRR was founded on the vision of an individual who saw the world becoming smaller every day. She saw students around the world benefiting from a world-class education and it was her vision to see American students receive the same world-class education. In addition, in this global village, American students inculcated in the global culture will succeed immensely in their future. This requires the best teachers from around the world bringing their rich personal experiences from other cultures to America's classrooms" (Global Teachers Recruitment and Resources, 2012).
Teachers Placement Group (TPG)	"Teachers Placement Group, founded in 1999, is a leader in helping teachers from the Indian subcontinent travel to the United States to participate in cultural exchange programs. . . . Our program will help your students receive world-class instruction from highly qualified teachers while learning about India's rich and vibrant culture. . . . We work to help you find highly qualified and culturally curious teachers for your schools" (Teachers Placement Group, 2012).
Visiting International Faculty (VIF)	"VIF helps K–12 schools build the 21st-century skills necessary for students to succeed in the global marketplace. As J-1 exchange teachers, VIF educators are uniquely positioned to bring a global mindset to the classroom, providing meaningful and memorable international education opportunities that influence the viewpoints of generations of students at home and abroad" (Visiting International Faculty, 2012).

Glendale's Small World

IRI, the agency used in Glendale, espoused a mission similar to those in the table, in both its focus and its language. Though IRI did not have a website, Ms. Jain summarized their mission during an interview:

> Our motto is that educators transcend borders, so we wanted to have, with the world becoming smaller every day, an education system that would be common throughout the countries. So if you have an educator in the United States, our idea is . . . that educator could go teach in India without any problems. The curriculum would not be very starkly different, so our mission, our goal is that, we have an exchange program for Indian teachers to come teach in the United States. We don't want physical borders to exist for the teachers.

Ms. Jain's mission was curious for several reasons. First, an "education system that would be common throughout the countries" does not yet exist, nor do I believe it ever will or even *should* exist. Cultural contexts should dictate what and how knowledge is transmitted, and what is important knowledge in one culture or country is not necessarily important in another. Yet Ms. Jain persists in exporting teachers as if a common education system or curriculum already exists. Her desire for an absence of borders does not mean there are, in reality, no borders. Second, there is a disconnect between her desire for teachers to transcend borders and her ability to provide for the teachers during this transcendence. Ironically, this disconnect only serves to reinforce the borders that *do* exist, creating more cultural clashes and confusion. Ms. Jain's refusal to acknowledge that education systems are different and that borders do exist, combined with her lack of support for teachers, is professionally irresponsible and endangers her employees. Brown (2013) found similar results in her study of overseas-trained teachers in South Carolina, as her participants were recruited under the premise of universal certification and practice, or what Brown calls "a borderless field" (n.p.).

As described in an earlier chapter, VIF, which was previously used in Glendale, used idealistic language to describe their acculturating mission:

> Imagine your students listening attentively as their South African-born teacher shares his experiences during the last days of apartheid; a German teacher discusses the fall of the Berlin Wall; or a Spanish teacher demonstrates Flamenco . . . to an after-school club. Extraordinary teachers sharing the world with your students—that's the essence of . . . VIF. (Visiting International Faculty, 2006)

The agency's perceptions of cultural diversity and globalization were interesting in their specificity; the countries and moments that it highlighted are those of success, moments that could not reflect poorly on the United States or lead to difficult discussions in the classroom. For example, VIF stressed a South African teacher's discussion of the *end* of apartheid, *not* apartheid itself, nor ongoing racial unrest and inequities. Noticeably absent from the VIF materials were stories from teachers who could remember colonial legacies, warfare, famine, or any other negative cultural experiences. Overall, the diversity that agencies promised to districts was superficial and based more on "heroes and holidays" and "food and festivals," or a "tourist" approach to multicultural education, rather than on a critical multicultural approach (Cochran-Smith, 1995; Grant & Lei, 2001; Ladson-Billings, 1997; Nieto, 1995).

Ms. Muller of the Glendale School District noted that the district stopped working with VIF because "cultural diversity dropped [as our priority] over the past several years; it is just no longer the focus when we really just need to find more teachers." Here, the official recognized the political rhetoric and rejected it in favor of the most honest, yet still frustrating, truth that international teachers were used primarily to fill job openings that American teachers were not willing to take. Cultural diversity was a side note; using agencies that were able to provide more teachers at a cheaper price, even if those teachers came from only one poor country, was more valuable than continuing to work with an agency that promised more nationalities. Ms. Dougherty from the American Federation of Teachers found this argument frustrating: "I am supportive of the vision of bringing more cultural diversity, but hiring only . . . to fill openings is not cultural diversity."

Despite Ms. Muller's admission that cultural diversity and increased global awareness was no longer the primary focus of international teacher recruitment, she suggested that any tangential diversity discussions would benefit Glendale students:

> It brings cultural diversity to the school. Children need to be aware that the world is built of all types of people, and they bring strengths into the classroom that are different. That's good for children to be aware of. Overall, they serve a good purpose for providing cultural diversity in our classrooms.

Yet, according to Principal Sutherland of Chisholm Middle School, the goal of "inculcating students in the global culture" (Global Teachers Recruitment and Resources, 2012) was far from achieved. "For my kids, who have never been outside these blocks . . . who don't know what a cow is . . . and these Indian teachers with this global knowledge, it is just a mismatch," he said. "When you have somebody with limited experience versus global experience, it just doesn't mix." He pointed to a critical disjuncture in the agencies' theories and the reality of urban schools. Simply because someone from another culture is in the classroom does not mean that she will be able to "bring a global mindset into the classroom" without appropriate preparation and support (Visiting International Faculty, 2012). Mr. Sutherland went even further to say that the cultural mismatch between teacher and students created a barrier, or a closing, rather than opening, of the figurative borders between them.

MEETING SCHOOLS' GOALS

School-level administrators were not responsible for hiring their own international teachers. Instead, Ms. Muller and Ms. Jefferson in the Glendale central office made those placement decisions. However, once the principals were notified of their new teachers, their primary goal became to provide students with high-quality education using the teachers' broad content knowledge.

According to IRI and other recruitment agencies, international teachers were highly qualified because they possessed advanced content knowledge, often in more than one subject. For example, an Indian teacher certified in math was also typically certified in science, according to Ms. Jain of IRI. Though the teachers themselves were confident in their academic backgrounds, the principals were equally divided on whether or not international teachers' content knowledge was effectively communicated to their urban students. Another contentious issue was what "highly qualified" actually meant to the schools and agencies, and whether or not American teachers fit this profile as well as international teachers.

Content Knowledge

When asked what international teachers' biggest strength was, all 15 participants in this study—from the teachers themselves to principals, district officials, agency officials, and union representatives—replied that it was "content knowledge." This was predictable because agencies touted their teachers as well educated in their subject areas, and popular press articles frequently discussed teachers' educational qualifications. For example, GTRR stated that their teachers "have an impeccable command of their subject matter" and all the agencies in the previous table required teachers to have at least a bachelor's degree in their main content area. Indeed, Ms. Muller stated that, in her interactions with teachers before they were hired, she was more concerned with "fluency" because "we already know the content is there . . . [because] they have so many degrees and education." Ms. Jefferson, the other district representative, elaborated:

> What I have noticed with the international teachers is that they are learned in their content areas and they have vast degrees within their content areas versus the teachers in America. If [U.S. teachers] have advanced degrees, often times they are in other areas. For example, if a science teacher has a doctorate degree here in America, it is usually in leadership. It is not in science, versus the international teachers that we work with oftentimes come with two to three master's degrees in those specific content areas. So they come with a great bit of knowledge in the content fields that they are teaching.

The argument that they would be successful if they were fluent and had content knowledge is reminiscent of the rhetoric of Teach for America, in which recent college graduates are recruited from prestigious colleges and universities and are presumed to be good teachers because of leadership skills and a good educational history (e.g., Dunn & Kavanagh, 2012; Kavanagh, 2010). There was no doubt that international teachers came with impressive academic credentials. Three teachers profiled here had both a bachelor's and a master's degree in their subject area, and several had a second degree in a related subject. What was less clear was whether teachers' content knowledge was enough to make them successful in the classroom. For example, did they also possess Shulman's (1986) concept of pedagogical content knowledge? Did they knew specific methods and strategies for teaching their particular content area?

Two principals argued that content knowledge was not only a strength promised by the agency, but one they had seen in practice. Mr. Clark said he had observed his international teachers, including Aleeza, and seen their knowledge in action, and students had given positive feedback. He posited that Aleeza's content knowledge made her well equipped to lead the school's after-school test preparation program, in which she offered tutoring for the state's high-stakes graduation exams in science. Mr. Norman concurred with Mr. Clark's assessment: "I have sat in on several classes and their grasp of the concepts is remarkable. A lot of the things that our [American] teachers are looking for and fussing around with books, they know." He said that Faria had grown into one of his most competent teachers.

For the two other principals, content was adequate, but teachers' delivery of content was impeded by other challenges. Mr. Scott described his experience, but did not include his teacher, Shrusty, in his analysis because he did not know enough about severe disabilities to effectively judge her content knowledge as a special education teacher. For other international teachers that he has supervised, he asserted:

> I have not seen any strengths. Because I would like to say classroom content, but I have not necessarily seen that. I am not saying that it has not happened somewhere, but I have not seen it. . . . Not to the point where I would have seen it as a strength. I have not necessarily seen it where it was such a deficit that they could not teach. I still do not consider it a strength, though. I think, like the ones that I have had, their content was okay. Like if you were rating them from an A to an F, [they would be a] C-slash-B. Not seen any with an A, but the classroom management has been such an issue that I have not been able to see anything as a strength, because they have not been able to give that content out.

Mr. Sutherland expressed similar disappointment that international teachers "know the content; however, it does no good if you know the content and you cannot have control of the classroom." Based on my classroom observations, the reality may fall in the middle of the principals' divergent assessments. Although I did not see any extraordinary content knowledge or anything that made me think the Indian teachers possessed more content knowledge than American teachers, I do not believe it is because they did not possess vast knowledge about their subject. For example, I have no doubt that Faria can teach quadratic equations without the aid of a textbook or that Aleeza can explain sound waves without difficulty. However, the classes that I observed did not require as much content knowledge as the teachers possessed. I saw evidence of basic subject-matter knowledge, but nothing that they required of the students or voluntarily shared with me approached the advanced scientific and mathematical abilities that their principals claimed they possessed. This is the case for many international teachers who, as the last ones hired with the least experience in American schools, are often placed in remedial or general-level classes, while more experienced American teachers worked with advanced, gifted, or AP levels. Further, as Mr. Scott and Mr. Sutherland similarly observed, there were several sessions where other classroom dynamics prevented me from assessing teachers' content knowledge at all. Thus, it was difficult to assess the true extent of my participants' knowledge because of mitigating factors such as class placement and management difficulties.

Highly Qualified Status

When the term *highly qualified* gained popularity after its inclusion in the No Child Left Behind legislation of the early 2000s, states were given considerable flexibility in determining qualifications for teachers in their state. Federal guidelines required only "1) a bachelor's degree, 2) full state certification or licensure, and 3) [proof] that they know each subject they teach" (U.S. Department of Education, 2010). Such "proof" could take the form of a state licensure exam, a graduate degree, or National Board Certification, depending on the state. Several states, like Connecticut and Massachusetts, added additional requirements, such as pedagogical preparation. For the state in which Glendale was located, requirements were only those three listed above, and the proof was a passing score on the Praxis II examination. Educational scholars disputed these requirements, arguing that such negligible qualifications were, in fact, producing teachers who were only minimally qualified to teach, especially in urban schools (Berry, 2003; Darling-Hammond, 2004).

These nominal requirements were what made it easier to recruit international teachers for U.S. schools. Like "graduates" of other alternative recruitment programs, such as Teach for America or Troops to Teachers, international teachers did not need any U.S.-based pedagogical knowledge. Requirements for acceptance into agency programs mirrored the state requirements, with only the addition of English proficiency and 2–3 years' teaching experience in their home countries. Ms. Jain of IRI maintained that these requirements were stringent enough to find the best teachers because "teachers who are successful in India are successful in the U.S.," ignoring not only the contextual factors that make one a good teacher, but also the possibility that preparation in pedagogical content knowledge, though not required by state law, would make a teacher more fully equipped to work effectively in urban schools.

According to Shulman (1986), pedagogical content knowledge (PCK) "represents the blending of content and pedagogy into an understanding of how particular topics, problems, or issues are organized, represented, and adapted to the diverse interests and abilities of learners, and presented for instruction" (p. 8). Though research has consistently shown that intelligence or education in an academic subject is not enough to make one an effective teacher, and that PCK is, in fact, a better indicator of a teacher's true abilities, states like the one that housed Glendale ignored such findings and preferred instead to retain minimum requirements (Ball, 2000; Darling-Hammond, 1990; Ladson-Billings, 1995). Research on PCK for math and science teachers has been especially abundant and has pointed to the necessity of preparing those teachers to communicate their often theoretical and dense subject matter to varied ages and abilities (Neiss, 2005). Yet, international teacher recruitment agencies, which most often recruited teachers for STEM subjects, did not require any PCK from their teachers. Though the teachers may have possessed PCK, because IRI and other companies did not require proof, it remained an afterthought for urban districts.

Thus, if the true goal of recruitment was to bring "high-quality" teachers to U.S. schools, and "highly qualified" was defined only as someone with a major in a subject, certification, and proficiency in English, the question remained why districts could not find American teachers to do these jobs. Districts were not requiring anything more from international teachers than they required from American teachers. As with American teachers, hiring became less about finding and supporting the most well-prepared teachers—with content knowledge, pedagogical knowledge, and pedagogical content knowledge—and more about saving money.

MEETING DISTRICT GOALS

The chief objective of international teacher recruitment was, for many districts, to satisfy what they viewed as a teacher shortage. Though Glendale, like many other urban districts, had a teacher retention and misdistribution problem, not necessarily a "shortage" of qualified educators, the key personnel in charge of hiring and teacher placement were divided on whether or not the shortage was real. They said international teachers were necessary because not enough qualified American teachers were applying for positions, or because those Americans were not staying in their positions. However, schools in the northern parts of the district consistently had more applicants than positions, even in subject areas such as math, science, and special education that were deemed "areas of critical need." According to district representative Ms. Muller,

We basically can find the teachers we need for the most part, so the shortage is not the problem. The problem is retaining quality teachers that we have. Basically, we still have some needs in those areas that we are able to fill quicker with international teachers. They help us to fill critical needs areas a little faster than we would ordinarily be able to do. Of course, they [the open positions] wouldn't sit open all year, either.

The principals with whom I spoke were unaware of how many international teachers were hired each year and in which schools they were placed. When asked what they thought about the fact that 73 of 74 international teachers were placed in the south side schools, all principals smiled ruefully and shook their heads. They then had four different responses:

Mr. Norman: Hmmm . . . [long pause] . . . I probably do not need to comment on that.

Mr. Scott: No, I didn't know that, but it's not a surprise to me. That's the way it works in [Glendale]. Are you surprised? I'm not.

Mr. Clark: I think that's because of the lack of, uh, a word that is politically correct . . . uh because of the lack of parent participation, the county can strategically place the teachers on this side of town. We know that happens, but I embrace it because they [international teachers] work for me. . . . But I do know and I am friends with principals on the north end of town, and if those parents . . . [think the] teacher has a language barrier, if kids do not understand a word, then that teacher is gone or transferred, not fired.

Mr. Sutherland: Well, of course, it's all about money. The parents in the north have enough money to get the best teachers every time they need them. We do not have that ability here, so we get the teachers placed by the county, and those are sometimes international teachers. [North side parents] have more power to make their own decisions.

The principals' comments, and even the long pause of the principal who did not comment, illustrate a deeper political struggle at work behind the seemingly innocuous placement of international teachers. They may have been hired to satisfy the teacher shortage, according to Ms. Jefferson, or to combat the teacher retention problem, according to Ms. Muller, but there were larger issues that caused shortages or attrition in the first place. The principals pointed to power differences as reflected in parent involvement, incomes, and longstanding district policies that all contributed to the majority of international teachers working in south side urban schools, where there was less expected resistance from "consumers."

Yet, regardless of whether the issue was one of a shortage or retention, neither problem was solved by international recruitment. International teachers sometimes left after their first year, and the majority of those who stayed were mandated by visa requirements to leave after their third year. Thus, recruitment was itself a stopgap measure that did nothing to solve systemic attrition and only temporarily eased employment problems in Glendale schools.

Trouble with Teacher Retention

New international teachers, like those profiled here, may experience a difficult adjustment period, similar to that for American teachers, where they struggle to learn new teaching methods, classroom management, and school procedures (Kauffman, Johnson, Kardos, Liu, & Peske, 2002; Ladson-Billings, 2001). Their struggles are frequently compounded by culture shock and lack of information about U.S. urban schools, as discussed in earlier chapters. Ms. Jain stated that "above 98%" of her teachers returned for all 3 years allowed by their visa, though she did not elaborate on how her teachers were tracked. Participants and district officials disputed this statistic, stating that some teachers left during or at the end of their first year. This further contributed to the revolving door of urban schools (Ingersoll, 2002).

Mr. Scott shared an experience of working with an international teacher whom he deemed "unprepared" for his U.S. school. He stated that her English skills were not what they should have been and that her lack of classroom management significantly prohibited student learning. He recalled IRI sending a support specialist to work with this teacher in her classroom, but the specialist was not there long enough to make a difference. "She [the support specialist] would have needed to be there every day, the whole time, for it to be effective," he said. "I didn't see any changes or think it made a difference." Mr. Scott acknowledged that his attempt to provide the teacher with a mentor was unsuccessful, because the mentor was consumed with planning for her own classes, and that additional support at the school level may have helped the teacher with her transition. As a result of these difficulties, and because Mr. Scott did not recommend renewing the teacher's contract, she returned to India at the end of her first year. Therefore, he argued that international teachers did not combat the attrition of teachers in Glendale because they were not prepared well enough to sustain long-term employment.

"Temporary" by Definition

The majority of teachers hired by IRI did not leave during or immediately after their first year, according to Ms. Jain. They did, however, leave after 3 years because of the restrictions of their visas and the program constraints outlined by IRI. This leaving mirrored the typical exodus of teachers from urban schools. Research has continuously shown that around one-third of the urban teaching force leaves within 3 years, and over 50% leave within 5 years (Ingersoll, 2002; Ingersoll & Perda, 2009; Nieto, 2003). International teacher recruitment did not provide teachers for any longer than American teachers would typically stay and, in fact, contributed to earlier teacher attrition.

Though the visa regulations for H-1B and J-1 visas appear strict, there are, of course, exceptions to the rule. Visa holders are allowed to apply for visa extensions, visa waivers, or transfers to other work visas, though there is no guarantee that their applications will be approved. For visa extensions, teachers need the release of their current employer, which in many cases is a for-profit recruitment agency. IRI did not commonly allow teachers to extend their stay past 3 years. This was not unique, as many other recruitment agencies also stated on their websites that they did not support waivers or extensions. What was unique, however, was the way my participants were treated by IRI when they requested extensions.

Further prohibiting long-term employment for international teachers was a stipulation in the IRI–Glendale contract. It contained a version of a "non-compete" clause. This clause prohibited Glendale from directly hiring or sponsoring a new visa for any international teacher previously employed by IRI, for 1 year after their visa expired. Thus, if teachers wanted to stay in the United States and find another sponsor other than IRI, as my participants' friends did, they had to find another school district to employ them. Teachers said they were told this when they first arrived, but did not remember until they were reminded by the district officials when principals attempted to step in on their behalf and asked the district to consider keeping the teachers past their 3 years.

This contract stipulation was somewhat understandable, as IRI and other agencies wanted their businesses to seem like "cultural exchanges" and not as paths to citizenship. Had they not done this, they might have faced even more attacks that claimed the program was taking American jobs. For example, one critic on the Right argued,

> H-1B visas (especially for teaching positions) should be eliminated immediately. There are more than enough American teachers for the available positions, HIRE THEM! With American unemployment at almost 10% why are we bringing in ANY H-1B workers? (Right Side News, 2009, p. 1)

Such a sentiment ignores the larger issue that there are schools in the United States where teachers do not want to work, instead placing the blame for unemployment on districts that hire international teachers. This same critic misinterpreted the 2009 AFT report's findings, arguing incorrectly that the report found that schools are "increasingly hiring international teachers over Americans" and that American teachers are being "displaced" (Right Side News, 2009, p. 1). However, as explained by district officials in Glendale and in popular press articles, the teachers were working in schools that many American teachers chose to avoid or in which they did not stay. Thus, if IRI allowed the teachers to remain in the United States with a visa waiver, it would not be "taking" an American's job, merely filling "the jobs they can't get enough locals to take on" (Coates, 2005, p. 64). The conflict persisted between support for globalization on one hand and anti-immigrant rhetoric on the other.

SHORT-TERM GOALS VERSUS LONG-TERM PROBLEMS

In 2002, the National Commission on Teaching and America's Future concluded, "short-term, quick-fix approaches to placing teachers in the classroom fuel high teacher attrition rates and diminish teaching quality" (p. 14). International teacher recruitment is one example of a "quick-fix" approach to larger urban problems. As a result, many goals of recruitment remained unmet. Teachers' personal goals were partially met, as in their acquiring improved pedagogical skills and developing relationships with individual American students. However, other goals such as saving money and living the "American Dream" remained largely unfulfilled because of program constraints and hidden fees. The goal of bridging cultures and providing urban students with exposure to global knowledge existed primarily in rhetoric and not in reality. Though discussed at length in the literature of the recruitment agencies, principals did not believe this goal was achieved. They argued that additional preparation was necessary to avoid a "cultural mismatch." Even if teachers were able to act as cultural ambassadors, their positions came at the risk of exploitation. Supposedly hired to "create bridges of mutual understanding" (Visiting International Faculty, 2010), they inevitably became part of the "efficient mechanism" (Avenida International Consultants, 2010) of the recruitment machine. Districts can do much to address this, and suggestions will be provided in a later chapter.

School administrators' goals of bringing highly qualified teachers were also only partially met, according to principals' testimonies and classroom observations, and it was difficult to truly assess the content knowledge of teachers because of the classes they taught and other distracting variables, such as classroom management issues. Finally, the most prominent goal of the program—to fill open positions in urban schools—was not met for more than a brief period of time because, by definition, the recruitment programs were temporary. International teachers were mandated to leave after 3 years, thus contributing heavily to the revolving door of urban teacher employment. Instead of addressing the long-term problem of teacher retention in its urban schools, Glendale officials were primarily focused on short-term solutions that saved them money, or as Merrow (1999) noted about other alternative recruitment programs, they "diagnos[ed] the problem incorrectly and then propos[ed] inappropriate cures."

FIVE

Pushing the Boundary and Crossing the Line

Hidden Purposes and Consequences of Recruitment

There is nothing more to say—except why. But since why is difficult to handle, one must take refuge in how.

—Toni Morrison, 1970

If we have learned nothing else from the 20th century, we should at least have grasped that the more perfect the answer, the more terrifying its consequences.

—Tony Judt, 2010

During her last month in the United States, Samina was struggling even more than usual. The bad days were greatly outnumbering the good days, and she was increasingly homesick for her family. After observing another class in which very little learning happened, I asked Samina how things were going.

It's a nightmare and it's getting worse. It was a bad day. . . . I'm trying my best. I try to help the students who are trying to learn. . . . As the days are passing by, it is getting worse. I do not know if I will be back next year. But I am glad I made it through 1 year. I miss my family very much. When you have something like this, these bad days, you feel it more. But I feel lighter when I talk to you, to talk is good for me. It is stressful, though. I have lost so much weight. . . . I used to teach in my son's school before he got there. I liked the environment, you know, it's a private school. He was so young that he didn't know that I was a teacher. He was just 5 when I left the country and now he wants me to come back so I can be teaching in his class. . . . I tell him I am in America now. All those words come to my mind. I just have to be patient, only a few more days.

Several weeks after making these comments, Samina returned to her family in India, having left Chisholm Middle School 20 days before the end of the year at the behest of her employer at IRI. Her difficult experience, including her early departure, is a prime example of how recruiters' hidden purposes lead to intended or unintended consequences. In this chapter, I argue that the goals for students and other stakeholders enumerated in Chapter 4 are inherently opposed to the hidden purposes of international teacher recruitment, including saving districts money, generating profit for recruitment agencies, and contributing to the political rhetoric that neoliberal school reform is beneficial. I also argue that the disquieting consequences of recruitment, such as exploiting dependent employees, undercutting the teaching profession and teacher education, controlling teachers and their practice, outsourcing, and draining human resources from source countries, undermine progressive education efforts to unionize and fight for social justice. Ironically, these consequences of recruitment were the conditions that made international recruitment both "necessary" and possible to begin with.

POLITICAL SPECTACLE

The theory of political spectacle is useful in helping us understand international teacher recruitment. Created to explain the political climate of the 1950s and 1960s, Edelman's (1970) discussion of symbolic politics posits the theory of political spectacle. For Edelman, "practically every political act that is controversial or regarded as really important is bound to serve in part as a . . . symbol. It evokes a quiescent or an aroused mass response because it symbolizes a threat or reassurance" (p. 7). The recruitment of foreign teachers is a response to the symbolic crisis of a teacher shortage and the looming threat (or promise) of globalization. As the literature has demonstrated, there is, in fact, not a teacher shortage, but rather a problem of teacher retention stemming from dysfunctional patterns of schooling. However, as Edelman (1988) states, "in a crucial sense, problems are created so that particular reasons can be offered for public acceptance . . . so that particular remedies can be proposed" (p. 18).

Edelman's theory of political spectacle argues that there is an "onstage" rhetoric about political reform and a "backstage" reality, which the general public may never see; often, this onstage rhetoric is turned into a "spectacle" perpetuated by news media. The spectacle is a political symbol aimed at accomplishing a political goal or solving a problem that may or may not be as dire as the symbolic language makes it out to be. Further, political spectacle may provide tangible benefits to the stakeholders of the policy, but only provides symbolic benefits to the recipients or the general public (Smith, 2004). International teacher recruitment as a solution may divert public attention from the more troubling issues at hand, the systemic failures of urban education in the United States. Explained by Edelman (1988):

> The emergence of any problem may divert public attention from a different one that can be more threatening. Such covert masking of ominous conditions is a property of discourse about public issues and often an explanation for the willingness of a large

public to accept an issue as legitimate even if they have no particular interest in remedying it. That attention to a conspicuous problem may reduce interest in a more troubling one is sometimes consciously recognized but more often subconsciously sensed. (p. 27)

Smith (2004) aptly applies Edelman's theory to educational reforms. She reveals a pattern of actions in educational reforms, such as high-stakes testing and school choice, that demonstrates how the "spectators" are being misled by onstage rhetoric when there are deeper issues taking place backstage. She concludes that, however pure the stated intentions of educational reforms and political reformers, "they serve political purposes and interests" (p. 154).

Some important elements of Smith's taxonomy include symbolic language; casting political actors as leaders, enemies, and allies, and plotting their actions; and the distinction between onstage and backstage actions. In this chapter, I analyze international recruitment in light of each of these categories and demonstrate that recruitment is yet another manufactured solution to the "problem" of teacher shortages and global competition. Edelman's (1970) theory is a good way to analyze what is happening to international teachers because it helps us understand the issue in a way we could not otherwise. It forces us to consider the political motivations and implications for recruitment and see such recruitment within a nexus of educational policies that jeopardize students and teachers.

HIDDEN PURPOSES

As I argued in the previous chapter, there are many justifications for international teacher recruitment. Urban school administrators and policymakers want to hire highly qualified educators, prepare their students for a competitive marketplace, and fill open positions. Behind the façade of promoting cultural ambassadorship, however, are other hidden purposes: International teachers saved districts money while increasing profits for recruitment agencies and added to the political spectacle of urban education reform. These goals benefited not the teachers themselves (nor even the students), but districts, neoliberal reformers, and, most of all, recruitment agencies.

"It's All About Money": Districts and Recruitment Agencies

To an outside observer, it would not seem possible that districts could save money by paying someone else to manage their hiring. Indeed, the Glendale School District agreed to pay $4.18 million to two recruiting agencies for the 2010–2011 school year; $2.65 million of that was going to IRI. The head of the district's human resources department explained that the money was for "teachers' salaries that range from $34,000 to $79,000." Yet, despite yearly administrative fees of $11,500 per teacher, districts like Glendale were still able to save money because they were not required to provide health-care benefits (paid for by the teachers themselves), disability insurance (supposedly paid for by the agency, but more likely by the teachers' fees), Social Security, or retirement benefits (because the teachers left after 3 years, which also reduced the number of unionized teachers). As a principal noted, "It's all about money," or else Glendale would not have continued hiring international teachers despite principals' misgivings and apprehensions.

In a depressed economy when urban schools were already cash-strapped, policymakers in urban districts like Glendale were looking to save money. While international teachers were employed in the district, Glendale had a fluctuating budget deficit of $84 to $110 million. For-profit recruitment agencies capitalized on districts' desire to cut costs by promising quality teachers for lower prices. That purpose is evident in this excerpt from the website of one of the agencies that is similar to IRI, Global Teachers Recruitment and Resources:

> With each passing year, the undeniable financial constraints and scarcity of reliable teachers for each school system is readily apparent. We at GTRR work with your mission in mind. GTRR teachers receive the same salary as other teachers with similar experience and equivalent degrees. Moreover, as GTRR makes benefits available for our teachers, the school is relieved of the burden of providing the same. Rather school systems pay an administration fee that is generally less than the cost of benefits. Collaborating with GTRR means quality teachers with savings to the school systems. (Global Teachers Recruitment and Resources, 2012)

Especially revealing was the idea that benefits would be a "burden" that public school systems would have to pay, rather than a right for public employees. Further, GTRR only "made benefits available" to teachers, which was a diplomatic way of saying that teachers could choose to pay the full cost for their own benefits from a variety of plans offered by the agency.

At the same time that districts were saving money, agencies were making it. Such "administration fees" quickly added up and made agencies profitable. In addition to system fees, IRI also charged teachers between $5,000 and $6,500 each for initial recruitment fees, which the recruiter Ms. Jain said included costs of applications, interviewing, miscellaneous paperwork, visas, and relocation assistance. These fees, paid before teachers left India, may have also paid for district administrators' trips to India for interviewing. Though no one from Glendale District went to India in 2009, Ms. Muller and Ms. Jefferson had both traveled abroad—at no cost to the district—in previous years to meet a pool of applicants.

Together, the four teachers with whom I worked paid Ms. Jain over $25,000, and when combined with the initial fees paid by the Glendale District for each teacher's recruitment, IRI made $70,000 from just four employees. Some of the things that Ms. Jain said were covered by the teachers' fees were not, according to the teachers; in addition to the application fee, teachers also had to pay for their own visa processing. Although according to the law for J-1 exchange visas, it is the responsibility of the employer to pay visa fees, according to two teachers, Ms. Jain did not tell her employees this, and instead required them to travel 10 hours across India to Chennai (which was an additional expense) to handle the visa process themselves.

Valuing profit over people took on a whole new meaning for me as a researcher when I learned of the struggle in which Aleeza found herself at the end of her 3-year visa. In March, Aleeza and several other teachers told Ms. Jain that they would like to extend their visas and continue teaching at their schools. In April, Aleeza gave birth to a premature baby girl. By the time Ms. Jain informed the teachers that they would not get an extension, it was May, and Aleeza's daughter was still in the hospital. Unless Aleeza was granted a visa extension, she would have to leave her daughter alone in the United States or stay illegally. Close to tears, she described the situation to me:

> I have to stay here because the doctor says I cannot travel for the next 6 months because of my baby. My baby cannot as she has breathing problem. I did send her [Ms. Jain] an email like twice . . . requesting her to see my situation is bad, "please do something for me." There was no reply. . . . She does not like to respond to people. I have three kids to take care of and then, because my husband is on a dependent visa, he cannot work too unless I get a work permission. . . . I did email her like you know "the doctor says she can give me the hospital papers or whatever we need but I need this extension because I am not leaving my baby here and going nowhere." . . . I told her that I am ready to pay whatever you are going to get if you hire a new teacher because my situation was I do not want to go back. At least not right now.

Aleeza said her employer never returned her emails or her phone calls, despite her extenuating circumstances that required immediate attention. She also explained that she was so afraid that her employer would not pay her for her maternity leave that she returned to work only 2 weeks after an emergency Cesarean section, despite a doctor's advice that she stay out of work for 6 weeks. Other questionable practices will be discussed in the section on the consequence of teacher exploitation, but it is important to note here that Aleeza connected all of Ms. Jain's misdeeds to her desire to hire a new teacher in Aleeza's place, thus increasing IRI's profit. Aleeza summarized, "If there are potential teachers here, then her company cannot bring any more teachers. . . . So that is why she does not want us to stay here."

"It's All Bluster": Political Spectacle of Education Reform

There were several ways that international teacher recruitment and, in particular, recruitment agencies contributed to the political spectacle of urban school reform. Though some examples are detailed at length in other sections and chapters, they are summarized in Table 5.1.

A school board meeting in July 2010 clearly exemplifies the way that Glendale policies contributed to the political spectacle. The director of human resources for the Glendale district called international teacher recruitment an opportunity that had served the district well in the past. In his plea to the board to renew IRI's contract for the upcoming year, he cited many reasons why the program should continue: International teachers brought 12–15 years of experience; they had experience teaching upper-level courses and could do so in Glendale; the district educated 85% of the state's refugees, so international teachers made sense; and there were no other teachers willing to take the jobs (Local newspaper article, July 12, 2010). These four arguments, although potentially true in other circumstances in other districts, were blatantly untrue for Glendale at the time. Instead, they were part of the political spectacle of urban reform and globalization. Such statements perpetuated the rhetoric of reform while keeping the public in the dark about the true realities of international teacher recruitment. Data collected directly contradicted each of the director's four reasons for continued recruitment.

First, the director argued that international teachers possessed much experience, more so than the average American teacher or teacher applicant. This was not true for the four teachers discussed here, only one of whom had more than 4 years of experience with adolescents. Further, an invoice that lists the yearly pay for each international teacher for the 2010–2011 school year demonstrates the situation. In Glendale, each teacher (American or international) was paid on an incremental and rigid scale based on years of experience. For example, $42,492 was paid to a teacher with a master's degree with 0–4 years of experience or a teacher with a bachelor's degree with 8 years of experience. Ten teachers on IRI's invoice received this amount of $42,492, meaning that one in four IRI teachers had less than 8 years of experience. This directly contradicted the director's statement that the teachers had 12–15 years of experience.

Second, the district maintained that international teachers' experience with upper-level classes would enable them to teach advanced courses, especially in math and science. Though this possibility was open, in actuality, most teachers taught lower-level courses. Aleeza, Faria, and Samina, three teachers of core academic subjects, did not teach any honors, advanced, gifted, or AP courses in their years in Glendale, and as previously noted, Faria's gifted certification was never utilized in her school and she left without having taught any higher-level classes. Further, an examination of the Glendale school websites revealed that courses assigned to international teachers were almost always lower- or general-level

Table 5.1. Evidence of the Political Spectacle of International Teacher Recruitment

Element of Political Spectacle	Evidence from the Study
Symbolic language	Recruitment agencies used language of "cultural ambassadors," "global competitiveness," and expanding the "global village" to symbolize neoliberal globalization.
Casting political actors as leaders, enemies, and allies and plotting their actions	Though recruitment agencies cast themselves as districts' allies in the fight to solve the teacher shortage and prepare urban students to be "global citizens," this study did not reveal any evidence of the casting of leaders or enemies in the recruitment process.
Dramaturgy: political stages, props, and costumes	Recruitment agencies engaged in dramaturgy when they created a "narrative" (Smith, 2004, p. 22) of the American Dream and sold this storyline to their international teachers. Additionally, IRI staged a "comprehensive" orientation for international teachers that was less than 2 days long.
Democratic participation as illusion	While the school board in Glendale did vote for the continued recruitment of international teachers, there was no democratic participation from citizens in the district. Principals acknowledged that they did not have a choice about whether to accept teachers into their schools. Additionally, the teachers themselves had no democratic voice, either in the district or in the agency.
Disconnect of means and ends	There was a substantial disconnect between the ends of international teacher recruitment—filling open positions and allowing international teachers the freedom to migrate to the United States—and the means to get there— exploitation of teachers and a lack of cultural relevance in the classroom.
Distinction between onstage and backstage action	There were practices that recruitment agencies claimed to follow and practices their teachers stated were actually followed. There was also the "story" provided to me by Ms. Jain in our interview versus the lived experiences of my teachers, and the story provided by principals versus the story provided by Glendale officials, illustrating a distinction between onstage and backstage action. In addition to symbolic language, this was the most evident example of the political spectacle.

Adapted from Edelman (1970) and Smith (2004)

classes. Although three teachers with doctorates were teaching advanced students, the vast majority of international teachers were not. This was not surprising, as American teachers in urban schools typically work many years before being "allowed" to teach advanced students, as in many schools it was seen as a "reward" for teachers' experience working "in the trenches." It would have been unusual for a temporary teacher to enter into an already-established culture of working one's way to the top and be automatically given higher-level courses.

Third, Glendale officials argued that, in a district that educated 85% of the state's refugees, international educators were assets. There were two key flaws to this argument. First, the teachers were not of the same ethnic background as the refugees. To be sure, there were many refugee and immigrant students in Glendale's schools, but they were from countries such as Burma, Bhutan, Somalia, Iraq, and Afghanistan. Seventy-three of the 74 teachers recruited in 2009–2010 were Indian, and one was Hispanic. Second, the teachers were not even placed in the schools with high refugee populations. My four participants were placed in schools with 99% African American students, and the three schools that had the highest concentration of refugee students, according to state records, had no more than five international teachers combined. In fact, the school with the highest percentage of refugee students in the entire district, with students from 54 countries who spoke 48 languages, had no international teachers from 2008 to 2011.

Finally, it was presumed that no other teachers would fill the open positions. Under "normal" circumstances, such as when the district first began recruiting international teachers around 2000, this may have been true because urban schools typically have difficulty recruiting and retaining educators. However, in the midst of an economic recession and massive teacher layoffs across the country and state, this was untrue at the time of this study, despite the director's claim that no other teachers were available. Districts surrounding Glendale laid off more than 600 teachers, and the one school board member who publicly vetoed the decision to renew contracts with IRI and another for-profit agency said it behooved the district to hire local teachers first.

All of these arguments for renewing IRI's contract were the same persuasive points that the agency used when selling districts on their services in the first place. Ms. Jain and IRI were able to capitalize on the political spectacle, so much so that a Glendale board member, while voting to approve the contract extension, echoed Ms. Jain's words almost verbatim from what she told me during our interview. The board member stated, "We live in a global world. We can't be so parochial in providing talent for our students. This is one of the features of the [Glendale] school system that I'm very proud of. Other international countries hire American teachers the same way for the richness and diversity they bring." Ms. Dougherty of the AFT concurred that the political spectacle of recruitment was taking the focus away from the true problems of urban schools: "All the focus on urban schools is just bluster if this [international teacher recruitment] is the solution."

HIDDEN CONSEQUENCES

While conducting this research, analyzing the data, and writing, I debated what I should "name" the consequences that the teachers in Glendale and their peers around the United States faced every day. Are they intended or unintended? Are they hidden from the public on purpose or for less malicious reasons? Does it matter? After much reflection and conversation, I was brought back to the opening line of Toni Morrison's *The Bluest Eye* that begins this chapter: "There is nothing more to say—except why. But since why is difficult to handle, we must take refuge in how." I cannot conclusively ascribe motives to the consequences; I cannot say *why* these things happened to teachers and students who deserved better and, even if I could, that would be literally and figuratively "difficult to handle." Where would I find people who are willing to come out and say they want to exploit others for profit and destroy the teaching profession? Yet, even if we cannot know for sure why these things happen, that does not mean we can ignore what is going on. As scholars, we want to understand, explain, and make sense of phenomena, but here I must resign myself to not knowing why and simply "take refuge in how."

Exploitation

Exploitation of international teachers is not limited to those working in Glendale. Other foreign educators around the United States experience daily exploitation— often described in very public venues like *The New York Times* and *The Washington Post*—similar to the hidden stories of the teachers in Glendale. In this section, I describe the exploitation faced by Glendale teachers and then share stories of similar practices in Baltimore and Prince George's County, Maryland; Baton Rouge, Louisiana; and New York City, New York.

Glendale

Tolstoy (1995) wrote that "there are no conditions of life to which a man cannot get accustomed, especially if he sees them accepted by everyone around him" (p. 696). That was certainly the case for the exploited international teachers in Glendale. Though the teachers I interviewed said they were unhappy with the treatment they received at the hands of IRI, they were not comfortable discussing their problems with others in the school system, including their principals. They presumed that everyone accepted such treatment, and so they accepted it, too.

The teachers accepted their circumstances out of fear. An examination of the contract between IRI and Glendale justified their fear. One provision of the contract was that teachers could be fired "with or without cause" for any reason, at any time, by either Glendale or IRI. If that happened, the teachers' visas would be revoked, and they would be deported. Thus, Aleeza said, many teachers were afraid to do what they had specifically been warned not to do. Their orientation to U.S. school culture may have been lacking, but there was no shortage of time spent educating these teachers about how to behave as employees. Among the prohibited behaviors that they were warned of before and upon arrival were not showing their contracts to Americans, not asking their American principals for letters of recommendation, and not discussing their situation, especially their pay, with strangers.

Questionable practices that led to the teachers being under-informed or misinformed enabled their exploitation. For example, though Glendale officially provided the teachers' salaries, IRI distributed the checks. Glendale paid the contractor IRI four times per year, and IRI paid teachers in nine monthly checks. Though Glendale's American teachers had the option to receive their pay through the summer, international teachers were not given this option. Also, the teachers did not receive itemized pay stubs, only one check. Thus, they did not know their gross pay, how much was deducted for taxes or insurance, or if any additional fees were taken by the agency. Aleeza elaborated:

> *Aleeza:* We do not know what [Glendale] is paying her [IRI] and what she is paying us. We do not know about that, but she said she is equating the amount of salary for June and July in our previous salaries. And she is not going to pay us for summer.
> *Alyssa:* She is putting it into the other one, into May for example?
> *Aleeza:* She started from January. She distributed it from January through May. Now she never explained how the distribution goes and nobody dared to ask her because we do not want to lose our paychecks. . . . I would like to know about it, but then you know, there are so many other things that we get deducted for, our health insurance and then our taxes. I do not know on what basis are the taxes cut, but you know at least if we have a basic idea. We know that we have to pay tax, but then you know what type of, how are we paying it? We have to know that, right? We do not know anything.

Based on the contract between Glendale and IRI (available through an open records request), if the teachers were correct, then IRI had breached the contract in multiple places. These partial (or minor) breaches and fundamental (or major) breaches contributed to further exploitation.

Partial Breaches. The four teachers provided anecdotes that did not match the contract's promises. In several instances, their anecdotes did not explicitly or directly contradict the contract, but the language of the contract concealed the reality of the teachers' circumstances. For example, the contract read that IRI "certifies that it provides and is responsible for . . . all recruiting and selection expenses."

However, the teachers in this study each paid between $5,000 and $6,500, which they were told paid for their recruitment and selection, including the trips that U.S. administrators took to India to interview them in person. Additionally, the contract maintained that IRI was responsible for "all benefits, including health, life, disability, and workers' compensation." Though I could not verify whether the teachers were covered by life insurance or workers' compensation, they did contribute to their own health and disability insurance. Their short-term disability, unlike that of the American teachers with state benefits, did not include provisions for paid maternity leave, or if it did include these provisions, the teachers were never informed. Aleeza found this out after she gave birth to a premature baby by emergency C-section and her doctor told her to stay out of work for 6 weeks. However, when she attempted to contact Ms. Jain at IRI, she realized that staying out of work was not an option for her:

> I email her [Ms. Jain of IRI] saying when do I need to go back to school, what dates, please let me know are we allowed to take this leave or we don't have this opportunity over there. Please let me know. She gave me [a] one-sentence reply: "It depends on your OB-GYN clearance; if she [your doctor] says yes, then you can go." I was like okay. I spoke to [my doctor] and she was like "You are supposed to stay, take rest for 6 weeks, stay at home." [Then] I emailed [Ms. Jain] saying, "Is this leave going to be unpaid? And if it is, please let me know." She never got back to me. Now what should I think about that? And if it was a yes, then I would lose pay for whole of April and May. . . . That is why I had to come back. I cannot leave my other kids starving . . . so I need to go back because I don't know if she is going to pay me or not because she is not replying.

A third partial breach of contract was IRI's claim that they provided "assistance with procuring a visa." As previously discussed, the teachers were required to pay for their own visa and visa processing, including a 10-hour journey to another city.

Fundamental Breaches. In addition to partial breaches of their contract with Glendale, IRI also explicitly violated several clauses, according to testimony from my participants. These violations, too, made the teachers susceptible to exploitation. The contract guaranteed that teachers would receive: "assistance procuring local transportation . . . an orientation following teacher's arrival . . . additional consultation and staff development, as deemed necessary . . . and a liaison/coordinator to assist in teachers' professional development needs and help resolve problems." For these four teachers, none of these provisions was met. As described previously, the teachers were given no transportation assistance past their first day in the United States, after which they had to procure their own local transportation by hiring drivers or relying on American colleagues. Further, only two of my four participants received an orientation upon arrival. One of the participants arrived with a group of 15 other international teachers, all of whom she said did not receive orientation.

Teachers and principals in this study disputed the fact that IRI provided consultation, staff development, and a coordinator to resolve problems. The principals stated they saw someone from IRI only once per year, if that, and that if problems arose, it was rare for someone to come to school. Mr. Scott stated that someone had come to work with one of his previous employees, but that this person only observed for one week and that he had observed no changes as a result of the intervention. None of the teachers recalled attending staff development with IRI, and even when they said a liaison would have been helpful in communicating with their superiors, Ms. Jain was not available. For example, at her first high school in the United States, Aleeza stated that her assistant principal unfairly evaluated her. Though she repeatedly asked Ms. Jain to assist her in her discussions with the administration, Ms. Jain never replied and never assisted. Finally, Aleeza felt she had to "fight" for herself to ensure that she was not forced to return to India for poor performance; later, upon reflection, she wished she had been able to tell Samina the same thing before Samina left:

> I would have advised her to go on your own and fight for yourself because your employer is not going to do that for you. . . . She is just going to blame you. You did something wrong. . . . [She should be] coming in and saying, "Okay, if you are getting these, you know, needs improvement [marks on an evaluation], here is what I can do to help you." I mean, it does not make sense to wait until the end and say "oh well." . . . So, as an employer what did she do? Nothing, nothing. She never spoke to any principal. She did not speak to anybody. She was just waiting; if they do not give me my contract, I am gone and there is somebody else [from her company] who is going to be in my place. That's all.

At the same time that my participants in Glendale were facing these challenges, other foreign educators around the United States were encountering similar obstacles, thus demonstrating the systemic nature of the international teacher exploitation.

Baltimore, Maryland

Between 2005 and 2009, the Baltimore City School System recruited Filipino educators to fill "the jobs they can't get enough locals to take on" (Coates, 2005, p. 64). By 2012, there were more than 600 Filipino teachers in Baltimore, or nearly 10% of the teaching population. They were brought over on H-1B visas. The teachers paid between $5,000 and $8,000 for placement, while the district paid nothing. Avenida International Consultants (AIC) handled all of the paperwork and arranged recruitment visits for Baltimore officials in Manila.

The Baltimore Sun ran a series of articles on the teachers after they first arrived. Neufeld (2005) presented the personal story of one Filipina teacher, Aileen Mercado, a 34-year-old special education teacher who was hired to teach language arts and mathematics in Baltimore City schools. The author explained that the Baltimore district recruited Filipino teachers in particular because of the country's surplus of qualified candidates and their large English-speaking population. The teachers were assigned jobs in the city's most difficult schools labeled "persistently dangerous." Mercado left a husband and three young daughters in the Philippines and, as part of the program, was living with four other foreign teachers in one apartment. As in Glendale, the Filipino teachers lived in one apartment complex close to the subway because they did not have cars.

Neufeld briefly described the orientation process for Baltimore's international teachers:

> The school system organized a "cultural transition week," during which the teachers learned about different family structures. Watching a video, they learned about families in which both parents are gay—a foreign concept in their Filipino, Roman Catholic, conservative culture. They attended a summer institute open to all 700 new city teachers, and they assisted veteran teachers in summer programs. (p. 4)

Neufeld tracked Mercado and her colleagues as part of a year-long series in *The Baltimore Sun*, including a special report when two Filipino teachers committed suicide within 6 months of each other during the 2006 school year. Mercado later became a founding member of the Filipino Educators in Maryland, a group designed to support Filipino teachers and protect their rights. Since their inception, the organization has had much to do to protect their vulnerable population.

For example, in 2010, one principal of a Baltimore City high school recruited 7 out of 12 Filipino teachers to buy and resell thousands of dollars' worth of Mary Kay products. The principal was an independent sales director for Mary Kay and asked the teachers to pay an initial $100 to get started in sales. The teachers knew that they would have to ask their principals to provide letters of support when it was time for their visas to be renewed, so they participated, though they never intended to use or resell the inventory (Bowie, 2010). After the initial start-up package, their principal continued calling and emailing the teachers to purchase $200 in products to maintain an "active status" as a consultant. Four of the teachers spent between $600 and $1,000. Three teachers, who asked not to be identified in Bowie's exposé for fear of revenge, collectively purchased over $2,000 worth of cosmetics. Though the principal remained at the school during the investigation and until the end of the 2010 school year, she was later removed from her position by the school board.

With the current economic recession showing no signs of abating, Baltimore no longer has a shortage, but a surplus of applicants (E. Green, 2011). According to immigration law, employers must prove that there are not enough qualified U.S. citizens or permanent residents to fill those slots, thus ensuring that U.S. workers are not displaced by foreign workers. By 2011, Baltimore could no longer prove a dearth of qualified U.S. applicants, though officials from the school system contend that Filipino teachers have been integral to the success of students and are important to their communities (E. Green, 2011).

Unfortunately for the longstanding and loyal Filipino employees, the district waited until the last minute to file paperwork to renew visas, and some teachers got anxious and decided to file on their own, which resulted in rejection letters (E. Green, 2011). And even though the district reported putting a lot of energy into renewals and appeals for the 200 teachers who started between 2005 and 2007, the results were minimal. In the summer of 2012, more than 100 teachers' visas expired and were not renewed, thus endangering not only the teachers' futures but the educational trajectories of their children (E. Green, 2011).

Though the city schools CEO said he sympathized with the teachers and their children, the results of a "market test" proved that American teachers could fill the positions. The children, many of whom were academically successful and had plans to attend U.S. colleges, said their lives were thrown into a tailspin when they learned of their parents' fate. According to Green (2011), the Filipino children were faced with "bitter ends and uncertain beginnings," and one young woman with a scholarship to a Baltimore university said, "This whole thing has shown that the American dream can be a lie" (p. 1). It remains to be seen what will happen to the international teachers and their families.

Prince George's County, Maryland

As in Baltimore, Filipino teachers have been recruited in Prince George's (PG) County, Maryland, for nearly a decade. PG County is a diverse district outside Washington, D.C., that serves more than 125,000 students. Originally hired to fill shortages in math, science, and special education, in 2011, more than 1,000 teachers were told that they were no longer welcome in the district. Though a strange turn of events, legislation that was supposed to address exploitation at the hands of for-profit recruiters left the teachers even further from achieving their dreams. After a 2011 U.S. Department of Education ruling that called for reimbursing the teachers for some of their exorbitant fees, many Filipinos actually protested the outcome (Brownback, 2011). That the teachers protested a decision that was designed to help them shows the tenuous nature of at-will foreign employment.

The ruling was the result of a 4-year investigation in which the Department of Labor found that PG County willfully violated the law by illegally requiring international teachers to pay visa processing fees during their recruitment. By law, the school district is supposed to pay for the visa and placement fees. However, the Filipino teachers themselves had been paying these fees. (Note that Glendale teachers were also required to pay their own fees.) While the public school system in PG County was ordered to pay $4.22 million in back wages and a $100,000 penalty to the U.S. Treasury, it was also barred from participating in the H-1B program for 2 years (Brownback, 2011; Van Roeckel, 2011).

After learning of the ruling in April 2011, nearly 100 Filipino teachers held two protests at the U.S. Labor Department, but to no avail. The teachers were angry because, though they would each be compensated approximately $4,000 in back wages, the ban on the visa program in PG County essentially terminated their employment. The Filipino protesters would rather the government place the ban on new visas and that they be permitted to renew existing visas. This would have given them time to work on securing green cards or citizenship. However, the immediate decision disrupted their realities and meant that their families would have to leave what they had known as home (Brownback, 2011; Van Roeckel, 2011).

Many teachers had school-age children who adjusted to their lives and schools in the United States. The teachers' spouses were allowed to work under the H-1B visas, as well. One Filipino teacher, who traveled with colleagues to Arizona to look for other job opportunities, called the ruling and its subsequent fallout "an emotional massacre" (Leitsinger, 2011). If teachers did not find alternative employment, as their visas expired, they would be fired from PG County and would have to go back to their home country, jobless and homeless (Brownback, 2011).

Although the protests did not prevent teachers' visas from expiring, they did open up the space for dialogue about the unfair recruitment practices and treatment of international teachers. Dennis Van Roekel, president of the National Education Association, responded that "we need a set of standards that address the employment needs of school districts while protecting the rights of teachers" (Van Roekel, 2011, n.p.). The victimization of international educators is bound to continue if, as Van Roekel argues, there is no standard or guideline for equitable and ethical recruitment.

Baton Rouge

The powerful effect of union membership is evident in a landmark case in Louisiana, in which a group of Filipino teachers sued their recruitment agency for mistreatment and exploitation. Without the support of the AFT, which they were allowed to join because they were technically employees of Jefferson Parish, East Baton Rouge Parish, and the Recovery School District (which, post–Hurricane Katrina, includes more than 100 schools that were formerly part of New Orleans Public Schools), the Filipino teachers may not have been able to stand up to their recruiter or win their case.

The Louisiana case revolved around infractions by Lulu Navarro, a Filipina woman who operated a recruitment agency in Los Angeles. She charged the teachers $15,000 in fees before they arrived, and then required them to sign new contracts upon arrival that allowed her to take 10–15% of their yearly salary for as long as they were employed in the United States. She threatened the teachers with deportation if they did not sign, withheld their passports and other legal documents, and warned them not to speak to Americans about their situation. They were also forced to live in substandard housing. After years of mistreatment, one Filipino teacher named Ingrid decided to join AFT. She recalled, "When I first signed up for the AFT, she [Ms. Navarro] tried to retract my membership. . . . I said yes so she would leave me alone, but still I kept my membership and I think that was one of the best decisions I ever made" (American Federation of Teachers, 2010). Though Ingrid had approached local and state officials with her grievances, "Only when AFT picked up our case and made formal complaints, it made things turn around" (American Federation of Teachers, 2010). The AFT, working with the state chapter, the Louisiana Federation of Teachers, filed complaints with the Louisiana Workforce Commission and the U.S. Department of Labor.

After the case ended with a victory for the Filipino teachers, they collectively formed the Filipino Educators Federation of Louisiana, modeled after a similar coalition of Filipino teachers in Baltimore. Other Filipino teachers, filmed by the AFT, shared the importance of collective support for their cause: "It makes us a lot stronger because we know someone is there for us, willing to fight for us." Another stated, "You feel the strength that they [the AFT representatives] have, and it transfers to you during that difficult time" (American Federation of Teachers, 2010). Many of the exploitative practices and breaches of contract that existed in Louisiana were carried out by IRI in Glendale, though Louisiana teachers were employees of both the district and the agency and Glendale teachers were solely employees of IRI. Had the Glendale international teachers been able to collectively bargain and seek union counsel, they may have been more successful in their fight for justice.

New York City

Facing a shortage of certified teachers, New York City (NYC) Public Schools began recruiting international teachers in 2001. At the time, 17% of NYC teachers were uncertified, and the state had previously sued the system because of their tendency to place uncertified teachers in high-needs schools ("Judge bars school", 2000). Thus, between 2002 and 2003, the NYC Board of Education launched a major overseas recruiting drive and, under Mayor Michael Bloomberg, went from having 53 international teachers from Austria and Germany to 725. Five hundred of the new teachers were from the Caribbean. By 2005, there were more than 3,300 international teachers in NYC; though they were from all over the world, the majority remained from Caribbean nations. The Board and Department of Education established a Caribbean Recruitment Initiative through the Center for Recruitment and Professional Development.

Caribbean teachers were promised New York State teacher certification, master's degrees, housing assistance, and permanent U.S. residency. More than 10 years later, the teachers have not received much of what they were promised (The Association of International Educators, 2011; Callaci, 2011). According to a group of Caribbean teachers who have spoken out about the injustices they faced, the most grievous are their lack of permanent residency status, legal fees, and related family issues (The Association of International Educators, 2011).

Initially, the Caribbean teachers were issued J-1 visas, similar to the teachers in Glendale. The Department of Education (DOE) gave verbal assurances that they would help teachers with applying for green cards. After 3 years, when the maximum time on their J-1 visas ran out, the teachers switched to H-1B visas and also initiated the application process to receive their green cards. To begin the permanent residency process, the teachers were required pass at least three certification exams, get their master's degrees, receive permission from their home countries to waive the 2-year residency requirement (that would have required them to return to the source nation for 2 years before leaving again under another visa type), and receive a satisfactory evaluation from their school principal each year.

There were, according to the teachers, several roadblocks throughout the process. First, they were required to pay out-of-pocket for their own master's degrees. Next, in order to qualify for the waiver from their home countries, they had to pay off student loan debts and bonds that they had in their home country. Instead of continuing to make monthly payments, some teachers had to pay off their debts in lump sums and had to pay early loan termination fees. Finally, the likelihood of receiving permanent residency status was also compromised by a DOE decision to classify the teachers as EB-3 workers. EB-3 workers are "unskilled," whereas the more appropriate classification would have been EB-2, for professional workers. It is more common for EB-2 workers to be given permanent residency status (The Association of International Educators, 2011).

Understandably, the teachers looked for ways to expedite their labor certification process. The DOE designated legal counsel for them. Curiously, however, the law firm that the DOE assigned to represent the teachers was the same firm that represented the DOE itself. Some teachers had difficulty obtaining copies of their records because they were told by the attorneys that the DOE was their client. From 2004 to 2007, when the DOE paid the law firm nearly $3 million, the Caribbean teachers were also were required to make payments. One teacher reported paying over $8,000 in legal fees (The Association of International Educators, 2011).

The third major concern for Caribbean teachers in NYC is the impact of their residency struggle on their families. Like the Indian teachers in Glendale and the Filipino teachers around the United States, many Caribbean teachers moved to

New York to pursue the "American Dream." However, their spouses are unable to work if they are on a dependent visa or, even if they have their own visas, have found it difficult to secure long-term and stable employment without a green card. Many of the teachers' children cannot get scholarships and "age out" of their dependent visas.

Teachers in NYC tried working with the Black Institute, a nonprofit organization devoted to impacting public policy related to people of color, and the United Federation of Teachers (UFT) to remedy the injustices faced during their 10 years in the United States. This collaboration has benefitted the teachers in small but important ways. For example, the process to begin permanent residency used to, in addition to all of the requirements listed above, include a principal recommendation requirement, in which a teacher's individual supervisor had to approve the green card application. This assessment was too subjective, and according to the Association of International Educators (2011), it was beyond the scope of the principal's control to determine whether or not a teacher could stay in the country. With UFT's help, that requirement has since been eliminated. Although many Caribbean teachers are members of UFT, their immigration status prevents them from having the full representation accorded to union members. The Black Institute and the UFT have challenged the labor unions in the Caribbean to get involved (Ashby, 2011).

Even with the support of these organizers, the Caribbean teachers remain in flux. From 2005 to 2010, only 20% of all international teachers in NYC schools were given permanent residency status. Out of the 641 that received green cards, only 276 were Caribbean teachers (The Association of International Educators, 2011).

Attacking and Controlling Teachers and the Profession

As do other reforms that fit squarely into the neoliberal agenda, international teacher recruitment undercuts the teaching profession and how teachers are prepared. It is the latest in a long line of alternative recruitment measures that portray teaching as an easy career that does not require any special training for U.S. educational contexts. Neoliberal policymakers and advocates champion alternative recruitment strategies because they believe that traditional teacher education programs are full of "burdensome" requirements.

Though such programs continue to bring underprepared teachers into urban classrooms, neoliberal reformers are primarily concerned that teacher candidates have a choice about if and how to be trained. They distrust traditional programs, which they say focus too much on pedagogy, because to them, the more important criterion for teachers is to be knowledgeable in their content areas (Cochran-Smith & Fries, 2001; Compton & Weiner, 2008). They argue that teachers' academic proficiency, especially in math and science, would secure the United States' position in the global market, using what Kumashiro (2008) calls conservative frames that serve as "the seduction of common sense." That is, instead of educational policy being framed through a lens of social justice, it is framed through a lens of fear that the United States is falling further behind other nations. Alternative programs that bring teachers into classrooms at a more rapid rate and that recruit from elite universities are touted as rational, commonsense solutions to these pressing issues. For example, during his tenure as Secretary of Education under President George W. Bush, Rodney Paige championed the development of alternative programs. In his 2002 report on teacher quality, Paige advocated a dismantling of certification systems that imposed "burdensome requirements" instead of focusing on high verbal ability and content knowledge, the two skills Paige viewed as most important for teacher success (pp. 8–14). In a later report, Paige stated that one of the main reasons for his push was because the "teacher shortage [was] experienced in many locations" where eased requirements could have ushered more teachers into the classroom (Paige, Rees, Petrilli, & Gore, 2004, p. 2). Paige explained that "many wonderful candidates with families and mortgages will have no choice but to say no" to teaching as a profession if they were required to undergo traditional preparation (p. v), and alternative programs held the promise of bringing "thousands of talented soldiers of democracy into our schools" (p. vi).

In addition to undercutting efforts to prepare effective teachers through teacher education programs, international teacher recruitment also weakened education reforms devoted to finding a long-term solution to teacher turnover in urban schools. Instead of focusing on the larger question of why teachers are dissatisfied with and disenchanted by urban schools, recruitment agencies allowed districts to take the easy way out. They supplied them with teachers on demand, who were willing to work in substandard conditions for little pay and few benefits. According to Ms. Dougherty of the AFT,

> I see it as an attack on the profession. It furthers the idea that anybody can teach and shows people are not committed to finding a long-term workforce. A lot of it is pragmatism. Where else could you find people willing to pay thousands of dollars to work in a persistently dangerous Baltimore school? What district wouldn't want that?

Continued recruitment of international teachers and other alternatively recruited educators can, thanks to their seemingly never-ending availability and relatively cheap labor, be used as a pawn in policymakers' attempts to destroy the job security and bargaining power of all teachers.

Controlling Teachers' Knowledge

In addition to using international teachers as a way to control the profession, various stakeholders also use tactics that controlled the teachers themselves. Many of the recruiting agencies willfully misled international teachers about U.S. teaching environments. IRI never informed the teachers of the type of school or exact location of their employment before the teachers arrived in the United States, at which point it was too late to effectively prepare them for urban schools and students. The orientations from the agency and the district were so general that teachers remained uninformed and underprepared until their first day and beyond. The result was that teachers did not know what they did not know. Though these examples may seem like only carelessness on the part of the employers, they are also examples of stakeholders making conscious choices to leave the teachers uninformed and control what they learned and when. Further, because teachers were private employees, it was especially difficult for them to unionize. As a result, they were dependent on their employers like IRI.

As previously discussed, only two Indian teachers attended orientation with IRI, and only three with Glendale. The teachers' orientations, when offered, were too brief and too focused on logistics to make a difference in their adjustment to U.S. student culture or to enable them to improve their instructional practices. Though she arrived with plenty of time before school began, Aleeza did not receive an orientation from the agency. She recalled:

> *Aleeza:* They told us we were going to have one [an orientation].
>   But I do not know why we did have not that. . . . We came in
>   two batches [of teachers]. So I guess the first batch had the
>   orientation, and we did not have a chance to have orientation.
> *Alyssa:* So how much time separated this first batch
>   from the second batch? A year?
> *Aleeza:* [Laughing.] No, it was like 15 days.

The Glendale orientation, held in conjunction with the regularly scheduled pre-planning for American teachers, did not substantially differ from a traditional new teacher orientation for American teachers and, as with IRI, concentrated by and large on rules and regulations. For example, with other American teachers, the teachers in this study who received a Glendale orientation learned about sexual harassment policies, special education interventions, payroll procedures, grading policies, and the current teacher evaluation system. Aleeza framed her brief orientation through Glendale as a list of what *not* to do: Do not lecture; do not touch a student; do not "handle a student and tell them that they cannot do that; you need to report it to somebody." Others who attended did not remember anything outstanding.

Although these facts were important for ensuring that international teachers were aware of school, district, and state policies, the orientation did not help teachers understand anything new about their students or the best ways to teach them. As one international teacher, previously employed by Visiting International

Faculty (VIF), explained, "International teachers were misinformed or under-informed about . . . the socio-cultural-racial-historical state of education in the United States" (Solano-Campos, 2010). Orientations that focused on the sociocultural context would have more adequately prepared the teachers for the challenges they would face teaching in urban schools. The need to improve orientation procedures will be discussed in more detail in the conclusion.

Controlling Teachers' Employment Rights

One of the ways that international teachers would have been able to advocate for better preparation and support was through participation in a union. However, in the case of these Glendale teachers, they were told that union membership was impossible. As I was reminded multiple times by Glendale administrators when I asked how they could help my participants receive equitable treatment, the administrators said the teachers are technically not employed by Glendale. They are employees of IRI, a private company, and as such, are not eligible to participate in a union for public school employees. Many of the conditions that a union would find deplorable, the district appeared willing to condone because the teachers were their subcontractors, not their employees. It should be noted that, while there are local and state unions that represent American teachers in Glendale, because the district is located in a "right to work" state, the union has effectively no negotiating power. It is a vicious cycle, as few teachers join because they know the union has no power, but the union continues to have no power because so few teachers join. Yet, even if the Glendale teachers had been allowed to join the union, the benefits that came with union membership would not be afforded to them and their participation would have been mainly symbolic. The difference between Glendale and places like Baltimore and New York City is that the teachers in those cities were considered public employees and not subcontractors. Thus, they were able to benefit from legal counsel and collective bargaining (though, as we saw, their participation was still wrought with conflict), whereas the Glendale teachers would have had only "symbolic" membership, according to Ms. Dougherty of the American Federation of Teachers, and would not have been able to take advantage of the majority of services.

As in the Louisiana case explained above, the international teachers in Glendale were dependent on their employers to such an extent that it made it possible for IRI to take advantage of them. In Louisiana, the teachers feared retaliation if they told anyone about their circumstances. Aleeza stated that IRI teachers, too, feared termination and deportation if they did not follow Ms. Jain's rules. One of the key arguments in the Louisiana Federation of Teachers (LFT) case, which confirmed that the Filipino teachers were forced into dependency on their employers, was that the contract language that stipulated the terms of teacher termination was unjust. The Glendale contract, obtained through an open records request, contains the same stipulation. Glendale may demand removal of a teacher (1) with cause, immediately; or (2) without cause, with 30 school days' notice. IRI may terminate a teacher immediately, with cause, if "that teacher's continued employment could harm [IRI's] reputation or economy." Further, the contract gave IRI the right to "terminate a Teacher's exchange visa at any time for any reason, with or without notice." If no cause was necessary for termination, any international teacher could, feasibly, have even been terminated for speaking with me. Mr. McNeil, the AFT lawyer responsible for the Filipino teachers' victory in Louisiana, noted that such a clause, while not expressly forbidding union membership, rendered union membership merely symbolic and the teachers more vulnerable as at-will employees.

Unfortunately for the Glendale teachers, there was also a contract provision that prevented them from seeking alternative employment. Had they, for example, wanted to leave IRI's employ because of their mistreatment, but wanted to stay in their original positions in Glendale, the county itself risked breaching the contract. As such, they would not take the risk of employing an international teacher who had previously worked with IRI. The contract read, "At any time while this Agreement is in effect, [Glendale] shall not retain the services of any Teacher unless it is through [IRI]. Should a teacher seek to circumvent the provisions herein without [IRI's] permission, [Glendale] shall notify [IRI] in writing immediately." The purpose of creating dependent employees, to sustain IRI's profit and their dominance over the supply of international teachers to the county, virtually guaranteed that the teachers themselves would have no voice in their recruitment, preparation, or professional development. Such a categorization of teachers as subcontractors was convenient and beneficial for the district, as well. Should the teachers ever complain about their treatment or should anyone uncover any violations of contract, as I discuss here, district personnel would have plausible deniability because the teachers are not technically their employees.

Teachers as Human Capital

In today's business world, human capital has come to mean understanding and valuing individuals' knowledge and skills. If companies hire "human capital managers" or invest in "human capital resources," they are said to be investing in the future. While I appreciate the focus on individuals, human capital theory still unquestioningly relies on the market. One is only valuable if the market deems one to be so, and one is only worth as much as one's skills are worth at a particular point in time. The guise of viewing people as capital for their own benefit is a convenient, strategic, and rhetorical distortion of human commodification. As international teachers and their skills are traded across borders, they, too, are treated as human capital. Host and source countries are then left to deal with either outsourcing or the brain drain.

Outsourcing. One of the consequences of globalization and free trade policies is the outsourcing of American jobs to other countries; in many cases, companies pay workers less than they would pay American workers to perform the same tasks, thus decreasing their expenses. "The recruitment agencies are using Tata [an Indian-based multinational company] as a model, where Indian tech workers come to the U.S.," explained Ms. Dougherty of AFT. "It is now an industry standard to save money through privatization and outsourcing." Indeed, Tata Technology had offices in 12 countries, including India, Singapore, Thailand, and Mexico, where skilled workers were often trained for work in the United States, and prided themselves on "operat[ing] where our customers need us to be, leveraging our global resources to maximize product value" (Tata Technologies, 2010). Ms. Jain explained in her interview with me that she, too, wished that IRI was able to branch out to more countries and "transcend borders."

Some opponents of international teacher recruitment use the "outsourcing" argument to justify their opposition. For example, the one school board member who voted against reapproving IRI's contract in the Glendale district for the 2010–2011 school year did so because she wanted to "care for our own before we start going to the outside" (Local newspaper article, July 12, 2010). The president of the local chapter of the National Education Association (NEA), a teachers' union similar to the AFT, concurred that it was a "slap in the face to the tens of thousands, if not hundreds of thousands, of teachers all over this country that have been laid off" (Local newspaper article, July 12, 2010). A concern for international teachers is that, if Americans see them as "taking" their jobs, the Americans will not look any further into their working conditions or care about what happens to them once they are in the United States. Thus, the outsourcing consequence is included here not to justify or assume agreement with the position that international workers "take" American jobs but to insist that *all* workers in the United States, whether they are American or not, deserve to be treated equitably and supported in their careers.

Brain Drain. Perhaps the most hidden consequence of international teacher recruitment is the impact that recruitment has on source countries, or the nations supplying the teachers. Colloquially, this loss of human capital is known as the brain drain. The brain drain occurs with the migration of educated doctors, engineers, and technology professionals; more recently, the trend extended to nursing professionals as well. In fact, in 2009, one in three nurses in the United States was international-born (AFT, 2009). This was a very real problem in the countries from which foreign teachers hail.

Most commonly, source countries are developing countries like the Philippines, where shortages in educated employees already exist. AFT (2009) reported that, during the last 10 years when Filipino teachers have been heavily recruited for U.S. positions, there was a 16,000-person teacher shortage in the Philippines.

A presentation given at the 16th annual conference for Commonwealth Education Ministers in Australia provided additional insight into the disturbing global effects of international teacher recruitment, especially the brain drain:

1. To achieve UNESCO's Education for All (EFA) initiative by 2015, there will be an estimated 18 million new teachers for primary and secondary schools needed around the world.
2. In a recent survey, 50% of Organisation of Economic Co-operation and Development OECD countries stated they were seriously concerned about attracting and retaining high-quality teachers, especially in high-demand subject areas.
3. In developing countries, such as the Philippines and Barbados, college graduates are six times more likely to emigrate than those with only a secondary education.
4. National and international improvements need to be made in order to learn the extent and impact of teacher mobility on source countries, as there is currently no systematic way to track teacher migration patterns. (Ratterree, 2006)

As residents of a developing country, Indians were acutely aware of the impact of teacher migration, and highly skilled migration in general. In 2003, Thomas noted,

> Though the union ministry of human resource development is typically unconcerned, a tremor of apprehension is beginning to run through the boards and councils of management of India's . . . schools that a mass migration of the best and brightest teachers from these schools in particular may well be in the offing. (p. 1)

By 2006, educational scholars like Paliwal argued that India's government and schools must act to combat international teacher recruitment: "Globalization and commercialization of education is becoming a reality and India being a prominent figure, in so far as the concern of human resources is concerned, cannot afford to ignore these changes" (p. 66). The teachers agreed that there existed a certain expectation that the best and brightest in India, whether they be engineers or teachers, would at some point work abroad. The trend, Shrusty stated, was growing in the education sector as it had in technology earlier.

More personally, the migration of teachers meant they had to choose between raising their own children and providing for them, even if temporarily. Filmmaker Ramona Diaz, while filming Filipino teachers in Baltimore, remarked:

> In a modern-day story of immigration and globalization, these young professionals are coming West in pursuit of economic advantages. . . . The irony is inescapable. The Filipino teachers—90 percent of them women—are leaving their own children

to the care and education of others in order to take jobs teaching inner-city children in schools abandoned by many of their American-born colleagues in favor of districts with better resources in the suburbs. (Quoted in Nepales, 2006, n.p.)

Indian teachers also had to leave their families in order to seek employment in the United States. Though Shrusty and Aleeza were eventually able to bring their families with them, Samina did not get that opportunity.

CHALLENGING THE SPECTACLE

The question remains: If international recruitment is, in fact, about finding the best teachers, or even about preparing students for the global marketplace, why is it that only urban districts are taking advantage of this opportunity? If teachers who are intelligent can teach any student anywhere as well as those teachers with pedagogical preparation, why do wealthy suburban schools not employ hordes of international teachers? Why are international teachers only in Washington, D.C., and not Alexandria, Virginia; in downtown Chicago and not Hyde Park; and in New York City and not Long Island? The reality is that the hidden purposes are equally as alluring for urban districts as are the stated goals, and suburban districts do not need to cut expenses and fill positions that no one will take because suburban districts are better-funded and positions are in high demand. Further, suburban parents and students have the social and cultural capital to ensure that their teachers are the most effective and can relate to their students.

The political spectacle of recruitment ignores the often negative consequences on teachers and students. This research adds to the theory of political spectacle by demonstrating the concrete effects of symbolic language and its other tenets on all the actors in the recruitment process. If teachers are exploited, and in many cases live in fear, they cannot educate students as well as can teachers who are treated well and who receive proper preparation, benefits, and support. "Just like we know that kids can't learn when they are hungry, teachers are only effective educators if they are being treated well," summarized Ms. Dougherty of the AFT. "If they are not being threatened, not always worrying about visa status or contracts and fees. All this worry and anxiety affects the quality of services they can provide." The AFT asserts that the public should be made aware of the employment conditions of international teachers and should aid them in fighting for equality of employment, in order to provide the best education for their children:

All teachers working within one school system should have the same requirements for certification, the same performance expectations, the same benefits and the same employer. These are fundamental union principles and should also be fundamental public expectations. (American Federation of Teachers, 2009, p. 19)

SIX

Charting a Course

The Future of International Teacher Recruitment

Good intentions may do as much harm as malevolence if they lack understanding.
—Albert Camus, 1942

Our lives begin to end the day we become silent about things that matter.
—Martin Luther King, Jr.

The teachers' last few months in the United States were wrought with stress and turmoil. For a variety of reasons, they did not want to leave and return to India. Thus, in March, Shrusty, Faria, and Aleeza—who were at the end of their 3-year visa allowance—applied for visa extensions. This would have allowed them to stay in Glendale schools and work for an additional 1 to 3 years. Ms. Jain told them she would apply for extensions on their behalf. However, Ms. Jain said that she never encouraged her teachers to apply for extensions and always told them "from the beginning that it is not possible." By the beginning of May, the teachers had not heard whether their extensions were approved, though they still had to finish the school year, sell their home furnishings, and buy plane tickets if necessary. Finally, on May 17, the teachers received an email from Ms. Jain, stating that their extensions had not been approved and they all needed to return to India by the end of May, a mere 2 weeks' notice to pack up their lives and families. The delay in response prompted some of the teachers to state that they did not believe Ms. Jain had ever truly applied for their extensions at all. Instead, they suspected she preferred that they return home, so she could hire new international teachers in their place, thus procuring more finders' fees from Glendale and more placement fees from her teachers. Remarkably, the teachers' friends who decided to apply for a visa waiver by applying to other school districts directly, which did not require employer approval, were granted waivers and were allowed to remain in the country. Thus, according to one teacher, "Those of us who stayed with [IRI] are all leaving now; but those who said 'no, we are doing this ourselves because we don't trust you,' they get to stay. So our loyalty to our employer did not get us anything but kicked out of [the] USA."

During what she thought was her last week in the United States, Shrusty's coworkers threw her a "retirement" party, complete with cake, pizza, a gold charm bracelet with the school mascot, and American flag balloons. She took photographs with her special education students, and those who could speak said, "Good-bye, Ms. Shrusty. We love you." She invited everyone to her apartment and prepared an Indian feast. "Everybody cried," she remembered, a bittersweet note in her voice. "Even Mr. Woods! And like, Ms. H., she is my American mom, you know, she is so approachable and she helps with everything. She can't even look at me anymore, because when she looks at me, she cries." Shrusty carried a handheld video camera with her, recording messages from her coworkers and friends, and even me. "I want to show this to my dad," she said, "to show him everything I have accomplished here. And I will keep it forever to show my American experience. This is more important to me than money; this is everything."

Meanwhile, with 2 days of school left, Faria finished accepting the last of her students' late assignments and entered their grades into the computerized system. "They always wait to the last minute," she remarked as she collected the papers. "But what can I do? It is better to have something late than nothing at all." She said that she would describe her American experience as "a challenging, good experience." Contrary to what Shrusty said, Faria did not believe that much had changed as a result of her experience. "Nothing has really changed," she said. "I [have] been teaching the same way the whole time." As she was summoned to the library for a teachers' meeting that was going to honor her and other departing teachers, she recalled the struggle to get her visa extended. Though she was very excited to see her family, she wished the extensions had worked out. She stated emphatically that she would love to come back to the United States as a teacher again, but hopefully not through the same agency because "things are not getting better; they are getting worse every year with [IRI]."

Aleeza's last week was filled with uncertainty and frustration. She had spent most of her time over the past several months trying to get her family's visas extended. They needed to remain in the country at least until her new baby was released from the hospital and was healthy enough to travel. She was most worried about her children:

My kids at home, they can make out that something is wrong and something is going on. . . . Because whatever the condition is, I never stopped cooking dinner, I always cook dinner for them. . . . When I am not cooking dinner, they know that something is majorly wrong and I am like, "See, I have to figure out how we can stay with [the new baby] here, my little one. . . . We need to figure out something, that is why I am not working, my mind is not working." They are like, "Mummy, we are praying."

Ms. Jain of IRI was no help in Aleeza's special situation. Aleeza argued that Ms. Jain was "mentally harassing" her by not responding to emails and phone calls, and that Ms. Jain may even have "sabotaged" the group of teachers who wanted to stay by lying about submitting their information for visa extensions. Some information, such as a passport number, was needed to apply for the extensions, which Aleeza found out when she called the immigration office herself; according to Aleeza, Ms. Jain did not have this information. Though Aleeza was fully aware that her program was for only 3 years, she insisted that her extenuating personal circumstances should have made Ms. Jain more receptive to providing individual attention and care, stating:

> I was prepared, like you know okay, we signed a contract for 3 years. . . . That's why I was trying other options, Australia, New Zealand, but now this situation. I didn't know that my baby was going to be premature and what we are getting here. I need her to survive for me. So I don't know how people can be so insane. She [Ms. Jain] is just trying to be like you know "Okay, you already knew this." Yes, I already knew this and I was preparing to get out. I had prepared my kids, you know like, after 3 years we need to go back to our country. But now here I come, I have a premature baby. I don't know what kind of facilities I have in India.

Unbeknownst to Shrusty, Faria, and Aleeza, their return to India would only be temporary. Shrusty sold her car, and all three teachers sold their furniture and other belongings. They purchased one-way return tickets to Hyderabad and left the United States at the end of May. Aleeza stayed illegally in the United States slightly longer until her daughter was well enough to leave the hospital and travel. Then unexpectedly, 2 months later, in July, Ms. Jain negotiated 1-year visa extensions. Shrusty, Faria, and Aleeza were given the choice of returning to the United States, purchasing airline fare for themselves and their families, buying new transportation and belongings, and paying more exorbitant fees in order to assume their former teaching positions. Despite previous statements that they did not want to continue working for Ms. Jain, the opportunity was too great for them to pass up, and all three returned to the United States. They should not have had to choose between their personal and professional happiness and their dreams for their children, but that is exactly what they did. When I found out that they were returning, I, like the teachers themselves, felt mixed emotions. They were returning to a broken system, further endangering their livelihoods and, though they were getting progressively more comfortable in their U.S. schools, they were still not culturally competent enough for me to feel comfortable with entrusting hundreds of children to their care.

And then there was the case of Samina, the middle school language arts teacher, who left earlier than expected. With 20 days remaining in the school year, Ms. Jain from IRI advised her to leave because, Samina said, "the year is almost over and it would be better for me to leave now instead of waiting to the end and not getting renewed." Samina did not know why her employer advised this, and Ms. Jain denied ever recommending that a teacher leave in the middle of the year. But other teachers suspected it was because Ms. Jain realized that, if Samina waited until the end of the year, the school would open her position for an American teacher. However, because of her early departure, Ms. Jain sent another international teacher in her place to complete the school year, perhaps in the hope that the new teacher would be rehired for the following school year, thus keeping IRI from losing money. In a startling example of valuing profit over personal support, IRI, as her employer, made a number of decisions that prevented Samina from lasting through her first year and into her second. This included not providing her with an orientation, not providing continuous professional development, and not acting as her advocate in asking the school administration to provide more support for her at the school level on a daily basis. Ms. Jain maintained that her agency provided all of these things for all of their teachers all of the time.

Samina's views about staying wavered based on what she was told by IRI. For example, in the middle of the spring semester, Samina was feeling slightly discouraged but still maintained her desire to return the following school year:

Samina: [I will come back] definitely, if I am given a chance. I would like to prove myself as a good teacher, internationally maybe, because I do not want to be called as a teacher who was not able to control her class. "She ran away."

Alyssa: So you would like to prove yourself to the administration?

Samina: To the administration, and to myself, too. That is more important than the administration. When I look in the mirror, "Oh, what did you do in America? You came out? You couldn't finish it? You couldn't control the classroom? You couldn't change yourself? You couldn't learn anything?" Even this is a learning process.

Yet, during an interview 3 weeks later, Samina indicated that she was more uncertain about her future than before. She said that student behavior was "getting worse" and that she did not know if she could handle another year. "I get excited to think about going into an Indian classroom again, and all the students saying, 'good morning' and being respectful," she mused. "But I am proud of myself that I made it this year. That I came back every day, that is good for me." However, only 1 week later, after speaking with IRI again, she decided to return to India before the end of the school year. Given her tenuous situation, it was clear that more support was necessary from the outset, especially if the true purpose of recruitment was to improve teacher retention.

Thus, on what should have been her last week in the United States, Samina was already back in Hyderabad. Though her departure had been abrupt and filled with secrecy, she let me know by email that she was pleased to be home: "I am doing good. My family is really happy to have me back. For now, I am relaxing at home and having loads of fun."

After I knew the fate of the teachers, it was time to make a decision about my own part in the research. What was I going to "do" with all I had learned? Several people who read my work suggested that it was "part research, part exposé" and that I should go to the media. Especially in the Glendale district, it often seems as if injustices are never discussed or rectified unless the media exposes them first. Yet the Indian teachers in Glendale, like the teachers in other communities around the United States, live in constant fear that they will do something (or nothing) that could warrant deportation. I did not believe I could take the chance that, even if I offered anonymous "tips" to the media and did not reveal my particular participants, it would get back to my teachers and hurt them or their peers in some way.

Instead, I decided to meet with the administrators at the central office in Glendale. I made an appointment to meet with Ms. Muller, Ms. Jefferson, and their boss, the director of human resources for the entire district. I prepared a summary of my findings related to the teachers' preparation, pedagogy, and professional development. Of particular importance, I believed, were the findings about how the teachers were exploited by the recruitment agency. I was excited about the meeting; after all, this was the way my research was going to "matter." The district would finally see what was happening and do something to resolve the problem. I assumed that they could not have known about what was happening because, if they had, the injustices would have been addressed already. Below is my researcher's memo from the day of the meeting. I wanted to include it in its entirety to show the way the district responded to my research and why, in part, this book is so important to me.

> I am sitting in my car in the parking lot of the central office in [Glendale.] I am too shaken to drive home, so I am sitting here writing instead. I am still physically shaking which is why this handwriting is so messy. I am still in shock about what just happened in there. . . . I went into the office, the posh suites with mounted televisions and plush chairs, only several miles from the schools that don't even have a rolling television cart and whose chairs are falling apart. I waited for 20 minutes before [Ms. Muller] came out to get me. I greeted her, and her first words were, "So how long do you think this is going to take?" I stammered as we walked down the hall, through the locked door to the Human Resources suite of offices. "Well, I have a lot to share with you, so how long do you have? I understood that we would have an hour for our discussion." She shook her head as she led me into a small windowless conference room. "We have about 10 minutes." No explanation of where my other 50 minutes had gone, though I suspect 20 of them were the minutes I spent waiting in the reception area. After a moment, [Ms. Jefferson] entered the room, shook my hand, and sat down. I was waiting for

[the director] to come in, so I didn't say anything, but then they raised their eyebrows like they were waiting for me to start. I asked if he was coming and they said, "No, he's not available today." I asked if we should reschedule because now, not only did we not have very much time, but I also thought it was important that he hear what I found. "We'll tell him," they said. They were smiling. Okay, I could do this. Smiles were a good sign.

I explained the context of my research one more time and thanked them both for participating. I reminded them that I had done interviews and observations of the teachers and talked with their principals, too. I decided that, since we had only 10 minutes, I would run very briefly through the pedagogy portion. After all, they had access to the teachers' evaluations and had already indicated in our interviews that they knew about some of the teachers' challenges with classroom management and instruction. After just a couple of minutes, I went on to tell them about the way the teachers were treated by [Ms. Jain and IRI]. I told them about the fees, the lack of orientations, etc. They did not react at all until one of them said (I can't even remember who now), "So how many teachers did you interview?" I told them four teachers and four principals. "Oh, only four? Well that's not very many. How do you know this happened to other people?" I paused, confused. Surely, they were not telling me that I did not have enough evidence because I "only" had stories of injustice from four people. Gathering my thoughts, I explained, again, the case study approach and how I trusted the teachers' testimonies that what happened to them was happening to the other teachers in the district as well. Without stopping for a breath (my 10 minutes were speeding away!), I tried to tell them about the pay issues, how the checks were not itemized, how the teachers got paid later than everyone else and didn't know what was happening to their money. I couldn't figure out why they weren't taking notes for [the director]. I tried to tell them about [Aleeza] and her premature baby and what happened with the visas. At this point, [Ms. Jefferson] put up her hand, literally put her hand in my face in a "talk to the hand" kind of moment, and said, "We're just going to stop you right there, Ms. Dunn. This is not our problem. They are not our employees."

At that moment, I believed that my hopes for my research mattering, at least to the people in Glendale, were naïve and unrealistic. I didn't know whether to laugh or cry. (Thankfully, I didn't do either.) Instead, I said, "But they are your employees. Technically yes, they are subcontracted through [IRI], but they still work in your schools. They work in classrooms next to American teachers, they teach [Glendale] kids." She shook her head and started shifting in her seat. "It doesn't matter. We don't have control over them." I looked to [Ms. Muller]; for what, I'm not sure. Help, maybe? She didn't say a word. "I understand the technicality," I persisted. "But they are teaching your children. This is where I live. If I had children, they would go to these schools. I don't want my children or any children I care about to be taught by someone who isn't supported and who lives in fear. I don't want any teacher that I know to be exploited." I was trying very hard to remain calm and rational. I never raise my voice, but this was difficult. They both shook their heads. There was nothing they could do, they insisted, and our time was up anyway. I said that I was hopeful we could continue the conversation and that I would send something by email to them and [the director]. "Not necessary," I was told. "We don't need anything in writing." I was ushered out. It had been only 7 minutes.

So, here I am in the car, angrier than I have been in a very long time. I am astonished at their refusal to acknowledge this as their problem. Even as I write, I am trying diligently to think about both sides—what would have made them so resistant to hearing what I had to say? Were they just saying it wasn't their problem because that is the party line, or do they really, honestly believe that? And why wasn't [the director] there even though he just confirmed yesterday? I hope it wasn't because they suspected what I was going to say and he didn't want to hear it. Maybe I'm being too cynical. But what was that about not wanting anything in writing?! I am still going to email the summary to them and see if there are others I can copy on it, too. Maybe someone will care. There has to be someone.

Of all the days I have spent researching and working with international teachers, that was one of the most difficult. I never did hear back from the district officials after I sent them the summary of my findings and my recommendations for future recruitment and support. Although the administrators in Glendale did not want to hear my findings, I realized that this is a story that all educators need to hear and understand. Maybe if enough people—teachers, students, parents, educational advocates, teacher educators, and more—recognize the injustice and speak up about it, then these administrators and others like them would have to listen. I hope that other voices will join with mine and with the teachers themselves to make their stories heard.

In addition to calling for action, in this chapter, I also offer suggestions for how districts, including Glendale, can do better to recruit, prepare, and support all teachers. Even if my teachers' inadequate cultural preparation, exploitative hiring practices, and difficulty connecting with students were limited to four teachers (and I do not believe they are), that is four teachers and nearly 300 students too many. Because research alone cannot solve the numerous problems faced by international teachers, school district stakeholders, researchers, teacher educators, and policymakers must take steps to improve their recruitment, preparation, and pedagogy.

IMPLICATIONS FOR PRACTICE: WHY SCHOOLS AND DISTRICTS SHOULD SUPPORT INTERNATIONAL TEACHERS

One group of stakeholders who can help chart a course for more successful and equitable international recruitment is administrators at the school, district, and state levels. As I have argued throughout the book, there are multiple pressures that international educators face, but the most immediate pressures are those they experience every day in their classrooms. They are presumed to understand U.S. schools simply because they have been teachers in another context; they are presumed to be highly qualified simply because they have advanced degrees in their content area; and they are presumed to be culturally relevant simply because they are from another culture. Whether or not these assumptions are sometimes true for individual teachers, at a systematic level, basing staffing choices and professional development on anecdotal evidence, exceptionalities, and stereotypes results in overwhelmed teachers and even more students being left behind.

Support for international teachers can take many forms. Any intervention should consider the multiple ways that international teachers learn about their new contexts—from media, friends, peers, and students—and build upon these resources to enhance teachers' funds of knowledge (Moll et al., 1992). In particular, districts and schools can better use their human and fiscal resources to use agencies selectively, improve orientations, execute summer institutes, nurture possibilities for cultural ambassadorships, establish cross-country partnerships and communication, and improve existing professional development and mentoring.

Selective Use of Agencies

It is the responsibility of each district that contracts recruitment agencies to ensure that these agencies are legitimate and honest in their hiring practices. The exploitation in Louisiana and the questionable practices in Glendale could most likely have been avoided if district officials had been more attentive to the practices of the agencies and the needs of their teachers. Whether or not a recruitment protocol is developed, districts should selectively choose and monitor agencies that commit to adequate preparation and support.

Until a policy is established, however, districts need to select agencies that allow teachers to be employees of the school systems, not the private employer. If international teachers are public employees, they will be afforded all of the rights and benefits that American teachers are afforded, including insurance, professional development, and the right to join a union. Employees who are treated well and are not living in a constant state of fear that they will be sent home for no reason will be better teachers. Though this means that districts themselves will have to be more accountable for their international employees and those of their contractors than they currently are, it is vital that, if recruitment continues, they undertake this task in order to prove they truly care about the teachers and the students in their system. Ensuring safety and success is more important than a guarantee of plausible deniability.

Orientation Improvements

If anyone asked international teachers for their suggestions, they would provide an extensive and detailed plan for how to better orient and prepare foreign educators before and upon arrival. Glendale teachers had several suggestions. All suggested that orientation begin before teachers depart from their homes. This orientation would be conducted by the agency's contacts in the source countries, but district personnel would play a key role in ensuring that appropriate topics are covered in detail. For example, all of the teachers said that learning about classroom management was important because they had no classroom management problems in India.

The idea of using videos was mentioned by all four participants, who stated that orientations, in addition to being too short, were not "realistic" because they did not show the true picture of U.S. urban classrooms. One potential solution is that, if the technology is available, teachers in other countries can also use real-time video technology, like Skype, to "look in" on real American classrooms as teachers are instructing their classes. They can virtually observe both international and American teachers in their content areas; even if their exact placements were not yet determined, showing them a video of a school with a similar student population would be an improvement over the current methods of orientation. Such videos, either in real time or recorded for later viewing, would provoke important discussions about pedagogy, content, and classroom management.

In addition to videos, a group of "alumni" international teachers and American teachers should also speak to the group before they depart. Shrusty emphasized that an orientation would best be conducted by an Indian teacher like herself who had experience in American schools, while a district official, Ms. Jefferson, argued that an American teacher would best be able to prepare a new group before their departure. Above all, a pre-departure orientation should be extensive and honest. It cannot be done in one afternoon, and it cannot concentrate solely on making travel arrangements, as it did for the teachers discussed here. A good model for the pre-departure and onsite orientation would be the cultural training offered by the Peace Corps, especially their detailed *Culture Matters: The Peace Corps Cross-Cultural Workbook* (Peace Corps, 2010).

The same detail and honesty is necessary for the orientations once the teachers have arrived in the United States. In Glendale, teachers were supposed to receive 1 day of orientation with IRI (though, as previously discussed, two of my four participants did not have such an orientation), plus a new teacher orientation with Glendale. Glendale administrators acknowledged that such brevity was not useful for international teachers. Mr. Scott and Ms. Jefferson offered suggestions for a new international teacher orientation:

> *Mr. Scott:* I would talk a lot about behavior, in terms of how to respond to different types of off-task behavior. I would talk a lot about how to motivate the unmotivated, . . . about differentiated instruction, how to get across concepts to kids who are below the grade level, below their reading level, or deficient in their math skills. I would do a lot of talking about how to deal with that. But then just kind of talk about what is acceptable in our culture, in Black culture or teenage culture, if there is such a thing, what is acceptable, what to expect.
>
> *Ms. Jefferson:* I would stress basically the instructional curriculums and how they are set up here. . . . I would make sure that they are aware of all of the strands and standards for their particular areas, whatever they are going to be teaching, for instructional purposes. And then I would do a very extensive training program on classroom management, expectations, discipline plans, and again the culture of the American classroom versus others.

Both suggestions highlight instructional strategies and classroom management. However, I would caution against framing the sessions using the language that Mr. Scott employs. I believe that approaching the orientation with a deficit perspective—using language like he does of "off-task," "unmotivated," "below," and "deficient"—would prejudice the teachers and lower their expectations before they have even met any American students. Mr. Scott and Ms. Jefferson also emphasize the need to "talk" about a variety of topics. My recommendation would go far beyond simply talking about instruction and management. For teachers to actually learn these topics, they must experience them, potentially through additional training in the summer before they begin teaching.

Summer Institutes

This experiential learning could take place in a 5-week Summer Institute. Such a program would require that teachers arrive 5 weeks before the beginning of the school year, as opposed to 1 or 2 days before, as is the custom for most international teachers. This would undoubtedly be more expensive, but because the agency makes at least $17,000 per teacher from school district fees and teacher fees, some of this revenue could be used to supplement the Summer Institute. The teachers would need to be paid for their time, the funds for which can come from multiple sources, including the agency, grants, or in-kind donations from a university partnership. Both recruitment agencies and districts would benefit from a longer orientation because the teachers would begin the year better prepared, thus increasing their effectiveness, their students' achievement, and the reputation of the agency. Of course, as research on Teach for America has shown, a brief summer program is not enough to fully prepare teachers for the multitude of new experiences they will encounter in urban schools. However, combined with pre-departure orientations and ongoing professional development, a thoroughly planned and collaboratively executed Summer Institute is a significant improvement over the nonexistent or ineffective training that international teachers currently receive.

A well-developed Summer Institute would combine classwork and practical experience. To prepare for the Summer Institute, teachers would be given a pre-reading list and materials before their departure. Then, district and agency officials would collaborate to place international teachers in a summer school classroom in their content area. Though summer school is not a true duplication of a traditional classroom, it is the closest approximation available if the teachers arrive between June and August. International teachers would assist an American teacher each morning for several hours, gradually assuming more responsibility for classroom activities, and then transition to a higher education setting where they would participate in seminars and workshops. Over the course of the workshops, the new teachers would learn the particulars of what Mr. Scott and Ms. Jefferson outlined, but would also delve deeper into the histories and sociocultural contexts of their future students and communities. Workshops could be co-taught by American teachers, veteran international teachers, and university faculty, and could include modules such as History of American Education; Culturally Relevant Pedagogy; Content Methods; Working with Special Needs Students; Cultural Diversity in the U.S. Classroom; Policies and Practices in Public Schools; and State and Local Policies.

Cultural Ambassadors

One of the stated goals for international teacher recruitment is to bring "cultural ambassadors" to urban schools. However, as discussed in Chapter 4, this goal is not often realized. Compared to the other recommendations offered here, this goal is easily implemented. For teachers to be "ambassadors," they need to share their culture and perspectives with the community, colleagues, and students. For example, according to Ms. Dougherty of the AFT, a group of Filipino teachers began a yearly culture show in which they discussed their culture with other teachers and community members and shared traditional music, food, and dance. As long as the teachers' cultural ambassadorship does not stop at this "food and festivals" approach to multicultural education, it is an easy, low-stakes way for a cross-cultural discussion to begin. Part of this community-building can also be the creation of a "host family" program, in which American students' families teach one international educator about U.S. culture and customs. The family's role would be similar to the American allies' roles described in Chapter 2, and the international teachers would reciprocate by sharing their own cultural experiences with the families.

International teachers could also share their culture by participating in panels or workshops on international and comparative education at nearby universities. For example, the Indian teachers in Glendale live 10 minutes away from two major research universities with programs in Southeast Asian studies, subaltern studies, postcolonial studies, and comparative education. Their emic perspectives could add to the knowledge already disseminated at the university level. This would also give the teachers a way to intellectually engage others in a discussion about their culture, because, as previously discussed, they were frustrated by their students' lack of knowledge about India. They would not be called upon to "speak for their race or ethnicity," as when one teacher was asked, "So what do Indians think about *Slumdog Millionaire*?" by an American teacher, but would be sharing their individual opinions and experiences in an intellectual fashion.

Transnational Communication

Districts, agencies, and the teachers themselves could facilitate partnerships between U.S. schools and English-medium schools in source countries. In a modern adaptation of pen pal letters, students in the United States and source countries could share stories by email or blogs. A concrete example of this international communication was the Freinet movement in France during the 1950s and 1960s (J. Dunn, 2013). Celestin Freinet, a progressive teacher and school founder, believed that student-produced narratives were more meaningful and beneficial to students than textbooks and, as such, his students wrote articles for "newspapers" that were sent among other Freinet teachers throughout France and the colonies, such as Algeria, Senegal, and Sudan. Students wrote individual articles about their lives, recent experiences, and educational topics of interest. For example, one newspaper might include a story about a trip to the Eiffel Tower, the ruins of a local church, or a description of a Gila monster. The teachers then led their classes in a group editorial process to revise the articles for publication, and students used their own printing press to print multiple copies of the newspaper to send through the country and the world. Indeed, Freinet's students were talking about the Algerian War before the educational establishment was, and the student-generated narratives created a "sense of the connectedness of the human family across continents" (J. Dunn, 2013, p. 49).

Freinet's method would be the ideal model for an intercultural exchange between American and international students. For example, in elementary, English, and social studies classrooms, the students could discuss culture, language, and customs with their international pen pals. In science or math courses, students in other countries could collect data and solve problems together. In any circumstance, the exchange could extend to the whole school community, beyond the individual international teachers' classrooms. A program called iEARN (International Education and Resource Network) adapts Freinet's model using modern technology like word processing, emailing, blogging, and Skype to connect students, materials, and ideas across borders. An exchange like iEARN would provide a concrete way for international teachers to integrate their personal experiences and stories into the curriculum, and it would allow students to learn more about the world around them, thus finally achieving the goal of bringing cultural ambassadors to U.S. urban schools.

Professional Development and Mentoring

In addition to extensive orientations and opportunities to share their culture, international teachers also need ongoing and relevant professional development. During the 2008–2009 school year, Glendale's international teachers attended a once-a-month professional development meeting at the district office. Attendance was mandatory, and teachers were supposed to receive stipends for attending, though Shrusty recalled that she had never received hers, even after numerous inquiries. Meeting topics, according to Glendale documents were "Coping with New Cultures and Behaviors; Classroom Management; Grades, Grades, Grades; Best Practices; New Teacher Celebration; Communicating with Parents; Assessing and Evaluating Student Performance; Journal Reflections; and Closing Out the School Year." The most illogical part of the meetings was that they were scheduled to begin before the school day ended for many of the teachers—which meant that they either had to miss the session and not receive their stipend or leave their school early (thus having to arrange their own transportation) and try to convince their principals to get them substitute coverage for the last period of the day.

The following year, international teachers' professional development was subsumed into the induction program required of all new teachers to the Glendale district. This induction program began with a New Teacher Orientation, lasting 1.5 days in late July. (Of course, most of the international teachers had not arrived in time to attend.) The orientation program involved 60-minute concurrent sessions on classroom management, co-teaching strategies, resources in the library media center, and instructional technology, plus a 2-hour session with content-area specialists. The induction program also involved monthly meetings on topics similar to those listed above as part of the initial international teacher program. As a slight improvement, the meetings were scheduled at 4:00 p.m., which was after the school day ended for everyone except middle school teachers. Although this induction program was a start, it was not nearly enough to provide the duration and type of support needed by international teachers. Further, it should not be assumed that international teachers need the same type of professional support as

American teachers. Just as teachers are encouraged to differentiate instruction for students with varying needs, districts should differentiate induction for teachers with different needs.

My recommendation is based on research about the most effective type of professional development: a reformed approach that is longer in duration, requires collective participation, focuses on content areas, engages teachers with active learning, and maintains coherence with school goals and standards (AERA, 2005; Birman, Desimone, Porter, & Garet, 2000; Speck, 1996). Four goals would be: (1) Familiarize international teachers with American school structure, students, and federal, state, and local reforms; (2) instruct international teachers in culturally relevant pedagogy; (3) utilize the personal, cultural, and academic skills of teachers; and (4) allow international teachers to collaborate and share best practices. In addition to the explicit instruction in educational history, pedagogy, and policies and practice that would build on the objectives of the 5-week Summer Institute discussed earlier, a new professional development program should also include in-school mentorship, professional learning communities, and co-teaching.

Mentors were one of Glendale's existing support structures provided to all new teachers, including international teachers. However, the current mentoring program was not as effective as it needed to be. For example, Samina said she had a mentor who was a librarian, as opposed to a fellow English teacher, and when her mentor went on leave, she was not given a replacement. Principal Scott recalled providing a mentor for a previous international teacher, but the relationship was not effective because the mentor got "caught up in her own world; they have their classes, their issues, and they do not have the time to really devote to that individual." Ms. Jefferson acknowledged the flaws in the current way the mentoring system was designed, in that the district "asked, encouraged, stressed" principals to provide a mentor, but that she "did not know what actually happens once they get there."

This "not knowing" is simply unacceptable. If a district thinks it is necessary to assign mentors, then it must take steps to ensure that mentoring actually happens. Under the guidance of the principal or assistant principals, and supervised by district personnel in charge of human resources and professional learning, a mentor should familiarize international teachers with school policies and procedures; provide daily support for working with diverse students; aid in developing curricular goals, lessons, and assessments; and ease teachers' culture shock by assisting with daily living questions and concerns. A good mentor would, in addition to these logistical duties, also possess certain dispositions, skills, and commitments: "commit to the role of mentoring . . . accept the beginning [international] teacher . . . be skilled at providing instructional support . . . be effective in different interpersonal contexts . . . model continuous learning and . . . communicate hope and optimism" (Rowley, 1999, pp. 20–22). Ideally, the mentor would currently teach or have taught the classes to which the international teacher is assigned.

In order to avoid the problem of having no time for relationship-building, as Mr. Scott noted in the quotation above, principals should schedule common planning time for the international teacher and mentor. The participants in my study who shared planning with their departmental colleagues agreed that this extra time together strengthened the relationship and improved their pedagogy. District officials can guarantee that international teachers and mentors who participate in this program will receive credit in the form of continuing education or professional learning units.

Mentoring should be supplemented with professional learning communities or critical friends groups (CFGs) (Ballock, 2009; DuFour, 2004). These communities, made up of American and international teachers, should be unique adaptations of CFGs that "make a commitment to meet together regularly to collaboratively inquire into teaching practice" (Ballock, 2009, p. 41). Building upon the unique voices and experiences of the teachers, and utilizing the key components of trust, commitment, action, and accountability inherent in CFGs, participants should nurture cultural similarities and differences. Each CFG should intensely investigate a shared and organically generated topic of interest, such as interdisciplinary lessons, media literacy, or performance assessments, keeping in mind what the international teachers want to study. Using the experiences, voices, and expertise of each group member will allow ideas and practices to evolve over time (Duckworth, 1997; Lieberman, 1998). They could also use the critical friends protocols to help each other analyze student work, their own writing or experiences, or other issues that arise in the classroom. As in the Summer Institute, international teachers could receive personalized attention with any issues they are experiencing and could use micro-teaching to practice new units and methodologies.

Finally, effective professional development should also include co-teaching. Each international teacher could be paired with one teacher from the same content area (potentially their mentor) and one teacher from a related subject, such as English–Social Studies and Math–Science. The pairs would collaboratively plan lessons that examine innovative cross-curricular topics. International teachers would give and receive peer evaluations, constructive criticism, and lesson modeling.

Overall, all interventions conducted at the school, district, and state level should be designed with the unique needs of the international population in mind. Improvements augment methodological proficiency and cultural relevance for international teachers, encourage collaboration between current and new teachers, and utilize international teachers' talents and global perspectives. Critics might ask why districts, schools, and other teachers should devote these kinds of resources (including time) to international teachers who are, by definition and law, temporary and whom they had no role in selecting or hiring. To them, I would say that these interventions are no different from other neoliberal policies that are supposedly designed with the needs of students in mind. Making these changes would ensure that districts' investments, to use the language of neoliberals, were more secure and were more likely to provide substantial returns in the form of student success. If these changes are made, then the most important goal of international teacher recruitment—to improve the achievement of urban students—will be closer to fulfillment.

IMPLICATIONS FOR FUTURE RESEARCH: WHY RESEARCHERS SHOULD INVESTIGATE INTERNATIONAL TEACHERS

As emphasized throughout the text, there is a severe lack of research on international teacher recruitment. I hope that the compelling stories of the Glendale teachers, as well as the similar experiences of international educators around the country, have demonstrated that the topic is both worthy of and necessary to research. It is heartening that, since I began studying international teachers in 2006, there has been a growing group of scholars from Illinois to South Carolina who have embarked upon their own research in this area. Districts and recruiting agencies are able to justify recruitment and continue making many spurious claims about its success because there is little to no research and what anecdotal evidence does exist is dismissed. A concrete body of empirical knowledge is vital to ensure the success of programs, teachers, and students.

I chose case study methodology for my research because I believe it allows in-depth exploration of one topic and participants. However, in future projects, I hope to blur the line between researcher and participant in an effort to make both my findings and my methodologies more socially just. Participatory action research is one way that I anticipate building upon the scholarship presented here. Further, I am extending my research aims to develop a grounded theory of globally responsive pedagogy (Dunn, 2012). In addition to more case study research in other districts with teachers from other countries, further research needs to be longitudinal, student-based, and comparative.

Longitudinal and Student-Based Research

Future researchers should study teachers from their first through third year (or sixth year, if the teachers are on H-1B visas). Beyond their time in the United States, research should continue once international teachers return to their home countries to evaluate the effects of U.S. experience on their classroom teaching. If teachers move to other countries, such as Australia, New Zealand, or the United Kingdom that also heavily recruit English-speaking educators, researchers could follow them into that additional cultural context. Above all, the longitudinal research should be classroom-based and should include interviews and observations. Multiple data sources will allow researchers to unearth findings that would not be revealed from only one source and, especially with international teachers who have much to lose, it is important to see them in multiple ways and to realize that there are aspects of their story that we may still not know to ask about. As Jonathan Kozol (2000) recalls, "The answers I remember longest are the ones that answer questions I didn't think of asking" (p. 22).

In addition to the need for longitudinal research on teachers, this book has confirmed the need to understand the role of students in international teacher recruitment, particularly their perceptions and their achievement. Future researchers could examine student perceptions of international teachers and focus on questions such as: How do students perceive international teachers' content knowledge, commitment to students, classroom management, cultural relevance, and connection to students? What is the effect of these perceptions on student performance?

Student achievement in international teachers' courses should also be measured in future studies. Certainly student test scores can be examined, but "achievement" should also be measured through a variety of other factors. Were students prepared for future courses? What new critical or analytical skills did students learn from international teachers, and how did these skills impact their overall school performance? Did students improve their global or cultural awareness and global citizenship, and if so, how (Quaynor, 2012)? For example, did they learn more about countries outside the United States, including the home country of their teacher? Did they learn more about their own culture as they reflected on the similarities and differences between themselves and their international teachers? How did learning about other cultures influence their out-of-school contexts, interactions with students from other backgrounds, and self-concepts? It is imperative that, as with all educators, test scores not be the end all and be all of what makes a teacher effective. There is so much more that international teachers can bring to students' lives if they are helped to do so.

Comparative Research

My research also raises many questions about how the specific contexts of international teachers' placements influence their job satisfaction, adjustment, classroom management, and teaching methods. Comparative research has the ability to answer some of these lingering questions. Researchers should investigate the experiences of teachers from different home countries; teachers from the same country who are placed in different types of schools (urban, suburban, rural) or in different states to see the contextualized effects of race, class, and culture on teacher success and satisfaction; and teachers from different countries in the same subject area. All of these findings will help uncover if and how teachers' countries of origin and placements influence their recruitment, preparation, and pedagogy.

Other comparative research should focus on recruitment in other countries, such as England and Australia. Such research can consider the effects of the Commonwealth Teacher Recruitment Protocol, the different source countries from which teachers are drawn, and other questions similar to those suggested for U.S. comparative research. Researchers in education, political science, international studies, or economics can also study recruitment agencies to learn how they choose which countries to recruit and place teachers, and how their practices are or are not beneficial and equitable for the teachers, host countries, and source countries.

IMPLICATIONS FOR TEACHER PREPARATION: WHY TEACHER EDUCATORS SHOULD CARE ABOUT INTERNATIONAL TEACHERS

In addition to engaging in research on and with international educators, teacher educators can also be specifically involved in their development as professional educators of U.S. children. Ineffective alternative recruitment efforts like this one compete with the viability of U.S. teacher education programs, and this is especially dangerous at a time when teacher education is under attack (e.g., Berliner, 2000; Zeichner, 2009). Alternative programs are able to be so successful because they claim that teachers do not need pedagogical preparation. Teacher educators need to continue their fight to show that not only do pre-service teachers need training, but that their jobs do not stop when students leave the university. In-service training is a vital component of teacher education (Dunn, Donnell, & Stairs, 2010); it is in these spaces of induction that teacher educators can engage with and support educators from abroad.

Additionally, the university-prepared educators will be working side-by-side with international teachers upon hire. If teacher educators are to fulfill their mission of creating teacher-leaders, then they must explicitly discuss the ways that American-born teachers can advocate for themselves and their colleagues.

Teacher educators' involvement with international teachers can take many forms: as researchers, as discussed in the previous section; as educational consultants to administrators and recruiters; as leaders of professional development; or as committed advocates for social change who help prepare American teachers to be allies in the struggle.

Teacher–School–University Partnerships and Professional Development

A mutually beneficial relationship should be developed between nearby universities and the districts and schools in which international teachers are placed. Many universities and local schools, especially those with NCATE accreditation, are already connected through partnerships or as professional development school sites. Many partnerships, unfortunately, are not as beneficial for individual teachers as they are for universities—that is, universities get to place pre-service teachers in the schools, conduct periodic professional development sessions, or arrange research projects, while teachers themselves may never see the benefits of this partnership or may see their participation as "just one more thing" that their administrators are making them do. A true partnership, then, would not be between the schools and universities only but would extend to the teachers and allow them to dictate what professional development and support is most important for their learning.

For example, international teachers should be able to enroll in extended education courses in their content area, educational studies, or a related area of interest. Even better would be tuition waivers or discounted rates if the international teachers participated in sharing their knowledge through workshops and class visits. University departments of education can offer in-service workshops for international teachers, in conjunction with their Summer Institute and other professional development, on culturally relevant pedagogy and other areas that the teachers deem necessary. In addition, faculty in education or international studies can conduct workshops with principals and other district administrators to share research-based strategies for intercultural communication. This would help administrators better understand the experiences and cultures of their new employees.

Commitment to Supporting and Being Agents of Change

The new teachers who are prepared at institutions of teacher education will be working in collaboration with international teachers, and teacher educators need to prepare them to support their foreign colleagues. They will be on grade- and subject-level teams, co-teaching, or in classrooms next to international teachers. They may share some of the same students. As discussed in Chapter 2, the development of American allies is a critical component in international teachers' ability to function in U.S. urban schools. How can teacher educators help nurture in pre-service teachers the dispositions that are necessary to become leaders and change agents in their schools and communities?

Many teacher education programs say they are committed to teaching new teachers how to be agents of change, and a multitude of programs even discuss change agency in their mission statements. However, the focus of this change is often about effecting change in and for students. This is laudable but not enough. Teachers need to also be prepared to "see themselves as responsible for and capable of bringing about change to make schools more equitable" for colleagues and staff (Villegas & Lucas, 2002, p. 20). Schools will only be equitable when teachers are treated fairly, given proper support and development, and treated as people and not as commodities. At present, though teachers "play a special role in the international knowledge economy," this same economy "is, in fact, dependent upon the very employees that it seeks to commodify" (Fitzpatrick, 2012). Especially when teachers are being bashed and scapegoated in the media and in politics (Kumashiro, 2012), it would be very easy for American-born teachers to concentrate on fighting for change for their students and themselves—and never look into the classroom next door to see if an international colleague also needs help. Potential American allies may also need help seeing that the problems that affect their fellow teachers and their students are intertwined. This would require even the American allies from Glendale who are presented in Chapter 2 to be more committed to their international colleagues. Change agency needs be about more than helping with parent conferences and rides to school; it needs to include giving voice to a problem when those affected are too afraid to speak for themselves.

Beyond just supporting new teachers in being agents of change, teacher educators need to be the agents themselves. It is up to teacher educators and the institutions for which they work to model for their students the ways to do this—by refusing to stay silent when they see injustices in their universities and communities. They should be committed to international teachers not merely because they happen to be in the profession of educating teachers, but because it is, at the core, an issue of human rights and justice.

The United Nations Academic Impact Initiative is one way to frame the responsibility of members of higher education. This program calls for institutions to demonstrate their commitment to human rights by formally endorsing ten principles, many of which are directly related to why schools, colleges, and department of education (and the faculty within them) should be committed foreign teachers' rights. Among the principles are those calling for "a commitment to human rights, among them freedom of inquiry, opinion, and speech; educational opportunity for all people regardless of gender, race, religion or ethnicity; encouraging global citizenship through education; promoting inter-cultural dialogue and understanding, and the 'unlearning" of intolerance, through education' " (United Nations Academic Impact, 2011, n.p.). If teacher educators pledge to fulfill these principles in their universities, pre-service teachers will see the positive impact that social justice and advocacy have on educational environments.

IMPLICATIONS FOR POLICYMAKERS:
WHY WE NEED POLICIES FOR INTERNATIONAL TEACHERS

There are currently no national or state procedures, standards, or protocols for international teacher recruitment. Were such policies in place, perhaps some of the difficulties encountered by my participants could have been avoided or lessened. While I understand that there are a multitude of educational struggles and challenges at all levels, the abundance of evidence on international teachers' difficulties can no longer be ignored. Indeed, other "bigger" problems, such as Race to the Top, charter schools, and teacher quality, are interrelated and share many of the same characteristics as alternative recruitment. To ignore this component of the neoliberal educational agenda is to leave even more teachers and students behind. By addressing international teacher problems, larger issues can be solved, and vice versa.

Note that I am not advocating for more federal involvement in local and state educational systems. However, the federal government is responsible for immigration policy and enforcement. Therefore, I acknowledge that federal policy may be the first step in ensuring justice for this particular group, as evidently no anecdotal or research-based evidence has been effective thus far. The American Federation of Teachers (2009) recommends policies related to:

> the development, adoption and enforcement of ethical standards for the international recruitment of teachers; improved access to the government data necessary to track and study international hiring trends in education; and international cooperation to protect migrant workers and mitigate any negative impact of teacher migration in sending countries. (p. 27)

Informed by the union's work, I argue that policymakers must establish equitable recruitment procedures, oversee states and districts, renew their focus on teacher distribution and retention, and develop alternatives to neoliberal educational policies.

Equitable Recruitment Procedures

The most important change that policymakers can make for the success of international teacher recruitment programs is to encourage agencies and districts to adopt equitable recruitment procedures. Currently, there is no standard protocol for the way agencies should treat their employees, and as a result, teachers all over the country are at risk of exploitation and other abuses. For justice to be served, policymakers in local, state, and national governments should collaborate with other stakeholders, such as state and district administrators, union leaders, recruitment agency representatives, and international teachers, to develop recruitment guidelines.

A good model for these guidelines is the Commonwealth Teacher Recruitment Protocol, developed in 2004 by 53 countries to adequately deal with their own teacher shortages and recruitment efforts (Commonwealth Secretariat, 2004). The purpose of the protocol is worth quoting at length:

> The Protocol aims to balance the rights of teachers to migrate internationally, on a temporary or permanent basis, against the need to protect the integrity of national education systems, and to prevent the exploitation of the scarce human resources of

poor countries. The Protocol also seeks to safeguard the rights of recruited teachers and the conditions relating to their service in the recruiting country. In doing so, the Protocol seeks to promote the positive benefits which international teacher migration can bring and to facilitate the sharing of the common wealth of human resources that reside within the Commonwealth. (pp. 3–4)

The document then outlines the rights and responsibilities of recruiting countries, source countries, and recruited teachers, as well as suggestions for monitoring and evaluation of recruitment processes and programs. Had such a document existed in the United States, international teachers in Glendale would have had an outlet for voicing their concerns and frustrations about IRI's practices. Once a similar protocol is developed and adopted in the United States, further policy action will be easier to initiate, including the oversight of states and districts.

Oversight of States and Districts

In centralized urban districts, there is no shortage of top-down policies and procedures. In Glendale, for example, curriculum standards, course pacing guides, benchmark assessments, and mandates for grading come to teachers from above, by way of state or district administrators. Yet amid all of these policies, there are none dealing with oversight of international teachers.

State personnel should be aware of which districts are using international teachers by tracking their yearly reports and spending. A national database of international teachers, similar to a database established for tracking international nurses, would help states track where teachers are placed. District policymakers should also be privy to information about international teachers in their community and should make certain that individual schools are properly recruiting and supporting their employees. Holding district- and school-level administrators accountable for their hiring procedures will ensure that no one is able to erroneously claim that international teachers are not their responsibility and that they have no control over their employment.

Focus on Teacher Distribution and Retention

Many urban districts in the United States "are continually spending human and fiscal resources on teacher recruitment when the emphasis should be on retaining those teachers who have the skills and dispositions to teach successfully in urban schools" (Waddell, 2010, p. 70). This book has illustrated the difficulty of solving teacher shortage and teacher attrition problems with stopgap, temporary measures like international teacher recruitment. Because some international teachers left after 1 year and because the nature of the program was inherently temporary due to visa and contract restrictions, there was no feasible way for international teachers to solve the more systemic issue of teacher distribution and retention in urban schools. The Commonwealth Teacher Recruitment Protocol by the Commonwealth Secretariat (2004) recognized similar issues abroad: "It is the responsibility of the authorities in recruiting countries to manage domestic teacher supply and demand in a manner that limits the need to resort to organized recruitment in order to meet the normal demand for teachers" (p. 9). Thus, authorities were charged with better recruiting, distributing, and preparing their teachers at home before recruiting from abroad.

In 2010–2011, Glendale was scheduled to pay IRI $506,000 for administrative fees, in addition to the teachers' salaries. This tremendous amount, especially when combined with the fees paid to the second agency Glendale used, could be more effectively put to use in a self-study or commissioned study on the district's teacher distribution and retention. By asking Glendale teachers and other professionals what drew them to the district, what keeps them there, or what caused them to leave, administrators would better be able to judge which interventions and resources are necessary to bring and keep quality educators in the district.

Imagine the Alternatives

For policymakers, and indeed for district and school administrators as well, the implications of this research extend beyond the factual and into the abstract. That is, for some of the problems revealed here, it is not enough to change the immediate exploitative practices. We must reimagine the basic goals of education so as to avoid further problems. According to Judt (2010), this imagination is the key to creating a more progressive society:

> Why do we experience such difficulty even *imagining* a different sort of society? Why is it beyond us to conceive of a different set of arrangements to our common advantage? Are we doomed indefinitely to lurch between a dysfunctional "free market" and the much-advertised horrors of "socialism"? Our disability is *discursive*: we simply do not know how to talk about these things any more. (p. 34)

It is time for a shift in political discourse, even a discursive revolution. Indeed, if policymakers were to listen to teachers, students, parents, and teacher educators, they would see evidence of this revolution already happening. This does not mean we have to imagine alternatives to international teachers—merely that we have to imagine alternative forms of support and mentorship so they can succeed. We have to imagine alternatives to a system that is "capable of shutting off the sun and the stars because they do not pay a dividend" (Keynes, 1933, n.p.). A more progressive and socially just education will not be achieved until policymakers' focus moves past economic goals and into interpersonal and cultural goals.

LOOKING FORWARD

Should these suggestions for practice, research, teacher education, and policy be implemented, foreign teacher recruitment could be a positive way of bridging cultures, giving international teachers the opportunity to explore new horizons and gain valuable professional experience and allowing U.S. urban students to learn about the world from cultural insiders. As it currently exists, however, international teacher recruitment is inequitable and ineffective for teachers, students, schools, and systems. With the upsurge in a neoliberal agenda that undermines teachers and detracts from the teaching profession's viability, recruitment efforts designed to address a recurring need in urban schools are instead usurped by unquestioned, potentially exploitive recruitment policies. Whatever good intentions the schools and recruiters had were marred by their lack of understanding of the teachers' complex experiences and their refusal to work toward solving critical problems.

So are teachers without borders a reality or a possibility? I would counter the neoliberal globalizing rhetoric that claims that there are no borders; such claims only fortify the cultural borders experienced between teachers and students. By pretending that cultures and nations to do not matter, we are only making them matter more. If we were more serious in our consideration of the borders that do exist, we could actually develop teachers who transcend them and start to break them down. That requires a commitment to challenging the political spectacle of neoliberal globalization and the master narrative of urban school reform that teaching is easy and that culture does not matter. We must do more than the Glendale administrators; we must do more than say that this is not our responsibility. Because of *course* it is our responsibility—they are working in our schools, living in our neighborhoods, and teaching our children. We must fight for the teachers and students whose voices have been silenced.

Methodology

The intent of this book was to explore the recruitment, preparation, and pedagogy of international teachers and illuminate the intersections between their practice and educational policies. The primary study discussed throughout the text utilized qualitative case study methodology. Specifically, it was a collective case study where "each case study is instrumental in learning about [the research topic and] important coordination between the individual studies" (Stake, 1995, pp. 3–4). People, organizations, and places were given pseudonyms to ensure confidentiality. As the primary researcher, I am solely responsible for the analysis presented here.

PARTICIPANTS

Participants in this research included four teachers (one middle and three secondary), four principals, two district officials, one recruiter, and three union personnel. They are described in Table A.1.

All of the principals and teachers granted me permission to research in their schools and classrooms within the Glendale district, an urban public school system in the southeastern United States. (More about the Glendale context is explained in the Introduction.) Overall, it is my hope that the discussions benefited the participants as much as the researcher, by enabling the international teachers to share goals, struggles, successes, and questions with a fellow educator in a way that positively impacted their classroom practice.

DATA COLLECTION

Data were collected through interviews, observations, and documents. Qualitative interviews formed the bulk and basis of this research. As stipulated by Rubin and Rubin (2005), interviews were structured as extended conversations with a responsive partner and utilized a conversational guide that allowed spontaneous discovery while maintaining a consistent overall structure (Gillham, 2005). The participants themselves generated many topics on the spot, and if the issue was of a general nature, I posed similar questions to the other participants in follow-up interviews. All interview questions were related to and developed from the research questions. Between February and May 2010, interviews with teachers and

Table A.1. Participant Profiles

Pseudonym	Occupation	Gender	Race or Ethnicity	School or Organization
Aleeza	Secondary science teacher	F	Indian	Tubman High School
Shrusty	Secondary special education teacher	F	Indian	Douglass High School
Faria	Secondary mathematics teacher	F	Indian	Woodson High School
Samina	Middle grades English teacher	F	Indian	Chisholm Middle School
Mr. Sutherland	Principal	M	African American	Chisholm Middle School
Mr. Scott	Principal	M	African American	Douglass High School
Mr. Clark	Principal	M	African American	Tubman Middle School
Mr. Norman	Principal	M	African American	Woodson High School
Ms. Muller	District official	F	African American	Glendale Central Office
Ms. Jefferson	District official	F	African American	Glendale Central Office
Ms. Jain	Owner of IRI	F	Indian	International Recruitment, Inc. (IRI)
Ms. Dougherty	International relations	F	White	American Federation of Teachers
Mr. See	Public relations	M	White	American Federation of Teachers
Mr. McNeil* *real name	Legal affairs	M	White	American Federation of Teachers

principals were conducted at their schools, and interviews with other participants were conducted in their offices or by phone. The sessions were digitally recorded and transcribed verbatim shortly thereafter to maintain the data's integrity. Transcriptions were shared with the participants for their review and clarification.

Formal classroom observations of each international teacher were conducted in the second half of the school year, depending on the teachers' schedule and availability. The formal classroom observations were designed to collect data on the learning environment and teachers' culturally relevant pedagogy, or their use of multicultural methods, work with diverse learners, and multicultural competence, as defined by Ladson-Billings (1997), Gay (2000), and Irvine and Armento (2001). During the observations, I took field notes and recorded descriptions of events that took place in the participant's classroom from the beginning of each period to the end. This record included descriptions of the classroom setup and environment, teacher instructions, student responses, and verbal and nonverbal interactions (Merriam, 1998). I also completed a checklist that listed examples of culturally relevant teaching. The checklist was based on the research of Gay (2000), Irvine and Armento (2001), and Ladson-Billings (1997).

From the teachers, I also collected any relevant documents, including lesson plans, handouts, or other materials. Additional documents included agency publicity materials, school board minutes, newspaper articles, websites, and other artifacts.

DATA ANALYSIS

I followed the recommendations of Miles and Huberman (1994) and Rubin and Rubin (2005) when analyzing data. All steps led to thematic coding, the process by which raw data are "mined" and concepts are unearthed (Corbin & Strauss, 2007, p. 66). All interviews were transcribed from their recordings, and, along with my field notes and observation guides, I wrote memos based on my findings from all of these sources. I examined each transcript individually to determine a first level of codes, or labels used to identify important themes or concepts. My theoretical frameworks and my review of the literature informed this first level of codes. Additionally, I utilized open coding to reveal any new themes that may not have emerged in previous research. This was especially necessary for my research because so little had been previously published. My highlighted, coded, and notated transcripts were then used for a second round of coding.

During this second level of coding, I systematically compared codes within and across all data sources and subjects. I determined a final list of emergent themes based on the patterns and commonalities between my interviews and observations. Throughout the coding process, I kept track of themes as they emerged and evolved in a researcher journal. The final codes are those presented in the many of the chapters as headings and subheadings.

METHODOLOGICAL CONSIDERATIONS

In order to ensure reliability, each participant engaged in member checks to verify the information in his or her interview transcriptions, observation guides, and any materials collected during the interview process (Miles & Huberman, 1994). Additionally, I kept a journal to act as a research trail; in it, I tracked changes in research questions, procedures, or coding.

Member checks and personal reflection also aided internal validity, or the study's ability to replicate the reality of the situation being studied (Court, 2006). Internal validity was further addressed when I conducted multiple observations and interviews of the teachers and their classroom practice. External validity, or the study's generalizability to other settings, was enhanced because I triangulated multiple data sources, including interviews, observations, and documents (Merriam, 1998).

RESEARCHER'S PERSPECTIVE

As a former teacher, my role as a classroom observer was an especially difficult position in which to find myself. This section is my attempt to situate myself in my study, to share the ways my story may have influenced my research and the ways my research influenced my personal story.

"Look, Nice White Lady's Back Again": My Place in My Research

Students are familiar with seeing visitors in their classrooms. Whether it is an administrator conducting an evaluation, a subject-matter coach, a district or state official, or even a parent of another student, it is not unusual for a desk in the back of the room to be occupied by an outsider when students enter class each day. My presence, however, was especially noticeable because I did not "look" like I belonged. I was in a suit and had a laptop or notebook on my desk. I was often typing or writing furiously as students entered the room and throughout the class period. And, of course, there was the most salient and obvious difference: I was White. My research was conducted in schools where 99% of the students were Black and where the majority of teachers and administrators were also Black. I told the participants that they could either introduce me or I could introduce myself, or if they preferred, they could just ignore me and continue with the lesson. I was only asked to introduce myself once. That time, I told students that I was a university researcher, working with their teacher, and was a former English teacher. I thanked them for allowing me to join their community. They clapped when I finished speaking, and one student said, "You must be really smart." Another student turned to a classmate and said, "Bet she's better than our English teachers here." What was it that made them assume I was a smart, qualified teacher: my race, my education, my suit and laptop, my university moniker? All or none of the above?

   The times when I was not introduced, individual students took it upon themselves to ask me who I was and what I was doing in their classrooms. They passed
the information on to their neighbors and, after one or two visits, they came to
know my position. They let each other know I was there, as exemplified by one
middle school student who announced to his classmates, "Look, nice White lady's
back again." Interestingly, *every* time in *every* class, at least one student said he or
she wanted to attend my university. Not many of the students were able to answer
what they would like to study there or "be when they grow up," but they all indicated that they knew of the university's reputation as a place where "smart people
go." One student came up to me as soon as I walked into the classroom, before I
was able to take a seat, and said, "I want to go to college in 2 years." He gestured
down at his dress pants and tie and said, "I can even dress for success. I would fit
right in." His teacher later told me that he was not passing her class. This was not
uncommon; the majority of students who began conversations with me about
college in general were not traditionally academically successful in their current
classes. Thus, I do not know if they were having such discussions because they felt
they *should* talk about college, they had misinformation about college admission
standards, they wanted positive reinforcement, or they simply wanted to have a
conversation with me.
   In addition to beginning discussions with me, students also reacted to my
presence in several other surprising ways. They flirted with me or shared unsolicited information about liking or disliking their teachers or the subject. During
one observation in which students were talking loudly and not paying attention
to the teacher, two boys began talking to me. Despite my attempts to redirect their
focus, they persisted until one said, "This class is such shit." The other student then
raised his voice and said, "Don't curse in front of the nice lady! Don't you have
any respect?" The debate went on, with three other male students getting involved
and telling the first boy to be respectful, until the first two boys stood up, and
one slapped the other. Though there may have been other issues at play, or a history between them, their argument turned physical because the young man would
not apologize for cursing in front of me. Ironically, the boy who did not believe I
should hear cursing began the altercation, in which I not only heard more cursing
but also saw fighting.
   The most significant dilemma I faced was when to become involved in the
class. Did I stop the two boys from fighting? Did I participate in class discussions if
a student said, "I wonder what our visitor thinks"? What if students were working
in groups, and one group needed some extra assistance? What if a student caught
me noticing her on her cell phone; did I give her a "teacher look" to get her to put
it away, or look the other way? (In the first two instances, I did; in the second two,
I did not.) I wondered about my participation in every aspect of the classroom,
even about something as seemingly minimal as providing a student with a pencil
and paper when he didn't have any. When I saw a student struggling with a math

problem, and then witnessed a collaborative teacher instruct him in the wrong way to solve the problem, I debated whether or not to say something to the student or the teacher. Inevitably, the problem solved itself when the student approached me and asked, "Can you help me with this? I don't think I am doing it right, and I don't think he is, either." Though I am no math teacher, I remembered that concept, showed him where he made his mistake, and walked him through the correct way to solve the problem. Then, the student seated in front of me "woke up" (she'd been "sleeping" the whole class), turned around, and asked if I could help her, too. I did. Later, I spoke with my participant about my uncertainty. As much as I did not want to jeopardize my research, I was even more concerned about intruding on her class and "stepping on her toes." She assuaged some of my fears when she said, "Please help them as much as you want. They need it all and I cannot be in all places at all times."

Far surpassing my desire to help students was my desire to help teachers, my participants. Several times I was asked, "Do you think I did a good job?" or "How does this compare to what you see in American teachers' classrooms?" Often, these questions were asked after a particularly difficult class, and the teachers said they were disappointed that I had to witness a "bad day." Unfortunately, as presented in the body of this work, there were manifold challenges, resulting in *many* bad days. Teachers said they felt helpless, discouraged, or unsure of themselves. Their difficulties made me want to help them with lesson planning, classroom management, and more. But, if I provided a teacher with additional materials, for example, would I truly be witnessing her lived experience as a teacher? Was I unduly influencing the results of my study if I discussed culturally relevant pedagogy too much, or if I shared some new classroom management techniques with her? During one observation, I met a curriculum specialist who was modeling a lesson in one of my participants' classrooms. She asked, "Are you here to help her?" I responded, "No, are you?" She was there to help, but only minimally, as she emphasized that "there are 16 other teachers I need to help, too."

Researcher Bias

As Ladson-Billings (1997) noted about her own groundbreaking research, it is difficult to separate one's own perspective from one's work. Citing Sirotnik (1988), she explains: "no inquiry is ever without initial values, beliefs, conceptions, and driving assumptions regarding the matter under investigation" (Ladson-Billings, 1997, p. 241). Thus, though it is important to examine my beliefs as a researcher, my personal investment in education does not have to be considered a limitation.

I believe that culturally relevant pedagogy is a desirable goal for all teachers in all schools, especially multicultural, urban schools, as supported by multitudes of research. I value teachers, systems, and policies that support a progressive view of education and allow students to be empowered and work for a more socially just society. But I also believe that there is no one "correct" way to teach and no one simple solution to schools' problems today. I entered into the study with an open mind and the goal to improve the education system for the desired audience of this study, including international teachers, school districts, policymakers, teacher educators, and recruitment agencies. As Court (2006) noted, a researcher "must be willing to externalize and critique her intuitive understandings and to write down and study these reflections throughout the course of a research project" (p. 1). Data triangulation, member checks, and my researcher journal served as the requisite externalization.

Notes

Introduction

1. The term *foreign teacher* is used interchangeably with *international teacher* in this work because that is what the participants call themselves. It is not meant to connote a sense of "othering" often associated with the word *foreign*, but merely to denote someone from another country.

Chapter 1

1. Selected agencies included Amity Institute; Foreign Academic and Cultural Exchange Services, Inc. (FACES); Global Teachers Recruitment and Resources, Inc. (GTRR); Intalage, Inc.; Superior Management Group; Teachers Placement Group; Universal Placement Services, Inc.; and Visiting International Faculty (VIF).

2. Countries included Argentina, Australia, Canada, Chile, Colombia, Costa Rica, Ecuador, England, Ireland, Mexico, New Zealand, Peru, the Philippines, Romania, South Africa, Spain, and Venezuela.

Chapter 3

1. Commonly known as *Mahatma*, meaning "great soul," Gandhi's given name was Mohandas.

Chapter 4

1. All of the agencies included were also studied by Barber (2003); several agencies from his list have been left off the table, however, because they did not have publicly available materials or did not include a mission statement on their website. At the time of writing, the website for AIC had been disabled in response to the allegations made against its owner, Ligaya Avenida. I believe it is important, however, to show that the trend of these mission statements is not only across agencies but across time—the mission statements were initially collected in 2006 and were updated every year since until this book went to press. Though some words were changed, the overall message was never altered.

References

Ahmed, I. (2002). The 1947 partition of India: A paradigm for pathological politics in India and Pakistan. *Asian Ethnicity, 3*(1), 9.

American Educational Research Association (AERA). (2005). Teaching teachers: Professional development to improve student achievement. *Research Points, 3*(1), 1–4.

American Federation of Teachers (AFT). (2009). *Importing educators: Causes and consequences of international teacher recruitment.* Washington, DC: American Federation of Teachers.

American Federation of Teachers (AFT). (2010). *American dream: Helping Filipino teachers.* [Online video]. Retrieved from http://aft.org/newspubs/videos

Amity Institute. (2012). *Amity foreign teacher recruitment.* Retrieved from www.amityteachers.com

Anzaldúa, G. (1983). Foreword. In C. Moraga & G. Anzaldúa (Eds.) *This bridge called my back: Writings by radical women of color.* New York: Kitchen Table/Women of Color Press.

Apple, M. W. (2001). *Educating the "right" way: Markets, standards, God, and inequality.* New York: RoutledgeFalmer.

Apple, M. W. (2006). *Educating the "right" way: Markets, standards, God, and inequality.* New York: Routledge.

Apple, M. W., Au, W., & Gandin, L. A. (Eds.). (2009). *The Routledge international handbook of critical education.* New York: Routledge.

Appleton, S., Morgan, W. J. Sives, A. (2006). Should teachers stay at home? The impact of international teacher mobility. *Journal of International Development, 18*(6), 771–786.

Ashby, G. (2011, November 15). Caribbean teachers cry foul. *Guardian Media.* Retrieved from http://www.guardianmedia.co.tt.

The Association of International Educators. (2011). *Broken Promises: The story of Caribbean international teachers in New York City's public schools.* Washington, DC: The Black Institute.

Avenida International Consultants. (2010). *International teacher placement program.* Retrieved from http://aiccorp.us.com

Axtman, K. (2004, March 5). Texas begs for teachers—with or without credentials. *The Christian Science Monitor.* Retrieved from http://www.csmonitor.com

Ayers, W. (2001a). *To teach: The journey of a teacher.* New York, NY: Teachers College Press.

Ayers, W. (Ed.). (2001b). *Zero tolerance: Resisting the drive for punishment in our schools.* New York: The New Press.

Ball, D. L. (2000). Bridging practices: Intertwining content and pedagogy in teaching and learning to teach. *Journal of Teacher Education, 51,* 241–247.

Ballock, E. (2009). What makes some small learning communities so effective, and how can I support my own? In C. J. Craig and L. F. Deretchin (Eds.), *Teacher learning in small-group settings: Teacher education yearbook XVII.* Lanham, MD: Rowman & Littlefield Education.

Banks, J. A. (1994). *Cultural diversity and education: Foundations, curriculum, and teaching.* Boston: Allyn and Bacon.

Banks, J. A. (Ed.). (2004). *Handbook of research on multicultural education,* 2nd ed. San Francisco: Jossey-Bass.

Barber, R. (2003). *Report to the National Education Association on trends in foreign teacher recruitment.* Washington, DC: Center for Economic Organizing.

Basu, M. (2002, August 21). Teachers from afar impart global feel. *Atlanta Journal Constitution,* pp. E1–3.

Bauman, Z. (1998). On glocalization: Or globalization for some and localization for others. *Thesis Eleven, 54,* 37–49.

Behizadeh, N. (2012). *Making writing meaningful: A sociocultural analysis of student perceptions of the authenticity of writing tasks.* Unpublished doctoral dissertation. Emory University, Atlanta, GA.

Berliner, D. C. (2000). A personal response to those who bash teacher education. *Journal of Teacher Education, 51*(5), 358–371.

Berry, B. (2003). *What it means to be a highly qualified teacher.* Retrieved from http://www.teachingquality.org

Bhagwati, J. (2004). *In defense of globalization.* New York: Oxford University Press.

Biggs, A. G., & Richwine, J. (2011, November, 1). Assessing the compensation of public-school teachers. American Enterprise Institute. Retrieved from www.aei.org.

Birman, B. F., Desimone, L., Porter, A. C., & Garet, M. S. (2000). Designing professional development that works. *Educational Leadership, 57,* 28–33.

Bonilla-Silva, E. (2006). *Racism without racists: Color-blind racism and the persistence of racial inequality in the United States.* Lanham, MD: Rowman &Littlefield Publishers.

Bowie, L. (2010, March 14). Principal signed a Filipino teachers to buy, sell makeup. *The Baltimore Sun.* Retrieved from http://www.articles.baltimoresun.com

Bowles, S., & Gintis, H. (1976). *Schooling in capitalist America: Educational reform and the contradictions of economic life.* New York: Basic Books.

Brown, K. (2013, April). *A borderless profession?: A critical vertical case study of the recruitment and use of overseas trained teachers in the U.S. southeast.* Paper presented at the annual meeting of the American Educational Research Association, San Francisco, CA.

Brownback, A. (2011, July 15). International teachers protest federal ruling against Prince George's County schools. Retrieved from http://www.gazette.net.

Callaci, D. (2011, March 10). International crisis: DOE's broken promises leave recruited teachers in limbo. *United Federation of Teachers.* Retrieved from http://www.utf.org.

Camus, A. (1942). *The plague.* New York: Vintage International.

Carroll, L. (1920). *Alice's adventures in Wonderland.* New York: The Macmillan Company.

Chakravarty, S. D. (2001). Multicultural education in India. In C. A. Grant & J. L. Lei, *Global constructions of multicultural education: Theories and realities* (pp. 59–89). Mahwah, NJ: Lawrence Erlbaum.

Charney, J. (2009). Hiring teachers from abroad. *School Administrator, 66*(3), 35–36.

Chomsky, N. (1999). *Profit over people: Neoliberalism and the global order.* New York: Seven Stories Press.

Coates, T.-N. P. (2005, November 21). Looking abroad for a few good teachers. *Time,* pp. 64–65.

Cochran-Smith, M. (1995). Color blindness and basket making are not the answers: Confronting the dilemmas of race, culture, and language diversity in teacher education. *American Educational Research Journal, 32,* 493–522.

Cochran-Smith, M., & Fries, K. M. (2001). Sticks, stones, and ideology: The discourse of reform in teacher education. *Educational Researcher 30*(8), 3–15.

Commonwealth Secretariat. (2004). *Commonwealth teacher recruitment protocol.* Retrieved from www.thecommonwealth.org

Compton, M., & Weiner, L. (2008). *The global assault on teachers, teaching, and teacher unions.* New York: Palgrave MacMillan.

Consortium for Research on Educational Access, Transitions, and Equity. (2008). *Access to Elementary Education in India: Country Analytical Review.* United Kingdom: R. Govinda & M. Bandyopadhyay.

Cook, S. (2000, August 22). Foreign teachers find a place in U.S. schools. *The Christian Science Monitor,* p. 18.

Corbin, J., & Strauss, A. (2007). *Basics of qualitative research,* 3rd ed. Thousand Oaks, CA: Sage Publications.

Council of the Great City Schools. (2012). *Urban school statistics.* Retrieved from www.cgcs.org

Court, D. (2006). *Research and validity in qualitative research.* Retrieved from www.findarticles.com

Darling-Hammond, L. (1990). Teaching and knowledge: Policy issues posed by alternate certification for teachers. *Peabody Journal of Education, 67,* 123–154.

Darling-Hammond, L. (2004). Inequality and the right to learn: Access to qualified teachers in California's public schools. *Teachers College Record, 106,* 1936–1966.

Darling-Hammond, L. (2010). *The flat world and education: How America's commitment to equity will determine our future.* New York: Teachers College Press.

Darling-Hammond, L., Holtzman, D. J., Gatlin, S. J., & Heilig, J.V. (2003). Does teacher preparation matter? Evidence about teacher certification, Teach for America, and teacher effectiveness. Stanford University Working Paper.

Delpit, L. (1995). *Other people's children: Cultural conflict in the classroom*. New York: The New Press.

DeParle, J. (2007). A good provider is one who leaves. *The New York Times*. Retrieved from www.nytimes.com.

Derman-Sparks, L., & Ramsey, P.G. (2006). *What if all the kids are White?: Anti-bias multicultural education with young children and families*. New York: Teachers College Press.

Duckworth, E. (1997). *Teacher to teacher: Learning from each other*. New York: Teachers College Press.

DuFour, R. (2004). Schools as learning communities. *Educational Leadership*, 61, 6–11.

Dunn, A. H. (2010). "We know you're black at heart": A self study of a white, urban high school teacher. In K. Donnell & A. J. Stairs (Eds.), *Research on urban teacher learning: Examining contextual factors over time* (pp. 29–40). Charlotte, NC: Information Age Publishing.

Dunn, A. H. (2012, April). *Is there a globally responsive pedagogy?: International teachers and U.S. urban students*. Paper presented at the annual meeting of the American Educational Research Association, Vancouver, British Columbia.

Dunn, A. H., Donnell, K., & Stairs, A. J. (2010). Urban teacher learning across the professional continuum: A review of related literature. In K. Donnell & A. J. Stairs (Eds.), *Research on urban teacher learning: Examining contextual factors over time* (pp. 11–25). Charlotte, NC: Information Age Publishing.

Dunn, A. H., & Kavanagh, K. (2012, April). *International teachers, Teach for America, and the political spectacle of recruitment for urban schools*. Paper presented at the annual meeting of the American Educational Research Association, Vancouver, British Columbia.

Dunn, J. K. (2013). *One hundred million no longer: Learning to be French in the era of decolonization, 1940–1992*. Unpublished doctoral dissertation, Emory University, Atlanta, GA.

Edelman, M. (1970). *The symbolic uses of politics*. Chicago: University of Illinois Press.

Edelman, M. (1988). *Constructing the political spectacle*. Chicago: University of Chicago Press.

Education Commission of the States. (2000). *ECS teaching quality report*. Retrieved from www.ecs.org.

Ellison, R. (1986). *Going to the territory*. New York: Random House, Inc.

Feistritzer, C. E. (2007). *Building a quality teaching force: Lessons from alternate routes*. Upper Saddle River, NJ: Prentice Hall.

Finney, P. B., Torres, J., & Jurs, S. (2002). The South Carolina/Spain visiting teacher program. *The Clearing House*, 76, 94–97.

Fitzpatrick, M. (2012, October). *Globalizing teacher labor for the knowledge economy: An overview of recent trends in overseas recruitment*. Paper presented at the Globalizing Education in the 21st Century: The Bologna Reform and Beyond conference, Urbana, IL.

Fitzsimons, P. (2002). Neoliberalism and education: The autonomous chooser. *Radical Pedagogy*, 2. Retrieved from http://radicalpedagogy.icaap.org

Ford, J. C. (2011). *Political socialization and citizenship education for queer youth.* Unpublished doctoral dissertation, Emory University, Atlanta, Georgia.

Freire, P. (1998). *Politics and education.* Los Angeles, CA: UCLA Latin American Center Publications.

Freire, P. (2000). *Pedagogy of the oppressed.* New York: Continuum.

Friedman, T. L. (2005). *The world is flat: A brief history of the twenty-first century.* New York: Farrar, Straus, and Giroux.

Gay, G. (2000). *Culturally responsive teaching: Theory, research, and practice.* New York: Teachers College Press.

Gillham, B. (2005). *Research interviewing: The range of techniques.* New York: Open University Press.

Giroux, H. (2004). *The terror of neoliberalism.* Boulder, CO: Paradigm Publishers.

Global Teachers Recruitment and Resources. (2012). *About GTRR.* Retrieved from http://gtrr.net

Govinda, R. R. (2002). Providing education for all in India: An overview. In R. R. Govinda (Ed.), *India education report* (pp. 1–20). Oxford, United Kingdom: Oxford University Press.

Graham, K. A. (2001, September 17). Schools tackle shortage of language teachers. *Philadelphia Inquirer.* Retrieved from www.philly.com/inquirer

Grant, C. A. & Lei, J. L. (2001). *Global constructions of multicultural education: Theories and realities.* Mahwah, NJ: Lawrence Erlbaum.

Green, E. (2011, June 11). Baltimore school system faces challenges in keeping Filipino teachers. *Baltimore Sun.* Retrieved online at www.baltimoresun.com.

Green, K. (2011). *Youth voices: Youth radio, literacy, and civic engagement.* Unpublished doctoral dissertation, Emory University: Atlanta, GA.

Gutierrez, R. R. (2012). *Teachers on the global market: U.S. recruitment of teachers from the Philippines.* Paper presented at the Globalizing Education in the 21st Century: The Bologna Reform and Beyond conference, Urbana, IL.

Hansen, B. (2001). Teacher shortages [Electronic Version]. *The CQ Researcher, 11.* Retrieved from http://library.cqpress.com/cqresearcher

Henry, T. (2001, July 16). Teacher shortage gets foreign aid. *USA Today.* Retrieved from www.usatoday.com

hooks, b. (1995). *Killing race: Ending racism.* New York: Henry Holt and Company.

Howard, G. (1999). *We can't teach what we don't know.* New York: Teachers College Press.

Hutchison, C. B. (2005). *Teaching in America: A cross-cultural guide for international teachers and their employers.* Dordrecht, Netherlands: Springer.

Ingersoll, R. (2002). The teacher shortage: A case of wrong diagnosis and wrong prescription. *NASSP Bulletin, 86,* 16–31.

Ingersoll, R., & Perda, D. (2009). *The mathematics and science teacher shortage: Fact and myth.* Retrieved from http://www.gse.upenn.edu/faculty/Ingersoll

Ingersoll, R., & Smith, T. M. (2003). The wrong solution to the teacher shortage. *Educational Leadership, 60,* 30–33.

Irvine, J. J. (1990). *Black students and school failure: Policies, practices, and prescriptions.* New York: Praeger.

Irvine, J. J. (2003). *Educating teachers for diversity: Seeing with a cultural eye.* New York: Teachers College Press.

Irvine, J. J., & Armento, B. J. (2001). *Culturally responsive teaching: Lesson planning for elementary and middle grades.* New York: McGraw-Hill.

Johnson, S. M., Birkeland, S. E., Peske, H. G. (2003). *Fast-track alternative certification programs: Opportunities challenges for participants and state officials.* Paper presented at the Association for Public Policy Analysis and Management Conference, Washington, DC, November 2003.

Joshee, R., & Sihra, K. (2009). Religion, culture, language, and education in India. In J. A. Banks (Ed.), *The Routledge international companion to multicultural education* (pp. 425–436). New York: Routledge.

Judge bars school from hiring uncertified teachers. (2000, August 2). *Albany Times Union.* Retrieved from www.timesunion.com.

Judt, T. (2010). *Ill fares the land.* New York: Penguin Press.

Kauffman, D., Johnson, S. M., Kardos, S. M., Liu, E., & Peske, H. G. (2002). "Lost at sea": New teachers' experiences with curriculum and assessment. *Teachers College Record, 104,* 273–300.

Kavanagh, K. (2010). *A dichotomy examined: Beginning Teach for America educators navigate culturally relevant teaching and a scripted literacy program in their urban classrooms.* Unpublished doctoral dissertation, Georgia State University, Atlanta, GA.

Keller, B. (2005, January 5). Company matches foreign teachers and U.S. schools. *Education Week,* p. 8.

Keynes, J. M. (1933). National self-sufficiency. *The Yale Review, 22*(4). Retrieved from http://www.mtholyoke.edu/acad/intrel/interwar/keynes.htm

Kopetz, P. B., Lease, A. J., & Warren-King, B. Z. (2005). *Comprehensive urban education.* Upper Saddle River, NJ: Allyn and Bacon.

Kozol, J. (2000). *Ordinary resurrections: Children in the years of hope.* New York: Crown Publishers.

Kozol, J. (2005). *The shame of the nation: the restoration of apartheid schooling in America.* New York: Crown Publishers.

Kumashiro, K. K. (2008). The *seduction of common sense: How the right has framed the debate on America's schools.* New York: Teachers College Press.

Kumashiro, K. K. (2012). *Bad teacher!: How blaming teachers distorts the bigger picture.* New York: Teachers College Press.

Ladson-Billings, G. (1995). But that's just good teaching!: The case for culturally relevant pedagogy. *Theory Into Practice, 34,* 159–165.

Ladson-Billings, G. (1997). *The Dreamkeepers: Successful teachers of African American children.* San Francisco: Jossey-Bass.

Ladson-Billings, G. (2001). *Crossing over to Canaan: The journey of new teachers in diverse classrooms.* San Francisco: Jossey-Bass.

Leitsinger, M. (2011, September 9). Foreign teachers' American dreams vanish in a flash. *Education Nation*. Retrieved from www.msnbc.msn.com.

Lewin, K. M. (2011). Access, equity and transitions in education in low income countries. *International Journal of Educational Development, 31*(4), 382–393.

Lieberman, A. (Ed.) (1998). *Building a professional culture in schools.* New York: Teachers College Press.

Madan, T. N. (1999). Perspectives on pluralism. *Seminar Magazine*. Retrieved from http://www.india-seminar.com

Mandela, N. (1995). *Long walk to freedom: The autobiography of Nelson Mandela.* Boston, MA: Back Bay Books.

Manik, S., Maharaj, B., & Sookrajh, R. (2006). Globalisation and transnational teachers: South African teacher migration to the UK. *Migracijske i etničke teme, 22*(1-2), 15–33.

McCarthy, C., Pitton, V., Kim, S., & Monje, D. (2009). Movement and stasis in the neoliberal reorientation of schooling. In M. Apple, W. Au, & L. A. Gandin (Eds.), *The Routledge international handbook of critical education*, pp. 37–50. New York: Routledge.

Mehrotra, S. (2012). The cost and financing of the Right to Education in India: Can we fill the financing gap? *International Journal Of Educational Development, 32*(1), 65–71.

Merriam, S. B. (1998). *Qualitative research and case study applications in education.* San Francisco: Jossey-Bass.

Merrow, J. (Executive Producer). (1999, September 15). *Teacher shortage: False alarm?* Washington, DC: Public Broadcasting Service.

Miles, M. B., & Huberman, A. M. (1994). *Qualitative data analysis: An expanded sourcebook* (2nd ed.). Thousand Oaks, CA: Sage Publications.

Mishra, P. (2007). Exit wounds: The legacy of Indian partition. *The New Yorker*. Retrieved from www.newyorker.com

Moll, L. C., Armanti, C., Neff, D., & Gonzalez, N. (1992). Funds of knowledge for teaching: Using a qualitative approach to connect homes and classrooms. *Theory into Practice, 31* (2), 132–141.

Morrison, T. (1970). *The bluest eye.* New York: Penguin Group.

Najar, N. (2011, October 13). Squeezed out in India, students turn to U.S. *The New York Times*. Retrieved from www.nytimes.com.

National Archives and Records Administration. (2012).*Visa regulations.* Retrieved from www.archives.gov

National Center for Education Statistics. (2011). *Digest of education statistics.* Retrieved from http://nces.gov

National Commission on Teaching and America's Future. (2002). *Unraveling the "teacher shortage" problem: Teacher retention is the key.* New York: National Commission on Teaching and America's Future.

National Council for Teacher Education. (2003). *Discrimination based on sex, caste, religion and disability: Addressing through educational interventions: A handbook for sensitizing teachers and teacher educators.* New Delhi, India: National Council for Teacher Education and National Human Rights Commission.

National Education Association. (2003, January 29). *Teacher retention key to teacher short-age crisis*. Retrieved from www.nctaf.org

Neiss, M. L. (2005). Preparing teachers to teach science and mathematics with technology: Developing a technology pedagogical content knowledge. *Teaching and Teacher Education, 21*, 509–523.

Nepales, R. V. (2006, August 5). *Only in Hollywood: After 'Imelda', Ramona Diaz tackles Pinoy teachers in U.S.* Retrieved from www.inquirer.net

Neufeld, S. (2005, August 28). Filipino teachers learn life lessons in Baltimore. *The Baltimore Sun*. Retrieved from www.baltimoresun.com

Nieto, S. (1995). From brown heroes and holidays to assimilationist agendas: Reconsidering the critiques of multicultural education. In C. E. Sleeter & P. McLaren (Eds.), *Multicultural education, critical pedagogy, and the politics of difference* (pp. 190–220).

Nieto, S. (2003). *What keeps teachers going?* New York: Teachers College Press.

Noddings, N. (2005a). *The challenge to care in schools: An alternative approach to education*. New York: Teachers College Press.

Noddings, N. (2005b). Caring in education. *The encyclopedia of informal education*. Retrieved from www.infed.org/biblio/noddings_caring_in_education.htm

Oberg, K. (1954). Culture shock. Presentation to the Women's Club of Rio de Janeiro. *Brazil, 1*–9.

Organisation for Economic Co-operation and Development. (2005). *OECD annnual report 2005*. Retrieved from www.oecd.org

Paige, R. (2002). *Meeting the highly qualified teachers challenge: The Secretary's annual report on teacher quality*. Washington, DC: U.S. Department of Education.

Paige, R., Rees, N. R., Petrilli, M. J., & Gore, P. (2004). *Alternative routes to teacher certification*. Retrieved from http://www.ed.gov

Paliwal, D. K. (2006). Globalization of Indian education. In S. Tiwari (Ed.), *Education in India* (pp. 60–72). New Delhi, India: Atlantic.

Payscale.com. (2010, August 1). *Salary snapshot for high school teacher job: Hyderabad, India*. Retrieved from www.payscale.com

Peace Corps. (2010). *Culture matters: The Peace Corps cross cultural workbook*. Retrieved from www.multimedia.peacecorps.gov

Peterson, J. (2005, June 13). Foreign aid for America. *Newsweek, 145*, 13.

Public Agenda. (2000). *A sense of calling: Who teaches and why*. New York: Public Agenda.

Purdy, M. A. (2011). Southern and independent: Public mandates, private schools, and Black students, 1951–1970. Unpublished doctoral dissertation, Emory University, Atlanta, GA.

Quaynor, L. (2012). Citizenship education in post-conflict contexts: A review of the literature. *Education, Citizenship, & Social Justice, 7*, 37–57.

Qureshi, S. (2010). Educational backwardness of Muslims: Causes and remedies. In A. Waheed (Ed.), *Minority education in India: Issues of access, equity, and inclusion.* (pp.42–51). New Delhi, India: Serials Publications.

Rajput, J. S., Kumar, P., & Walia, K. (2002). *Teacher education in India*. New Delhi, India: Sterling Publishers Private Limited. Ramachandran, V. (2009). Systemic barriers to equity in education. In P. Rustagi (Ed.), *Concerns, conflicts, and cohesions: Universalization of elementary education in India*. (pp.124–152). New York, NY: Oxford University Press.

Ratterree, B. (2006). *Globalisation and teacher employment: Teacher shortages, migration, and mobility*. Presented at the annual Commonwealth Conference of Education Ministers, Capetown, South Africa.

Right Side News. (2009). *New report shows schools increasingly hiring foreign teachers over Americans*. Retrieved from http://www.rightsidenews.com

Roberts, M. A. (2010). Toward a theory of culturally relevant critical teacher care: African American teachers' definitions and perceptions of care for African American students. *Journal of Moral Education, 39*, 449–467.

Robertson, S. L. (2008). "Remaking the world": Neoliberalism and the transformation of education and teachers labor. In M. F. Compton & L. Weiner (Eds.), *The global assault on teaching, teachers, and their unions: Stories of resistance* (pp. 11–30). New York: Palgrave Macmillan.

Rowley, J. B. (1999). The good mentor. *Educational Leadership, 56*, 20–22.

Rubin, H. J. & Rubin, I. S. (2005). *Qualitative interviewing: The art of hearing data*. Thousand Oaks, CA: Sage Publications. Rustagi, P. (2009). Towards universalizing elementary education: Emerging issues and challenges. In P. Rustagi (Ed.), *Concerns, conflicts, and cohesions: Universalization of elementary education in India*. (pp. 3–32). Oxford, UK: Oxford University Press.

Sack, K. (2001, May 19). Facing a teacher shortage, American schools look overseas. *New York Times*, p. A8.

Saltman, K. (2007). Corporatization and the control of schools. In M. Apple, W. Au, & L. A. Gandin, (Eds.), *The Routledge international handbook of critical education*. New York: Routledge.

"School districts import teachers." (2001). [Electronic Version]. Retrieved from http://fyi.cnn.com/2001

Shapira, I. (2005, April 3). Foreign teachers a quick fix. *Washington Post*, p. C3.

Shulman, L. (1986). Those who understand: Knowledge growth in teaching. *Educational Researcher, 15*, 4–14.

Siddle Walker, V., & Snarey, J. (Eds.) (2004). *Race-ing moral formation African American perspectives on care and justice*. New York: Teachers College Press.

Sirotnik, K. A. (1988). Studying the education of educators: Methodolgy. *Phi Delta Kappan, 70*(3), 241–247.

Skiba, R. J. (2008) Are zero tolerance policies effective in the schools? An evidentiary review and recommendations. *American Psychologist, 63*(9), 852–862.

Smith, M. L. (2004). *Political spectacle and the fate of American schools*. New York: Routledge Falmer.

Solano-Campos, A. (2010). *International teacher recruitment in Costa Rica*. Paper presented at the annual conference of the American Educational Research Association, New Orleans, LA.

Speck, M. (1996). Best practice in professional development for sustained educational change. *ERS Spectrum*, 14(2), 33–41.

Srivastava, P. K. (2006). Quality measures in teacher education. In S. Tiwari (Ed.), *Education in India* (pp. 168–173). New Delhi, India: Atlantic.

Stairs, A. J., Donnell, K., & Dunn, A. H. (2011). *Urban teaching in America: Theory, research, and practice in K–12 classrooms.* Thousand Oaks, CA: Sage Publications.

Stake, R. (1995). *The art of case study research.* Thousand Oaks, CA: Sage Publications.

Tata Technologies. (2010). *Better foundation, better future: About us.* Retrieved from www.tatatechnologies.com

Teach for America. (2012). *Our organization.* Retrieved from http://www.teachforamerica.org

Teachers Placement Group. (2012). *Background of Teachers Placement Group.* Retrieved from www.teachersplacement.com

Thomas, B. S. (2003). *Disturbing teacher migration tremors.* Retrieved from www.indiatogether.org

Tilak, J. B. G. (2009). Universalizing elementary education: A review of progress, policies, and problems. In P. Rustagie (Ed.), *Concerns, conflicts, and cohesions: Universalization of elementary education in India.* (pp. 33–71). New York, NY: Oxford University Press.

Tolstoy, L. (1995). *Anna Karenina.* London: Wordsworth Classics.

United Nations Academic Impact. (2011). Academic impact. Retrieved from http://academicimpact.org/engpage.php

United Nations Educational, Scientific and Cultural Organization. (2010). *EFA global monitoring report: Deprivation and marginalization in education.* Retrieved from http://www.unesco.org/fileadmin/MULTIMEDIA/HQ/ED/GMR/html/dme-1.html

U.S. Department of Education. (2010). *Definition of highly qualified.* Retrieved from http://www2.ed.gov

U.S. Department of Labor. (2012). *Work authorization for non-U.S. citizens.* Retrieved from http://www.dol.gov/compliance/guide/h1b.htm.Vaishnav, A. (2001, August 21). Teachers from Philippines arrive for duty. *Boston Globe.* Retrieved from www.bostonglobe.com

Van Roekel, D. (2011, April 6). Statement by NEA president Dennis Van Roekel on the Department of Labor's investigation of Prince George's County Public Schools. Retrieved from http://www.nea.org

Villegas, A. M., & Lucas, T. (2002). *Educating culturally responsive teachers.* Albany: State University of New York Press.

Visiting International Faculty Program. (2012). Retrieved from www.vifprogram.com.

Waddell, J. H. (2010). Fostering relationships to increase teacher retention in urban schools. *Journal of Curriculum and Instruction.* 4, 70–85.

Weber, E. (2007). Globalization, "glocal" development, and teachers' work: A research agenda. *Review of Educational Research, 77*(3), 279–309.

Wells, A. S., Slayton, J., & Scott, J. (2002). Defining democracy in the neoliberal age: Charter school reform and educational consumption. *American Educational Research Journal, 39*(2), 337–361.

Wise, T. J. (2010). *Colorblind: The rise of post-racial politics and the retreat from racial equity* San Francisco, CA: City Lights Books.

Wolff, A. H., & Glaser, H. S. R. (1986). West Germany and other nations can ease the U.S. teacher crunch. *The American School Board Journal, 173*(9), 27–28.

Young, A. J., & Young, D. B. (2001, March 7). Foreign teachers have much to offer. [Letter to the editor]. *Education Week*. Retrieved from www.edweek.org

Zeichner, K. M. (2003). Adequacies and inadequacies of current strategies to recruit teachers. *Teachers College Record, 105*(3), 490–519.

Zeichner, K. M. (2009). *Teacher education and the struggle for social justice.* New York: Routledge.

Index

About the Author

Alyssa Hadley Dunn, Ph.D., is an assistant professor of urban teacher education at Georgia State University. She is the co-author of *Urban Teaching in America: Theory, Research, and Practice in K–12 Classrooms* (Stairs, Donnell, & Dunn, 2011). Her research focuses on urban schools, students, and teachers, and on the intersections between social justice, multicultural education, and educational policy. She has published her scholarship in peer-reviewed journals and edited volumes, presented at numerous national and international conferences, and received awards for her research, teaching, and service. She is the recipient of the Distinguished Dissertation in Critical Education and Social Justice award from the American Educational Research Association and the Carl V. Patton's Presidential Award for Outstanding Faculty Community Service and Social Action from Georgia State University. A former high school English teacher, she received her Ph.D. in educational studies from Emory University.